Introdu ~~DATE DUE~~ ...llege Writing

Jean Reynolds
Polk Community College

Prentice
Hall

Upper Saddle River, New Jersey 07458

AVP, Editor in Chief: Leah Jewell
Acquisitions Editor: Craig Campanella
Editorial Assistant: Joan Polk
Managing Editor: Mary Rottino
Production Liaison: Fran Russello
Project Manager: Marianne Hutchinson, Pine Tree Composition
Prepress and Manufacturing Buyer: Ben Smith
Art Director: Jayne Conte
Cover Designer: Bruce Kenselaar
Marketing Manager: Rachel Falk

For permission to use copyrighted material, grateful acknowledgment is made to the
copyright holders on page 327, which are hereby made part of this copyright page.

This book was set in 10/12 Times Roman by Pine Tree Composition, Inc.,
and was printed and bound by Courier Companies, Inc.
The cover was printed by Phoenix Color Corp.

Prentice-Hall International (UK) Limited, *London*
Prentice-Hall of Australia Pty. Limited, *Sydney*
Prentice-Hall Canada Inc., *Toronto*
Prentice-Hall Hispanoamericana, S.A., *Mexico*
Prentice-Hall of India Private Limited, *New Delhi*
Prentice-Hall of Japan, Inc., *Tokyo*
Pearson Education Asia Pte. Ltd., *Singapore*
Editora Prentice-Hall do Brasil, Ltda., *Rio de Janeiro*

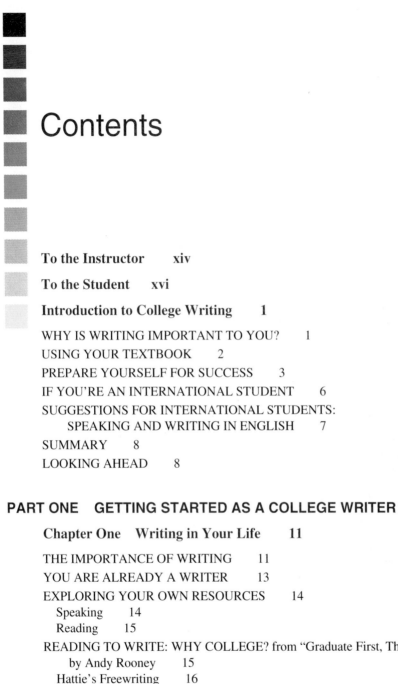

Contents

Chapter Five   Writing with a Plan and a Purpose   75

Chapter Six   Organizing Your Essay   89

Chapter Seven   Drafting Your Essay   110

To the Instructor

This book is the product of both research and classroom experience. I have benefited from years of teaching, reading, and exchanges of ideas with colleagues who share my enthusiasm about teaching developmental writers. As I planned this book, seven principles shaped the content and organization:

1. Effective learning experiences stimulate the human brain to restructure itself in exciting ways analogous to the rewiring of computer hardware. During active learning, dendrites are formed, brain cells form complex alignments, and new neurological connections are made. Research shows that writing, talking, and reading activities stimulate these important changes.

2. Developmental students benefit when motivational material is presented early in the semester. Many developmental students enter college unaware of the relationship between writing skills and professional success. Class discussions of real-world writing activities instill a positive attitude about college writing requirements.

3. A process approach to writing often works well with developmental students. They usually like the idea of writing by steps rather than tackling an assignment in a single strenuous effort. Because many students suffer from "writer's block" when they face a blank piece of paper, discovery activities are especially helpful.

4. Students like to write about a variety of topics: personal experience, career and consumer information, and current issues. Sharing personal writing helps build cooperation and trust in collaborative groups. When students have learned how to work together, they enjoy sharing information and opinions about more public topics.

5. Student writing should have a purpose. Too often students merely write out a list of causes and effects, or annotate the steps in a process, without demonstrating how this information will benefit readers. By contrast, on-the-job writing always has a purpose—exploring the causes of a successful advertising campaign, or explaining the steps in a medical procedure. "Making meaning"—a phrase coined by author Anne Berthoff—is important to all writing instruction.

6. Writing assignments for developmental students should vary in length and complexity. Students usually prefer to tackle single paragraphs first: As they gain confidence and fluency, they can move on to essay assignments.

7. The conventions of written English present a particular challenge. Many developmental writers lack confidence with punctuation, spelling, and other usage issues—and they are intimidated by sophisticated grammatical terminology.

Special Features in This Book

- Active learning is promoted through structured collaborative activities and a variety of reading and writing tasks.
- Students learn how to work effectively in groups—a skill helpful both in college and professional life.
- Motivational material in the Introduction and Chapter One demonstrates why writing is important to today's college students.
- This book offers unusually broad coverage of the writing process. One entire chapter is devoted to Discovery Activities because students produce better writing when they've found an intriguing topic to write about. An additional benefit is that the reading tasks and Thinking Tools in this chapter can be carried over to other academic subjects.
- Students are guided through the transition from single paragraphs to essay-length writing. Chapters One and Two focus solely on single-paragraph writing; Chapter Three helps students move from paragraphs to essays. Chapters Ten through Fifteen, which cover modes of development, all begin with one-paragraph assignments and move on to multiple-paragraph essays.
- In Part One (Chapters One through Nine), students practice using details, examples, and description to develop their ideas, and they are introduced to word processing and the World Wide Web. In Part Two (Chapters Ten through Fifteen), students learn about additional types of development: processes, classifications, comparison/contrast, cause/effect, narration, and definition.
- Methods of development are always tied to the writer's purpose. For example, students are asked to describe a process for an informative or persuasive purpose—explaining how to perform a task more efficiently, or convincing readers to stop a harmful practice.
- Usage problems are covered extensively. Part Three, Editing Skills, reviews fragments, run-together sentences, and sentence variety. In Part Four, three chapters are devoted to punctuation; Part Five includes chapters on verbs, word choice, and pronouns. Wherever possible, explanations are worded clearly and simply. Ample practice material is included. Each usage chapter stands alone so that as needed, instructors can select the content most important to their students.

Supplemental Material

An instructor's manual containing a syllabus, an answer key, teaching suggestions, and additional classroom activities is available.

To the Student

This book was written with you in mind. I tested many of its ideas, activities, and assignments in the first-year writing courses I teach at a community college. Through these classes hundreds of students—many of whom may have writing backgrounds like yours—have become successful college writers.

You might be surprised to learn how many writing experiences you and I share. I've often had to search for writing topics. Parts of this book had to be rewritten over and over, and often I've struggled to find time for writing in my busy daily schedule.

Feedback has been helpful to me, as it is to all writers. I've discovered that it's wonderful to receive compliments about my work, but it's equally important to hear ideas about making it better.

I've learned that anyone who has the desire to succeed, along with access to professional writing instruction, can become an effective writer. If you didn't excel in your high school writing classes, you're not alone. Many proficient writers (including me) weren't stars either. What counts is willingness to work on your writing.

If "work" makes you think of boring and repetitious drills, think again. Much of what writers do involves imagination and critical thinking. Finding subjects to write about, and ideas and examples that develop your ideas, can be a fascinating challenge. As you complete the exercises and assignments in this book, I encourage you to sharpen your observation and thinking skills. What intrigues you? What are your interests, likes, and dislikes? What is unique about you and your life?

My experiences and interests have influenced much of what you will be reading. For example, several years ago I bought a copy of ballerina Suzanne Farrell's book *Holding on to the Air* because I'd been thrilled when I saw her dance on stage in New York. When I read her life story, I was surprised to learn that she had lived in a building in my old neighborhood—the aging Ansonia Hotel, which I remembered well. One of her stories appears in Chapter Four.

I've always been intrigued by news stories about the astronauts living at space station Mir. What, I wondered, is it like to live for months in a weightless environment far from earth? To find out, I borrowed Peter Smolders's *Living in Space* from the library. Now a section of that book appears in Chapter Ten.

Anything you find interesting—current events, a summer job, romance, favorite sport, or friendship—has the potential to become a thought-provoking essay. Some of my students use a small notebook to jot down ideas gleaned from news stories, college events, family life, and the working world. In this book I've suggested many ways to discover subjects for writing, along with practical suggestions for developing and organizing your ideas. There are model essays to study, tips for avoiding usage errors, and checklists to guide you as you write and revise your work.

Most important, remember that every professional person is also a professional writer. At work you are likely to find yourself writing letters, reports, proposals, evaluations, presentations, and speeches. Keep your career goals in mind as you develop your writing skills in this course.

I wish you success both in college and your life after graduation. My deepest hope is that this book will help build your confidence and contribute to that success.

Acknowledgments

It has been a joy to work with Prentice Hall. I especially want to thank Craig Campanella, Leah Jewell, Corey Good, Maggie Barbieri, and Joan Polk. I am grateful to Pine Tree Composition, Inc., especially Marianne Hutchinson, for expertly transforming my manuscript into a published book. Many other people assisted me, including Hugh Anderson, Dean of Arts, Letters, and Social Sciences at Polk Community College; the Learning Resources staff at PCC; and Margaret Gorenstein, Vickie Nelson, and Virginia Read.

I am especially grateful to the reviewers for their thoughtful and helpful suggestions: Harvey Rubinstein (Hudson County Community College), Stanley Coberly (West Virginia State University at Parkersburg), Lisa Berman and Maria C. Villar-Smith (Miami-Dade Community College), Spencer Olesen (Mt. View College), Miriam A. Kinard (Trident Technical College), Margo L. Eden-Camann (DeKalb College-Clarkston Campus), Elaine Chakonas (Dominican University), Donald Judson (Providence College), Amanda S. McBride (Durham Technical Community College), and Thomas Beery (Lima Technical College).

My husband, Charlie Reynolds, has provided encouragement, humor, and support throughout my writing career. I extend my loving thanks to him.

Jean Reynolds

Introduction to College Writing

Preview

1. This course is designed to help you meet the challenges of college writing.
2. Your college offers many resources to help you succeed as a college writer.
3. If English is not your first language, you can benefit from some special study practices.

WHY IS WRITING IMPORTANT TO YOU?

If you studied American literature in high school, you've probably heard of Ralph Waldo Emerson (1803–1882), one of America's most brilliant writers. But Emerson did not rate himself as highly as the public did. Instead he insisted that a neighbor of his, Bronson Alcott (1799–1888), was a much more gifted thinker.

Unfortunately, Alcott's writing skills were poor. Because only wealthy families sent their sons to college in those days, Alcott never studied with a professional writing teacher. Unable to write for large audiences, Alcott could not publicize his extraordinary ideas about education, politics, and philosophy. As a result, he missed the opportunity for an important place in American literary history.

You enjoy many advantages undreamed of by ambitious men and women in the past. First, you have access to electronic writing aids. Your college probably has a computer laboratory where you can learn word processing. Even if you're not a skilled typist, a computer can help you improve your writing. Corrections and revisions can be done quickly and neatly. Many computer programs even have built-in spellcheckers, dictionaries, and grammar aids. Your college may offer other resources such as tutors, a writing lab, workshops, and computerized instruction. If you're an international student, you may be able to participate in special programs to increase your knowledge of English.

Most important, you are the beneficiary of recent research about writing. Experts have studied successful authors and teachers to learn the best ways to produce effective writing. Your professor has a wealth of writing experience and knowledge to share with you. Throughout this course you will be introduced to new ideas and strategies, and you'll receive expert feedback on your own writing.

Collaborative Activity: Explore Resources on Your Campus

1. On your own, make a list of campus resources for writers. Your list may include tutors, a writing lab, computerized writing instruction, writing workshops, a word processing lab, and other services. The college catalog, bulletin boards, and brochures may be good sources of information about writing services.

2. At your next class, meet with three or four other students to compare your lists and combine them into a master list of campus writing resources.

3. Divide the items on this list among group members so that each person has at least one resource to investigate. At your next class meeting, each member will present a brief (two or three minutes) oral report about these resources. For example, one student might visit the writing lab to learn about the services there. Another might visit the computer lab to find out when workshops on word processing are held.

4. Visit the resources assigned to you. Talk to staff members, and pick up any brochures that are available. Write down the names of staff members, hours the facility is open, and services offered. These questions may be helpful: Are appointments necessary? Is special equipment required? Do you need your student identification number to check in?

5. At your next class meeting, present your report. Hand out any brochures you have collected, and answer questions from group members. In addition, learn as much as you can from the presentations by other members of the group. Talk about the information all of you have gathered. Which resources will be helpful to you? How do you plan to take advantage of them?

USING YOUR TEXTBOOK

In any college course, it's a good idea to spend a few minutes examining your textbook to see how it is set up and learn about its helpful features. This book is designed to help you meet many of the challenges of college writing. You begin by writing paragraphs and then move on to essays. The earlier chapters feature personal writing—paragraphs and essays about your ideas and experiences. Later you will write about topics related to careers and public issues. Throughout this book, you'll be encouraged to build confidence and increase your knowledge by talking to other students about your writing.

This book uses a "process" approach to writing. Instead of trying to write a perfect essay all at once, you'll be encouraged to write in steps. A writing task begins with *planning* (making a writing plan, discovering ideas, and organizing them). Next is *drafting*—putting your ideas into sentences so that you have a complete essay when you finish. Drafting is often a messy process. First drafts are usually rough and incomplete; you may need to go through several drafts before you're satisfied with what you've written. The final step is *revising*—making improvements in organizing and development, and editing your work—correcting punctuation, spelling, and other usage problems.

Each step in the writing process has its own challenges. Most students appreciate help with finding ideas, developing them, and revising their work. One whole chapter in this book focuses on discovering ideas for writing. Several chapters offer suggestions for using descriptions and examples to develop your ideas. The latter part of this book suggests ways to avoid errors and make your sentences more polished and effective.

Collaborative Activity: Explore This Book

Instructions: Working with one or two other students, spend a few minutes browsing through this book. Look at the Table of Contents and Index, and thumb through the other pages. As you explore this book, look for answers to these questions:

1. What kind of writing instruction is offered in each of the five parts of this book?
2. Using the Table of Contents and Index as a guide, find pages that discuss these topics.
   • Using subordinate conjunctions
   • Drafting an essay
   • Avoiding sentence fragments
   • Using causes and effects to develop an essay
3. Find an example of each of these features:
   • Reading to Write
   • Collaborative Activity
   • Preview
   • Freewriting Activity
   • Writing Assignment
4. Using the Table of Contents, find the following three charts:
   • How to Discover Ideas (Chapter Three)
   • Revision Checklist (Chapter Eight)
   • Usage Checklist (Chapter Sixteen)

PREPARE YOURSELF FOR SUCCESS

Success begins with your attitude and beliefs about writing. First-year college students often worry needlessly about their ability to succeed as writers. The comments in the list below reflect their concerns—and, perhaps, some of yours as well.

1. "I'm not sure why writing is important to my future."
   No matter what major you choose, you can expect to hand in many written assignments before graduation, including research papers, lab reports, book reviews, essay exams, and compositions. In professional life, written reports are required from anyone who manages personnel, budgets, or ideas. As you advance professionally, and acquire greater responsibilities, the amount of writing will increase also. As a first-year college student, you have an excellent opportunity to begin preparing for future success.
2. "I have trouble finding ideas for writing."
   Writing topics are all around you. In Chapter Two, you'll practice discovering ideas through specialized thinking activities (called Thinking Tools); you'll also learn how to find them through structured writing and reading activities. Since many college students are uncomfortable about writing at first, there are also activities that don't require extended writing: drawing, clustering, and a listing technique called the journalist's questions.

3. "I can't spell."

    Neither could Franklin D. Roosevelt, thirty-second president of the United States and an extraordinarily powerful writer. Poor spelling can be overcome by resolving to check your final draft for spelling errors before you hand it in. Keep a dictionary handy, invest in a handheld electronic spellchecker (such as the Franklin Speller), or use the spellchecker on a word-processing program. Another good strategy is to carry a small notebook and label each page with a letter of the alphabet. Write down the spellings of words that cause problems for you, and refer to the notebook often.

4. "I get upset when my writing is criticized."

    Substitute the word "feedback" for "criticism," and remember that all good writers seek opinions from others about their work. (Every published book, including this one, is the result of much feedback and many revisions suggested by outside readers.) The collaborative experiences in this book will help you feel comfortable about feedback. Remember too that feedback should always have a positive component. Ask your classmates to tell you what they like about your writing, and be sure to praise the good qualities of their work as well.

5. "Writing is lonely."

    It doesn't have to be. One good trick is to picture your readers in your mind's eye as you're writing; another is to read your early drafts to friends and family members whom you can trust to give you encouragement and helpful suggestions. And you don't have to write alone. If writing tasks seem lonely, consider meeting regularly with a friend to write together. Author Natalie Goldberg regularly joins with friends to write, read, and talk about work in progress: You can do the same.

6. "I'm not talented."

    Successful writing is the result not of talent, but of knowledge, practice, and patience. To write well, allow yourself enough time to find an interesting subject, organize it effectively, and develop it thoroughly—and still more time to construct effective sentences and correct errors. Every college offers resources (such as tutors, software, and videos) to assist student writers. Make use of these resources (which you'll explore later in this chapter) to ensure your success.

7. "I put off getting started till the last minute, and then I run out of time to do the job well."

    Everyone struggles with procrastination now and then. Fortunately there are some simple tricks to get you started on a writing project early. A blank piece of paper or empty computer screen causes some writers to freeze: They're so afraid of writing badly that they can't get started. You can overcome this by doing some warm-up activities that will help you discover and organize ideas. Another good warm-up is making a writing plan (Chapter Three). In the drafting stage, write quickly. Remember that you can always make changes later. Having a complete draft in front of you—even if you're not satisfied with it—gives you something to work with.

8. "I make errors when I write."

    Most writers do. Successful writers go over their work to make corrections as many times as needed. The Usage Checklist in Chapter Sixteen will help you make sure a writing task is in the best possible shape when you hand it in. If you are unsure about punctuation or other usage areas, refer to the Table of Contents and Index of this book as you make corrections. Ask if your college learning center has software or tutors to help you. And remember that regular practice builds competence. At the end of this course you can expect to see many positive changes in your writing.

Exercise 1: Get in Touch with Your Writing Habits

Effective writing is the result of a number of day-to-day writing practices. This activity will help you evaluate your writing habits and decide which behaviors to start working on now.

Instructions: Read the following list of writing behaviors. Write "yes" in front of any practices that are already part of your life. Put a check in front of those you want to start practicing now.

_____ 1. I write in several steps rather than just one.

_____ 2. I start working on an assignment well before the due date.

_____ 3. I make a writing plan before I begin my first draft.

_____ 4. Before I start drafting an essay, I use one or more discovery activities to generate ideas.

_____ 5. When I'm planning an essay, I let ideas flow freely, without worrying about grammar and spelling.

_____ 6. I write at least one rough draft before I start writing my final draft.

_____ 7. During the drafting stage, I write several drafts if necessary.

_____ 8. I take all the time I need to revise an essay before I hand it in.

_____ 9. Before I hand in an assignment, I make sure every word is spelled correctly.

_____ 10. I look up any usage rules I'm unsure about.

_____ 11. I share my writing with others.

_____ 12. When an assignment is returned to me, I read the instructor's comments carefully.

_____ 13. I ask my professor to explain any comments I don't understand.

_____ 14. I'm looking forward to seeing my writing improve while I'm in college.

Collaborative Activity: Share Your Experiences

Instructions: Meet with a small group of other students to share your answers to the previous exercise. Which questions did you answer differently, and why? What writing experiences do you have in common, and which have been different? Discuss any memories about writing you wish to share with group members.

Collaborative Activity: Get Ready

Instructions: Which of the challenges in the following list will you be dealing with this semester? Meet with a small group of other students to compare your answers and discuss strategies for success in this course.

1. Which of the following demands on your time will you be facing this semester?

_____ family life

_____ a part-time job

_____ a full-time job

_____ a heavy course load

_____ other responsibilities (such as church and community commitments)

_____ other interests (such as student government, sports, the arts, and other hobbies)

_____ maintaining friendships and enjoying social activities

2. How will you ensure that you have enough study and writing time to succeed in this course?

_____ make a study schedule and stick to it

_____ cut back on working hours

_____ ask others to share some of the work you've been doing

_____ make success in college writing a priority in your life

_____ say "no" to some of the activities you've been doing

3. How much writing knowledge are you bringing to this course?

_____ thorough knowledge of the writing process

_____ extensive previous writing experience

_____ success in other writing courses

4. What kind of support system do you have?

_____ friends and family members who encourage you to write

_____ familiarity with college writing services, such as a writing lab

5. Which of these skills have you already developed?

_____ word processing skill

_____ typing skill

6. Which of these learning behaviors will you be practicing this semester?

_____ regular class attendance

_____ participating during class

_____ taking a thorough set of notes each day

_____ scheduling two hours of preparation for each hour of class

_____ following directions carefully

_____ completing all assignments punctually

IF YOU'RE AN INTERNATIONAL STUDENT

International students sometimes face special challenges in college. If your native language is not English, the following suggestions may be helpful to you:

1. Make a special effort to develop friendships with American students. Don't let shyness hold you back. Many American students are fascinated by life in other countries and are glad to have friends from around the world.

2. Don't be embarrassed to ask questions about the English language. Many American students will be happy to answer your questions, especially if you're willing to answer their questions about your own language and native land.

3. Expose yourself to as much English as possible. For the time being, immerse yourself in the English language. Get your news in English from radio broadcasts, TV programs, and newspapers. Watch English-language entertainment, and speak only English with friends, even if they're fluent in your native language. Remember that you're not giving up your own language: You can always go back to it when you're fluent in English.

4. Be patient with yourself, and maintain your sense of humor. Most people make many mistakes while they're learning another language. Usually several months or a longer period are necessary before you can clearly hear the sounds of English that are different from your native language. Pronunciation and grammar can be challenging as well. If you have good friends who are native English speakers, try teaching them a little of your language. You'll soon see that their struggles are no different from yours.

5. If you studied English in your native country, remember that American English may be different from what you learned in school. Your English teachers at home may not have known some of the expressions and grammatical constructions that Americans use. Be willing to keep learning more about English.

6. Carry a small English dictionary with you, and use it often. Make sure it's recent: English, like all living languages, is always changing. The definitions, spellings, and pronunciations may not be correct if your dictionary is more than ten years old. Buy a large English-language dictionary for your study area: It will give you more detailed information. You should also have a translator's dictionary written in your native language and English.

7. Remind yourself often of the advantages you enjoy as an international student. Your experiences with two countries, two languages, and two cultures can provide many ideas for college essays and research assignments. You will have much to offer during class discussions, and American students may seek your friendship. After graduation, your knowledge of the English language and American customs may lead to desirable job offers.

SUGGESTIONS FOR INTERNATIONAL STUDENTS: SPEAKING AND WRITING IN ENGLISH

Because every language is different, it's difficult to generalize about the challenges you'll face while perfecting your English. For example, the Welsh language uses "there is" constructions far more often than English does. The Korean and Japanese languages don't have plural noun forms, and rules for articles are different in Spanish and English. Many students have found the following suggestions helpful:

1. Be cautious with word endings. Word endings in English are extremely important. Often it's necessary to add an *s, t,* or *ed* to the end of a word. It may take you some time to start hearing, saying, and writing these endings. When you write an essay, check it carefully to make sure all the endings—especially the letter *s*—are placed where they belong.

2. Be aware of the differences between conversational English and standard English, which is used in school and professional life. Some rules in standard English may not apply to conversation. For example, it's important to write in complete sentences, but Americans often use short phrases when they speak.

3. Practice using *a, an,* and *the* correctly. *An* is used with nouns that begin with vowel sounds: *an* eagle, *an* hour, *an* umbrella. *A* is used with nouns that begin with consonant sounds: *a* European vacation, *a* house, *a* uniform. The more English you read and hear, the easier it will be to use these small but important words correctly.

4. Pay close attention to word order. In English, the subject usually comes first, followed by the verb and its object, if it has one. Other languages use a different word order, and some—such as Arabic—don't require a verb in every sentence, as standard English does. (Americans often omit verbs in conversation.)

5. Learn the plural forms of English nouns. Most words use *s* for the plural. If a noun ends in *x, s, sh, ch,* or *ss,* the plural will end in *es.* Some words have special plural forms: *women, men, children.* Refer to your dictionary to learn more about these plural forms.

6. Study English verb forms. In some languages, such as Chinese and American Sign Language, verb forms never change. A few languages, such as Arabic, don't require verbs at all. But in standard English, every sentence must have a verb, and you must understand how and why verbs change. Many verbs add *ed* or *d* to show that an event happened in the past. Some verbs, however, completely change when a sentence is about past events: *saw, taught, was.* English verbs also use helpers, such as *has* or *had,* with special past-tense forms. Chapter Twenty-two in this book, along with your dictionary, can help you master English verb forms.

Fluency in two or more languages is an impressive achievement that can enrich your life in many ways through friendship, travel, and cultural experiences. You're likely to feel some frustration and discouragement while you're mastering English. But be assured that the effort is well worth it: For the rest of your life, you'll often be thankful for the extra effort you expended to learn English.

SUMMARY

1. Thinking about writing experiences and your attitude towards writing can help you succeed in this course.
2. Your college offers many resources to help you succeed as a college writer.
3. Special study techniques can help you master English if it is not your first language.

LOOKING AHEAD

In Chapter One, "Writing in Your Life," you'll see why writing is so important to college and your professional life. You'll explore campus resources for student writers and practice some of the reading, writing, and thinking skills you've brought with you to college.

PART ONE

GETTING STARTED AS A COLLEGE WRITER

CHAPTER ONE

Writing in Your Life

Preview

Writing is one of the most important subjects you'll be studying in college. In this chapter you'll write several paragraphs and share them with other students. You'll see how talking to others and reading can help generate ideas for writing. You'll also practice "freewriting"—spontaneous writing, for your eyes only, that helps you explore ideas.

THE IMPORTANCE OF WRITING

Writing is vital to success both in college and your professional life. In college you'll need writing skills for essays, tests, research projects, lab reports, book reviews, case studies, and other assignments. Writing is equally important in professional life. Responsible, well-paid positions involve managing money and people—tasks that require writing.

And writing is vital to citizenship. Your language skills empower you to take your ideas to the people who make decisions—and to become a decision-maker yourself. Whether you're a dissatisfied consumer, a neighborhood activist, or an advocate for people on the other side of the world, words make events happen. Even the U.S. Constitution recognizes the importance of language by guaranteeing everyone—including those who are not American citizens—freedom to communicate.

■ ■ ■ Language Saves a Species

Many citizens have used their language knowledge to work for political change. About seventy years ago, Floridian Kirk Munroe promoted a bill to protect the manatee, a large aquatic mammal sometimes called a "sea cow." Fearing that the name "sea cow" would not impress legislators, many of whom were farmers, Munroe used the scientific name: Trichecus latirostris. One senator declared, "If there is a beast with any such name as that in the State of Florida, it ought to be protected." The bill passed.

Exercise 1: Writing in Your Life

Instructions: Read the list of writing tasks below. Put a check in front of any tasks you have already performed one or more times. Put an F (for future) in front of any tasks you expect to perform in the future.

Writing a letter to:

____ 1. a relative

____ 2. a friend

____ 3. a newspaper

____ 4. a government official

____ 5. a business representative

School tasks:

____ 6. an essay

____ 7. a book report or book review

____ 8. a research project

____ 9. a lab report

____ 10. a case study

____ 11. an essay examination

On-the-job writing:

____ 12. a memo

____ 13. a business letter

____ 14. an article for a professional publication

____ 15. a business report

____ 16. an employee evaluation

____ 17. a budget proposal

____ 18. a proposal promoting a new idea

____ 19. a book

Writing about current issues:

____ 20. a letter to a newspaper

____ 21. a letter to a radio or TV station

____ 22. a letter to a public official

____ 23. a committee report about an issue in your community

____ 24. a speech

Creative writing (short stories and poems) for:

____ 25. your own enjoyment

____ 26. a publication

____ 27. sharing with one or more friends

____ 28. sharing with one or more family members

Exercise 2: Look Ahead

Instructions: Think of a career that interests you—it does not have to be a definite career choice. Then list the writing tasks you think might be involved.

Collaborative Activity: Share Your Experiences and Expectations

Instructions: Meet with a group of three or four other students to discuss your answers to Exercises 1 and 2. Do you have similar expectations about college and professional writing? What can you conclude about the importance of writing to your future plans?

Collaborative Activity: Writing and Technology

Instructions: A list of kinds of technology related to writing appears below. Meet with a small group of other students to discuss this list. First, make sure the whole group understands each item. Use a dictionary or ask your instructor to explain anything unfamiliar to you. Use one check for any item a group member has used; use two checks for items you expect to use in the future. If you think of other types of writing technology, add them to the list.

____ 1. Typewriter

____ 2. Fax machine

____ 3. Photocopier

____ 4. Computerized word processing program

____ 5. Handheld spellchecker

____ 6. Electronic grammar checker

____ 7. Electronic mail

____ 8. CD/ROM dictionary

____ 9. CD/ROM thesaurus

____ 10. Computerized desktop publishing program

After you've discussed the entire list, talk about its significance. Is language technology important to group members now? Will it be important in the future?

YOU ARE ALREADY A WRITER

Chances are you've been writing throughout your school years. You may also have writing experience from the working world: a resumé, reports, business correspondence, memos. In college you will sharpen your skills, add others, and discover new ways to express yourself through language. At the beginning of this course you will write personal essays that draw upon the unique life story you bring to college and your special outlook on life. Then you will move on to academic writing tasks that challenge you to sort, organize, and develop ideas about the world around you.

Some students are so worried about grammar that they forget one of the main purposes of writing: producing something stimulating for others to read. Even before you enrolled in college, you observed, experienced, and analyzed the world around you. Writing lets you examine life and share your insights with your readers. For many students a course like this one is the first opportunity to make a powerful connection with others through writing.

Writing Activity: Describe Yourself

Instructions: Write a list of at least five positive words that describe the kind of person you usually are, such as loyal, energetic, fun-loving, truthful. Think of an experience you've had that illustrates how one of those words fits you. Write what you remember about the experience.

Collaborative Activity: Share Your Description

Instructions: Meet with two or three other students to read your word lists and talk about the experience you described. How has what you wrote helped you understand one another better?

Writing Activity: What Kind of Writer Are You?

Instructions: Four statements about writing from famous writers appear below. Choose one statement that reminds you of a past writing experience you've had. Write a few sentences describing the writing experience you remember.

"Writing is the hardest work in the world not involving heavy lifting." (Pete Hamill)

"Mastery of language affords remarkable power." (Fritz Fanon)

"If anyone's gonna write about me, I reckon it'll be me/myself." (Langston Hughes)

"Making a decision to write [is] like deciding to jump into a frozen lake." (Maya Angelou)

EXPLORING YOUR OWN RESOURCES

In addition to the campus services you learned about in the previous chapter, you have resources of your own that will help you develop as a writer: the reading, speaking, and thinking skills you brought with you to college.

Speaking

Ideas for writing often spring up in conversation. College friends may have grown up in a family very different from yours, or developed different political viewpoints, or traveled to places you've never heard of. Conversations about jobs, religion, romance, and other subjects may stimulate you to reexamine ideas you once took for granted.

Don't shy away from disagreements while you're exploring a topic in a discussion. Often a person with a different opinion can challenge you to think more deeply about your own position and discover stronger reasons to support it—or to convince you to modify your opinion. And there may be another unexpected benefit: You may hear yourself expressing an idea you'd never thought of before. So when you're discussing ideas in preparation for writing, have paper and a pen or pencil nearby. As new thoughts appear, write them down.

Collaborative Activity: Talk about Making College Friends

Instructions: On your own, write a list of suggestions that might be helpful to a student who has just arrived at your college and is eager to make friends. When you're finished with your list, meet with three or four other students to compare your ideas and combine them into a master list. If new ideas occur while you're talking, add them to the master list. When your list is finished, discuss the following questions with the other group members: How does your group's master list compare with each person's original list of suggestions? Did new ideas occur to any of you during the group discussion? How did the discussion feel to each of you? Did group members learn anything new from the activity?

Reading

Reading can stimulate you to discover new subjects and ideas to explore in writing. As you increase your knowledge through reading, the familiar complaint that there's "nothing to write about" becomes less of a problem. And reading can help you improve your writing style. You'll learn new words and absorb writing patterns that can enhance your own writing. Thoughtful reading teaches you how other writers organize and develop their ideas.

READING TO WRITE: WHY COLLEGE?

This book contains many "Reading to Write" activities that encourage you to mark up a reading selection and answer questions about it in preparation for writing. It's always a good idea to mark up a reading selection. For example, you might underline key ideas and circle new words that you want to look up in the dictionary. Writing questions and comments in the margins can stimulate you to think more deeply about what the author is saying and how it applies to your own knowledge and experience. Exclamation marks can indicate ideas that surprise you; question marks can indicate ideas that you find challenging or difficult.

Many students find it helpful to ask questions like these as they're reading: What does the passage mean to me? Did I agree or disagree with what I just read? Did the passage spark a thought, a memory, or an emotion? Reading "actively" in this way increases your comprehension and stimulates your thinking.

In the following example, a first-year student named Hattie responded to this excerpt from a newspaper column by Andy Rooney, an author and television commentator.

Why College?
adapted from a column by Andy Rooney

College ought to be for learning all the wonderful things in the world that have nothing to do with making money. You never have another four years like it in your life. There are books you'll never read if you don't read them in college.

There are subjects you'll never know anything about if you don't take the time to find out in those years. In college, everything about everything is laid out and available to you. It's like a buffet table with good food. You can take what you want. All you need is the appetite. There's always time later to learn how to make a living.

Here is how Hattie marked up Rooney's column:

College

by Andy Rooney

How can anyone spend 4 yrs in coll not thinking about money?!

Yeah! College life is special

College ought to be for learning all the wonderful things in the world that have nothing to do with making money. You never have another four years like it in your life. *Most students aren't rich.* There are books you'll never read if you don't read them in college. There are subjects you'll never know anything about if you don't take the time to find out in those years. In college,

True—there are lots of great opportunities on campus

everything about everything is laid out and available to you. It's like a buffet table with great food. You can take what you want. All you need is the appetite. There's always time later to learn how to make a living. *Well, some students can. I'm busy!*

Not for most people. Who's going to pay for school later for job training?

And here are the questions Hattie wrote down, along with her answers:

What does this passage mean to me?
College introduces students to wonderful new ideas and experiences.

Do I agree or disagree with Andy Rooney?
He's probably right as far as most students go. But earning money now and after graduation takes first place for me.

What memories, emotions, and ideas did this selection stimulate in me?
Sometimes I envy students who sit in the student center for long talks. I wish I could go to more of the things listed in the college newspaper. Last week there was a free jazz concert that sounded like fun. I've made only a few new friends. But I'm glad to earn money for college and to help Mom.

After Hattie had read and marked up the column, she responded to Rooney's ideas by "freewriting" about them—jotting down her thoughts freely, as they came to her, without stopping for changes or corrections.

Hattie's Freewriting

I disagree with Andy Rooney. He seems to think everyone is rich. I'm not. I have other people to think about, like Delonda. She needs more than high school, and it takes money to go to college, even a community college. Keshia should go, too. But she's too young to care yet.

It feels good to help Mom. I can read and have experiences later. I don't have to do everything now. Money comes first. Last month I paid the electric bill. I enjoy working at the mall, and my discount helps. So what if I miss out on some fun? I have my whole life ahead of me.

Freewriting Activity: Responding to What You Have Read

Instructions: Freewrite your own response to Andy Rooney's ideas. Don't try to produce a polished essay: Just write any thoughts and feelings that occur to you.

Hattie Prepares to Write

Here are the steps Hattie followed to develop her freewriting into a short college essay about her reasons for coming to college.

She began by rereading her freewriting and thinking about the main point she wanted to make (called a topic sentence). It took her several tries to write a topic sentence she liked. Here are two she rejected, along with her comments:

> I came to college because I want a better life.
> ("Better life" is too general. What I really want is a career that pays well.)
>
> My reason for coming to college is that I want to earn a good living.
> (Too wordy. The first eight words say very little.)

Hattie finally decided that this sentence accurately stated why she had come to college: *I came to college to increase my earning power.*

Next, Hattie listed the ideas and details she expected to include in her paragraph. To keep the list simple, she wrote in phrases rather than complete sentences. Instead of making a random list, Hattie grouped similar ideas and details together. She decided not to mention Andy Rooney, since her essay would be about her life rather than his ideas. Here is her list:

Hattie's List

What I'm missing by working hard:

> parties and fun
> new experiences
> having lots of friends
> things to remember

What I'm gaining:

> I can afford college
> I can help Mom
> setting an example for my two sisters
> working experience

Then Hattie planned her paragraph. She placed her topic sentence, along with some background information, at the beginning. Her groupings of ideas would follow. Here is her plan:

Hattie's Plan

I came to college to increase my earning power. (Topic sentence)

I know I'm missing some things. (First supporting idea)

I don't mind because now I can afford to go to college. (Second supporting idea)

I'm helping Mom, too. (Third supporting idea)

My sisters will have a good example to follow. (Fourth supporting idea)

I'm glad I'm taking college seriously. (Conclusion)

Hattie Drafts Her Paragraph

After Hattie had put her ideas in order, she felt comfortable writing her rough draft. She wrote quickly, reminding herself that she would make changes later. She knew that writers usually get a burst of confidence when they've completed their first draft because it's satisfying to see an essay taking shape.

Hattie's First Draft

I came to college to increase my earning power. I'm studying electronics and working part-time, not going to parties or having fun. I'm too busy to spend much time on those things. I've made some good friends but not lots of them, like some other people have. Working hard means I can go to college. I have a scholarship, but it doesn't pay for everything. Also I can help my family. Seven years ago my father left our family. He never sent us money. My mother works hard for me and my sisters. I help with the bills at home. I'm setting a good example at home. My sisters are very interested in what I'm doing. They're learning to take school seriously. I don't think college should be a vacation or a free ride. When I earn my degree, life will be better for all of us—me, my mom, Delonda, and Keshia.

Hattie rewrote her draft several times, marking it up each time with changes and additions. She made her ideas more clear and made her paragraphs longer. During a group activity in class, other students offered ideas for the essay. At their suggestion, Hattie added details—where she worked, her college major, and a few facts about her family. Here is Hattie's final draft, with her thesis statement (main point) underlined:

A Better Future

<u>I came to college to increase my earning power.</u> I'm studying electronics and working part-time at Radio Shack to make life better for myself and my family. Although I've made some good friends in college, I've been to only two parties since I started here. I know I'm missing out on some college experiences, but I don't mind. My hard work makes college possible for me. Seven years ago my father left our family per-

manently. He's never paid any child support. By working hard I can keep my schol-arship and cover my school expenses. I also want to help my mother, who has struggled to raise my sisters and me all these years. There's a little extra money left over every month that I put towards our electric bill. It feels good to know that I'm helping Mom. My sisters Delonda and Keshia will benefit from my example. Delonda is in junior high, and Keshia is in sixth grade. I've already seen improvement in their study habits. When I earn my A.S. degree, life will be better for all of us. Then I'll have more time for fun, friends, and new experiences. In the long run I don't think I'll have missed anything important at all.

Writing Activity: Respond to Hattie's Paragraph

Instructions: Write a short response to Hattie's ideas about college. After you have finished writing, reread your work. Can you find a main point the way Hattie did?

A Closer Look at Freewriting

Hattie used "freewriting"—spontaneous, ungraded writing—to prepare for her essay assign-ment. Freewriting "for your eyes only" is good preparation for a writing task because it liber-ates you from the restrictions of organization, punctuation, usage, and vocabulary rules. In most cases, no one will read your freewriting except you. It's an opportunity to explore ideas and feelings without worrying about someone else's opinion.

Freewriting offers you three important benefits. First, it is a comfortable way to start a writing project. You can approach a subject in any way that interests you, without worrying what readers will think. The blank piece of paper in front of you is less threatening when you can write freely. Second, freewriting develops fluency—ease and speed. If putting words on paper is usually slow and frustrating to you, freewriting can make you feel more comfort-able. Most important, freewriting helps you discover ideas and examples to write about. In-teresting ideas may appear unexpectedly, just as they often do in conversation.

You can learn more about freewriting from the following reading selection, by author and writing teacher Peter Elbow.

READING TO WRITE: LEARNING MORE ABOUT FREEWRITING

In the following selection, an experienced teacher of writing offers advice about freewriting. Before you begin reading Peter Elbow's ideas, answer the following questions.

1. Do you usually prepare for a writing task, or do you try to write a polished draft right away? Do you make corrections while you're writing, or do you go back later to fix what you've written?
2. College is going to introduce you to new ways of finding ideas for writing. Do you enjoy exploring new writing activities? Why or why not?
3. Have you ever tried freewriting before? If so, how did you feel about it?

After you've read the selection once, mark it up (see page 16) and write down any questions that come to mind as you read. Look up any new words in the dictionary. After you've read this selection, answer the questions that follow.

Vocabulary:

garbled   (adjective) mixed up, meaningless

coherent   (adjective) meaningful, understandable

compulsive   (adjective) repeated and automatic, not controlled

Freewriting
from Writing without Teachers *by Peter Elbow*

Don't stop for anything. Go quickly without rushing. Never stop to look back, to cross something out, to wonder how to spell something, to wonder what word or thought to use, or to think about what you are doing. If you can't think of a word or a spelling, just use a squiggle or else write, "I can't think of it." Just put down something.

The next time you write, notice how often you stop yourself from writing down something you were going to write down. Or else cross it out after it's written. "Naturally," you say, "it wasn't any good." But think for a moment about the occasions when you spoke well. Seldom was it because you first got the beginning just right. Usually it was a matter of a halting or even garbled beginning, but you kept going and your speech finally became coherent and even powerful. There is a lesson here for writing: trying to get the beginning just right is a formula for failure—and probably a secret tactic to make yourself give up writing. The habit of compulsive, premature editing doesn't just make writing hard. It also makes writing dead.

Responding to What You Have Read

1. What is freewriting?
2. According to Peter Elbow, how can freewriting help you develop as a writer?
3. How is freewriting similar to speech? How is it different?
4. Were you surprised that a writing teacher encourages students to write without stopping to make corrections? Why or why not?
5. What benefit of freewriting do you expect to be most helpful to you?

READING TO WRITE: FAMILY LIFE

The following reading selection will give you more practice with freewriting. This time the topic is family life. Maya Angelou (whose name was "Marguerite Johnson" as a child) is an African-American poet, singer, and actress. In this selection she describes an important railroad trip she took with her brother Bailey when both children were small. This selection offers many clues about her family members—mother, father, grandmother.

Before you begin reading, answer the following questions:

1. What does "family" mean to you? Write the names of the people you consider family members, along with their relationship to you. Did your list include anyone besides your parents, brothers, and sisters? Why or why not?

2. What people do you feel connected to outside of your family? Write down the names of both individuals and groups (such as a church congregation or club membership) who are important to you.

After you've read the selection once, mark it up, and write any questions that come to mind. A freewriting activity after the reading selection will help you explore your own memories, emotions, and ideas about family life.

Vocabulary:

calamitous	(adjective) disastrous
plied	(verb) offered vigorously
affluent	(adjective) wealthy
reneged	(verb) failed to keep a promise

The Train Trip
from I Know Why the Caged Bird Sings *by Maya Angelou*

When I was three and Bailey four, we had arrived in the musty little town, wearing tags on our wrists which instructed—"To Whom It May Concern"—that we were Marguerite and Bailey Johnson Jr. from Long Beach, California, en route to Stamps, Arkansas, c/o Mrs. Annie Henderson.

Our parents had decided to put an end to their calamitous marriage, and Father shipped us home to his mother. A porter had been charged with our welfare—he got off the train the next day in Arizona—and our tickets were pinned to my brother's inside coat pocket.

I don't remember much of the trip, but after we reached the segregated southern part of the journey, things must have looked up. Negro passengers, who always traveled with loaded lunch boxes, felt sorry for "the poor little motherless darlings" and plied us with cold fried chicken and potato salad.

Years later I discovered that the United States had been crossed thousands of times by frightened Black children traveling alone to their newly affluent parents in Northern cities, or back to grandmothers in Southern towns when the urban North reneged on its economic promises.

Responding to What You Have Read

1. Marguerite and Bailey were the only members of the Johnson family on the train. What did you learn about other members of the Johnson family? List as many facts as you can.

2. What emotions were experienced by the Johnson children? The other passengers? Other members of the Johnson family?

3. Although Marguerite and Bailey were traveling alone, they were connected in a variety of ways to many other people, some of whom they would never meet. List as many of those people and connections as you can.

4. What do you think Angelou was trying to accomplish in this selection?

Freewriting Activity: A Family Story

Instructions: Freewrite "for your eyes only" about your family. Which people do you think of when you use the word "family"? What conflicts separate your family members, and what bonds draw them together? How do the older members of your family relate to the younger generation? What interests, problems, values, and memories unite you? Dig into your memories of vacations, crises, and celebrations as you choose your story.

Paragraph Assignment: A Family Story

Instructions: Write a story about your family to share with other group members. Select a story that makes a point about your family—a special quality that you have. When you are finished, read your story aloud to other group members. Be sure to save it—you will be using it again in Chapter Three.

Writing Activity: Advise a Friend

Instructions: Imagine that next year a friend will enroll in your college. Write a letter explaining what to expect and offering suggestions about making friends on campus.

SUMMARY

1. Your writing skills can help you achieve success in college and your career.

2. Speaking and reading activities can help you develop your writing ability.

3. "Freewriting"—informal, spontaneous writing—is a good way to "warm up" and discover ideas for a writing task.

LOOKING AHEAD

In this chapter, you practiced using reading selections to discover material for writing. In Chapter Two, "Discovering Ideas," you'll experiment with other ways to find topics.

Discovering Ideas

Preview

Writing is "making meaning"—choosing experiences and ideas for writing, and determining their meaning for your readers. Discovery Activities help you choose an interesting topic and select ways to develop it. Discovery Activities include freewriting, clustering, drawing, talking, reading, and Thinking Tools.

MAKING MEANING

Ann E. Berthoff, an authority on writing, says that writing is "making meaning." When you write, you decide what *meaning* your experiences and ideas will have for your readers. For example, an embarrassing or scary incident from elementary school may seem funny now when you remember it. Or, on the contrary, some of the pranks your classmates laughed about then may seem tasteless or cruel now. A family story can inspire readers to imitate a special quality your family has, or it can persuade them to avoid problems your family has had to face. It's up to you to decide what meaning you want to communicate to your readers.

Writing Activity: Making Meaning

In this activity you will discover one or more meanings in a personal story.

Instructions: Freewrite for ten minutes about an experience you enjoy remembering. Include the thoughts and feelings you had at the time. Then write about the experience again as if you were someone else involved in the story (a parent, teacher, or friend, for example). Did the meaning of your experience change the second time?

Collaborative Activity: Sharing Meanings

Instructions: Meet with two or three other students to read and discuss what you wrote for the previous exercise. What meaning does each experience have for you? Is it the meaning the writer intended?

DISCOVERING IDEAS FOR WRITING

Before you can "make meaning" for your readers, you must find something to write about. In this chapter you will learn more about using reading as a springboard for writing. In addition, it will introduce you to a variety of other strategies for discovering ideas: journal writing, clustering, drawing, and Thinking Tools.

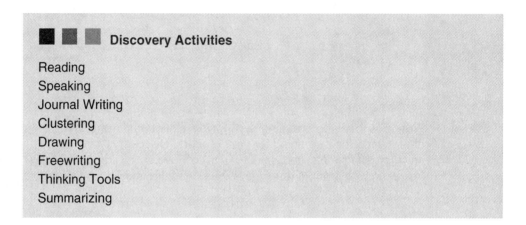

■ ■ ■ **Discovery Activities**

Reading
Speaking
Journal Writing
Clustering
Drawing
Freewriting
Thinking Tools
Summarizing

FINDING WRITING IDEAS IN YOUR UNCONSCIOUS MIND

Often students are surprised to learn that ideas for writing may already be hidden inside their minds, waiting to be discovered. Have you ever had a new thought come into your head in the middle of a conversation? Psychologists say such ideas aren't really new. Hidden mental processes in your mind, called the "unconscious," are always at work without your knowing it. While you're walking the dog or shopping for groceries, your "unconscious" may secretly explore a new idea or solving a problem. Many writers say that subjects for writing occur to them at just such moments; some even report waking in the morning with ideas for writing projects that developed during the night.

Many successful people—consultants, business leaders, artists, writers, psychologists—have learned to use the unconscious in a variety of ways to increase their creativity and meet new challenges. The strategies they use, which you will practice in this chapter, can help you discover ideas for writing.

Although you'll probably like some Discovery Activities more than others, don't settle into a habit of using only one or two. Successful writers routinely use two or more strategies to explore ideas: You'll benefit by following their example.

No matter what discovery strategy you're using, it's important to set aside enough time for your unconscious mind to work. Waiting until the last minute to begin writing blocks the unconscious and its flow of ideas. You can also help your unconscious by making sure that you understand any special requirements and have all the information you will need. Asking questions in class to clarify the assignment will make you feel more confident as you begin writing.

The Discovery Activities presented throughout this chapter will help you transfer new ideas from your unconscious into your conscious mind. It's important to be active when you're exploring ideas: Psychologists say that writing and talking are good ways to stimulate your unconscious to produce ideas. And drawing works especially well for many students because it adds another dimension to writing. Consider sketching, drawing, cartooning, or doodling when you're looking for writing ideas.

Above all, don't judge the ideas you discover, even if you don't like them. Judgments stop the movement of ideas, as you've probably noticed when you've been criticized during a conversation. If you're writing, keep your pen or pencil moving, even if you just write "I can't think of anything at the moment." The more you explore and experiment, the more satisfied you're likely to be.

■ ■ ■ Where Does Writing Come From?

Writing teacher Max J. Herzberg explains, "Possibly the strangest phenomenon in the process of writing is the fashion in which the writing creates itself, so to speak." According to Herzberg, many writers do much of their thinking and planning with the aid of a piece of paper or a computer screen: "The act of writing begets writing."

Set aside ample time for freewriting and other Discovery Activities. New ideas often appear as your pen or pencil moves across the essay. If you're sitting at a computer, the machine's hum may start words and ideas to flow. Your job is to be there, ready to write, so that the process can begin.

READING TO WRITE: THE HIDDEN WORKINGS OF YOUR MIND

This selection is from *The Hidden Persuaders,* a book about the psychology of advertising. Author Vance Packard describes an advertising study that reveals the workings of the unconscious mind. As before, mark up this reading selection, and write down any questions that come to mind.

Thinking about Colors
from The Hidden Persuaders *by Vance Packard*

The Color Research Institute gave consumers three different boxes filled with detergent. It requested that they try them all out for a few weeks and then report which was the best for delicate clothing. The consumers were given the impression that they had been given three different types of detergent. Actually only the boxes were different; the detergents inside were identical.

In their reports, the consumers stated that the detergent in the brilliant yellow box was too strong; it even allegedly ruined their clothes in some cases. As for the detergent in the predominantly blue box, they complained in many cases that it left their clothes dirty looking. The third box, which contained what the Institute felt was an ideal balance of colors in the package design, overwhelmingly received favorable responses. The consumers used such words as "fine" and "wonderful" in describing the effect the detergent in that box had on their clothes.

Responding to What You Have Read

1. Why did the color of the packaging have such a powerful effect on the consumers in the study?
2. What did you learn from this reading about the workings of the unconscious?

Freewriting Activity: A Special Color

Instructions: Freewrite about a time when a color had a special meaning for you. Possibilities include a gift, a place, an article of clothing, a favorite possession, a journey, or a crisis.

WRITING IN A JOURNAL

Journal writing is an expanded form of freewriting "for your eyes only" without attempting to polish your ideas or grammar. A journal is a personal notebook set aside for regular freewriting—perhaps every day, several times a week, or weekly. Regular journal writing is an excellent discovery activity that puts you in touch with the hidden workings of your mind.

Many writers develop the habit of spending a few minutes every day writing informally about something they've observed and thought about: The journal gives them the freedom to let ideas and feelings flow. When a writer needs a topic for a writing project, the journal provides a storehouse of ideas.

You'll get the maximum benefit from journal writing if you date each entry and go back from time to time to reread what you've written. You'll have all your ideas in one convenient place, and the dates make them more interesting as time passes and you review what you have written. Keeping a journal also helps you measure your progress as a writer, for you will probably notice improvements when you reread your entries later: a larger vocabulary, greater ease in writing, and—most important—the discovery of more interesting ideas and experiences.

Here are four selections from students' journals. As you read what each student wrote, ask yourself how you would have responded to the situations they observed. Try writing your own response to any situations you find particularly interesting. How are your responses similar—or different?

Students' Journal Entries

1. *The situation:*
    A new family with two young boys moved into a student's neighborhood. The student drove past the house one Saturday morning and saw the two boys pulling weeds from the flowerbeds in front of the house. When she drove by again an hour later, the boys were still working. She didn't see any adults.

What she wrote:
I can't believe the boys are working so hard without an adult making them do it. I wonder what this family is like. Are the boys getting paid? Were they threatened? Did the parents bring up the boys to believe in cooperation? I wonder if I could be that kind of parent. It really appeals to me. My parents aren't like that. My father especially really thinks kids should listen to adults because adults are in charge.

2. *The situation:*
A student on a track scholarship went to the college store to buy lab supplies for the biology course he was taking. He noticed the large number of snack foods sold there—many high in sugar and fat.

What he wrote:
Why does the store tempt us with all that junk food? I couldn't train if I ate that stuff every day. I wonder if the student government could get the store to stock better snacks. Maybe a lot of students would appreciate the change. Maybe not.

3. *The situation:*
An exchange student came to the United States from a Mexican town where his family had lived for several generations. Grandparents, aunts, uncles, and cousins lived close by. He became friendly with several American families that lived far away from their relatives.

What he wrote:
I miss my family desperately. I can't imagine living hundreds of miles away from them year after year. They're a part of me. My friends are wonderful, but I'm not as close them as to my family. When I have a problem, I can trust family more than friends. And I want my family to celebrate with me when good things happen.

4. *The situation:*
A student felt that his mother's college courses were disrupting his life; he missed having her around to cook and run errands for him. After he wrote several journal entries about the problem, his feelings changed.

What he wrote:
I was mad today when I had to do a load of clothes and fix my own dinner in the microwave. But now I feel better. I went to the Athletic Stop before Mom came home. I didn't have to tell her where I was going. She hasn't bugged me about my room lately!

Collaborative Activity: The Benefits of Journal Writing

Instructions: Meet with a small group of students to discuss the journal entries you've just read. How would you have responded to the situations they wrote about in their journals? If you wish, share one or more of the journal entries you wrote. Write down any writing topics you and your group members develop during your discussion.

From Journal to Paragraph

The final journal entry you just read, by a student named Jeff, is a good example of "making meaning" through writing. Because Jeff allowed himself to write freely, he discovered new ideas about his mother's return to school.

Jeff was unhappy at first when his mother enrolled in college. Her return to school meant "inconvenience." He had to do the laundry, shopping, and cooking that she used to do for him. But soon these changes had a new "meaning": freedom. His relationship with his mother improved, and he was enjoying more independence and privacy. After he explored his feelings in his journal, he wrote an effective paragraph that you'll read a little later on. Like Jeff, you too may discover new "meanings" within your experiences and memories when you experiment with freewriting and other planning activities. Here is Jeff's paragraph:

Back to School

I'm glad Mom decided to sign up for college. Although I expected to hate having her on campus, I'm surprised how well it's working out. The first shock is that we enjoy each other much more now. She loves talking about the new things she's learning, and she's genuinely interested in my ideas. Last night she, my dad, and I spent two hours talking about psychology. I've also become more independent since Mom enrolled in college. She doesn't keep the household on a regular schedule anymore, so I have more control of my time. It feels good to eat when I want to and run errands at my convenience. Last night I ate at the food court at the mall, and I didn't have to call first to tell Mom that I wouldn't be home for dinner. The best change is that Mom is giving me more privacy. Because I'm an only child, she always used to watch me closely. Now that she's busy with college, she's not so interested in my personal problems and social life. I've noticed that she's not asking as many questions about my college friends as she did when I was in high school. At last I'm beginning to feel like an adult.

Discovery Activity 1: Write Journal Entries

Instructions: Every day for the next week, freewrite about the topic listed below. After each entry, list any related writing topics that come to your mind. Don't be concerned about spelling, punctuation, and usage.

Your Journal

Day 1
Topic: Someone (a student, instructor, or staff member) you've met at college who intrigues you

Possible writing topics:

Day 2
Topic: A favorite place you've discovered on campus

Possible writing topics:

Day 3
Topic: A goal you're working on that's important to you

Possible writing topics:

Day 4
Topic: Something you've been wondering about lately

Possible writing topics:

Day 5
Topic: Behavior you've seen recently that you admire

Possible writing topics:

Day 6
Topic: Behavior you've seen recently that you dislike

Possible writing topics:

Day 7
Topic: An issue that's important to your family right now

Possible writing topics:

Collaborative Activity: Share from Your Journal

Instructions: Meet with a small group of other students to discuss any entries you wish to share. During your discussion, new writing topics may come to mind. Write them down, and consider using them in future journal entries and writing assignments.

Keeping a Journal

If you enjoyed "making meaning" through writing journal entries on the previous pages, consider continuing the practice. Set aside a notebook for this purpose, and make a habit of writing daily, if possible, about your thoughts, observations, and experiences. Be sure to date each entry. When you reread your entries later on, add and date any additional ideas and comments that come to mind.

CLUSTERING

Many students like the clustering technique because it doesn't require writing complete sentences. A *cluster* is a series of lines and circles that lead you from one idea to another. To make a cluster, write your topic in the middle of a piece of paper, and draw a circle around it. Then draw another circle close by and connect it with a short line. Inside the circle, write a word or phrase related to the previous one. As you think of other ideas, draw more lines and circles. Clustering is particularly useful when you're collaborating with others, since it's easy for everyone to contribute ideas: You simply keep adding lines and circles.

Patricia, a first-year college student, used clustering to discover writing ideas about a problem she'd noticed in some of her friends. The first person who came to mind was Patricia's friend Linda, who made excuses for not mastering the math skills required in her college program. Patricia wrote LINDA in a circle in the middle of a blank sheet of paper. Then she drew short lines around the circle, added other ideas, and circled them. Patricia continued the process until she ran out of ideas. Here is the result:

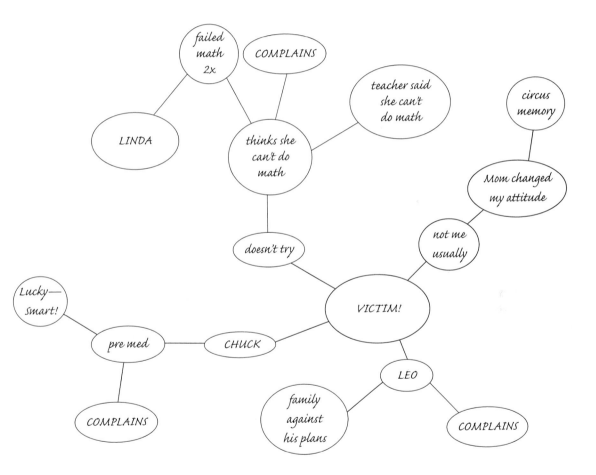

In Chapter Six you will see how Patricia developed the ideas in her cluster into a college essay.

Exercise 1: Make Clusters

Instructions: Three partly finished clusters appear below. Complete each one by adding ideas and details. Be as free as you wish.

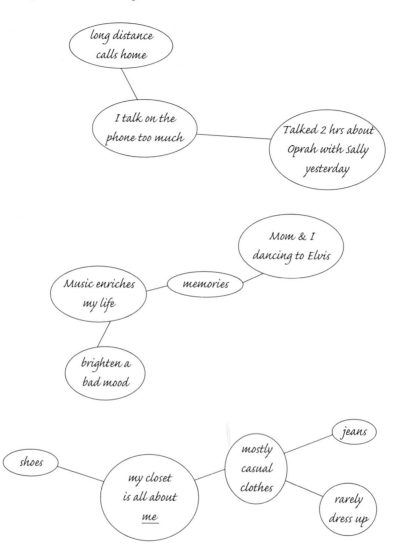

Discovery Activity 2: Clustering

Instructions: Reread the possible writing topics you listed after the journal entries on pages 28–30. Choose three that you find especially interesting, and make a cluster for each.

DRAWING

Drawing is another popular discovery activity with students who prefer pictures to words. You don't need artistic ability to discover ideas through drawing: Just let your imagination flow without judging the results. (If you've had artistic training, set aside your skills and focus on creativity during this activity.) Draw stick figures to represent people you know; make a cartoon about a current problem in your life, or sketch a place that's important to you. Moving a pencil, crayon, or paintbrush across a piece of paper may help you get in touch with new ideas. Here's a sketch one student drew when she felt lonely at college:

I'm lost and lonely.
How will I ever make
friends here? Everybody
else fits right in except
me.

C'mon! Talk to us!
We're always glad
to make new friends.

Discovery Activity 3: Make a Sketch

Instructions: Look again at the topics you listed with your journal entries (pages 28–30). Choose one topic (it can be one you chose earlier or a different one). Get out a blank sheet of paper and draw a simple picture or cartoon about your subject. In the space below, freewrite about any ideas that occurred to you while you were drawing:

Your drawing:

Discovery Activity 4: Other Ways to Discover Ideas

In the previous chapter you practiced freewriting, brainstorming, and talking in order to discover ideas for writing. In this activity you will choose one of these familiar activities and try it again.

Instructions: Look again at the results of Discovery Activity 2 (page 32) and Discovery Activity 3 (above). Using one of the topics you chose for these activities, try freewriting, brainstorming, or talking to discover more ideas about it.

Collaborative Activity: Talk about Discovery

Instructions: Meet with a small group of other students to compare the results of your Discovery Activities. Which activities did you like best? Why? How did the activities help you "make meaning" of experiences you've had? Take notes on your discussion in the space below.

Writing Assignment: From Discovery to College Paragraph

Instructions: Develop the ideas from one of the Discovery Activities you've done (journal writing, clustering, or drawing) into a paragraph. Share your final draft with a group of other students; consider making any changes they suggest.

FINDING TOPICS THROUGH READING

In Chapter One you saw that Hattie used one of Andy Rooney's columns to spark ideas for writing. Thoughtful reading can often help you discover ideas and "make meaning" from them. A checklist of questions can stimulate additional ideas to write about. The box below contains a list many students find helpful:

■ ■ ■ **Reading Checklist**

1. What was the author's purpose?
2. Did the author successfully fulfill this purpose? Why or why not?
3. Do I agree or disagree with the author? Why?
4. Did anything in this reading match my experiences—or contrast with what I've experienced?
5. Did this reading prompt me to change my thinking in any way?
6. If I could talk with the author, what would I say?
7. Does the reading stimulate me to change my thinking in some way?

In the following "Reading to Write" activity, you'll use a similar checklist to discover ideas for writing. You're about to read about an incident in the life of entertainer and educator Bill Cosby. After reading and marking up the selection (as Hattie did in Chapter One), write any questions that came to mind. You may find yourself asking two types of questions—those about your own attitude and beliefs, and those requiring research. If you want more information about Cosby's night-club career or involvement with civil rights, consider visiting the library. Then answer the questions that follow the selection. Your responses will help you discover ideas for writing.

READING TO WRITE: A MOMENTOUS EVENT

Author Ronald L. Smith is describing the impact of a momentous event—the death of Dr. Martin Luther King, Jr.—on one person, Bill Cosby. When you're finished reading, write down any questions that came to your mind, and answer the questions in the Reading Checklist that follows.

Aftermath of a Murder
from Cosby by Ronald L. Smith

At a concert in Kansas on April 4, 1968, Cosby received the news that the Reverend Martin Luther King, Jr., had been shot. It was hell night all over the country—a night of fear, anger, tension, and grief. Some people were burning inside, a raging fire of pain or a flickering candle of sorrow.

Cosby's own feeling of depression began to envelop him. He'd done his first show, not yet knowing more than the sketchy rumors. Now, facing the late show, he had heard the worst. King was dead.

Bill sat in the dressing room, weary from phone conversations with a tearful Harry Belafonte, confused and depressed, as tense as all of America, wondering what would happen next.

The crowds were filing in. Time for the show. He could hear the buzz out front. Then he came out onstage and the spotlights hit him. He began to do the show, shutting off the tragedy. But it wasn't working; he couldn't concentrate. He couldn't stand there in front of that small group of people when so many millions were getting the news that was coming fast and furious over the radio.

Cosby faltered. He told his fans that he couldn't continue. The audience was stunned.

Slowly, they began to applaud. The applause reached a crescendo, swelling louder, until it seemed they couldn't applaud enough. The audience stood as one, standing and applauding.

And they let Cos go, audience and performer sharing a moment of understanding and pain, and wondering what the rest of the nation would do with their own sense of loss.

READING CHECKLIST

1. What was author Ronald L. Smith's purpose when he wrote about this incident?
2. Do you think Smith successfully fulfilled this purpose? Why or why not?
3. Did anything in this reading match your experiences—or contrast with something you've experienced?

4. Did this reading prompt you to change your thinking in any way?

5. If you could talk with Cosby, what would you say? What questions might you ask?

6. Does the reading start you thinking about a particular idea or experience?

Collaborative Activity: Share Your Questions

Instructions: Meet with a small group of students to share the questions you wrote about the *Cosby* selection and your answers to the Reading Checklist. Take notes during your discussion. What new ideas did you hear? What thoughts occurred to you while you were talking and listening? Make a list of possible writing topics related to your questions, answers, and discussion.

Writing Activities: Respond to the Cosby Story

Instructions: Complete one of the following activities.

1. Imagine you were at the nightclub in Kansas the night Dr. King died. Write a paragraph as if it were going to appear in your campus newspaper, describing what you might have experienced there. Include your personal thoughts and feelings as well as what you would have seen on stage.

2. Talk to a person who vividly remembers Dr. King or one or more important events from the Civil Rights movement; take notes during your conversation. Develop the conversation into a paragraph as if it were going to appear in your campus newspaper.

3. Develop one of the topics you listed in the Collaborative Activity above into a paragraph.

Writing Assignment: Recall an Important Event

Instructions: Freewrite for ten minutes about an important event you remember. (The list that follows may help you choose a topic.) Read your freewriting and decide one important point you want to make about the event. Did you learn something important? Draw closer to family or friends? Change your attitude about an important issue? Begin a new relationship? Develop that point into a paragraph.

Suggested Topics

Family events: birth, adoption, death, marriage, divorce, vacation, holiday

School events: graduation, an award, performance, athletic event, classroom memory, celebration, contest

Job: getting hired, fired, or promoted; quitting, learning something new, a pleasant or unpleasant task

Weather: a hurricane, snowstorm, flood

Political events: an election, political demonstration, speech, convention, meeting

Friendship: a party, argument, trip, special day

THINKING AND WRITING

Writing and thinking naturally occur together. If you can discover interesting ideas for a writing task, readers are likely to enjoy and appreciate what you have written. Activities that sharpen your thinking skills can make you a more effective writer.

READING TO WRITE: THE IMPORTANCE OF THINKING

In this selection, Canadian author Stephen Leacock offers some ideas about the connection between writing and thinking. Mark up this selection with lines, arrows, stars, question marks, or other markings. Write down any questions that came to mind while you were reading. When you have finished reading, complete the activities that follow.

> *Vocabulary:*
> requisite   (adjective) required, necessary
> acquired   (verb) learned, developed

Writing and Thinking
from How to Write *by Stephen Leacock*

Writing is essentially thinking, or at least involves thinking as its first requisite. All people can think, or at least they think they think. But few people can say what they think, that is, say it with sufficient power of language to convey it to the full. But there are some people whose thoughts are so interesting that other people are glad to hear them, or to read them. Yet even these people must learn the use of language adequate to convey their thoughts; people may sputter and gurgle in a highly interesting way, but without the full equipment of acquired language their sputters won't carry far.

Responding to What You Have Read

1. List the points Leacock was making. Then write *yes* in front of each point you agree with and *no* for those you disagree with. If you're not sure, write a question mark.
2. Do you think it is possible to think *without* language skills? Give examples (stories if possible) to make your point.
3. Think of someone you know whose thoughts are usually interesting. Write a paragraph describing the person and the kind of thoughts he or she talks about.

Collaborative Activity: Talk about Thinking and Writing

Instructions: Meet with a small group of students to discuss this statement from Leacock's reading selection: "But there are some people whose thoughts are so interesting that other people are glad to hear them, or to read them." What ideas have you heard recently that you'd like to read or hear more about? What ideas of your own would you like to share with others? Take notes on your discussion.

Writing Activity: Explore an Idea

Instructions: Choose one of the incomplete sentences below. Fill in the blank, and then write several more sentences about the idea you've chosen.

1. I've always wondered _____

   _____ .

2. An idea that intrigues me is _____

   _____ .

3. A dangerous idea I've heard recently is_____

   _____ .

4. An idea I've found useful is_____

   _____ .

THINKING TOOLS

Thinking Tools are mental tasks that help you look at information, ideas, and experiences in a different way. Often they are useful when you're trying to discover and develop ideas to write about. In this chapter you'll experiment with eight Thinking Tools for discovering ideas. Here are the first six:

1. *Take something away.* To get a fresh perspective on your everyday life, imagine what would happen if something or someone familiar were absent: your roommate, telephone, car. What if you didn't live on campus? Suppose you didn't have a part-time job, an athletic scholarship, a class schedule. How would your life be different? Don't be afraid to play with an apparently impossible idea. For years people assumed that heating elements were required for cooking, cash or checks were needed for shopping, and paper was essential to writing. Microwave ovens, ATM cards, and computers could not be invented until creative people imagined new possibilities. Using your imagination in this way can help you discover new ideas for writing.

2. *Add something more.* The addition can be a person, fact, idea, or thing. Imagine what your life would be like if you won the lottery, had a roommate, or owned a business. One student freewrote about what his life would be like if he were married. When he reread his freewriting, he noticed that the ideas *privacy* and *freedom* appeared again and again. The result was a paper not about marriage, but about how much he enjoyed his single lifestyle.

3. *Put yourself into a situation you've read or heard about.* Pretend you're a member of Bill Cosby's audience at the nightclub or in another situation you've read or heard about. The next time a friend tells you about an event in his or her life, put yourself into the story to see if new ideas occur to you.

4. *Change one factor.* Think for a moment about Jeff, the student whose mother enrolled in college at the same time he did. How might his journal entry have been different if it had been his *father*, rather than his mother, who enrolled in college? Changing a factor in a remembered story can give you a new perspective on a person, group, institution, or situation.

5. *Focus your attention on anything that surprises you.* Since civil rights has not been a central issue in Bill Cosby's career, you might wonder why Dr. King's death was so important to him. A trip to the library to read more about Cosby—or Dr. King—could help you learn more. Hattie could have written an interesting paragraph about details of college life she hadn't anticipated. Looking for the unexpected in your own stories—and those told by friends and family members—can trigger ideas for writing.

6. *Ask what's missing.* The Cosby story didn't mention what happened to the audience that had paid to come to his second show. Did they receive a refund? If so, who supplied the money? Did the night club manager agree to let Cosby leave? Andy Rooney, in the reading selection in Chapter One, didn't mention students with financial responsibilities. Sometimes the untold part of a story can lead you to an excellent subject for writing. After reading the Cosby story, you might write a paper about an on-the-job struggle with a boss who disagreed with your beliefs about an important issue.

Thinking Activity: Use the Thinking Tools

Instructions: Topics related to the first six Thinking Tools are listed below. Choose three of these suggested topics, and use freewriting, clustering, or drawing to explore them.

1. Take something away.
   Suggestion: Imagine what your life would be like if one element were taken away—a possession, a task, a person.

2. Add something more.
   Suggestion: Imagine how your life would be different if something were added, such as a pet, car, job, or scholarship.

3. Put yourself into a situation you've read or heard about.
   Suggestion: Imagine that you're part of a movie, book, or TV show that's familiar to you—or part of a current event that's been in the news.

4. Change one factor.
   Suggestion: Change one fact about yourself, such as your age, nationality, ethnic group, sex, or financial status. Imagine how your life would be different.

5. Focus your attention on something that surprises you.
   Suggestion: Describe what surprised you most when you graduated from high school, landed your first job, or enrolled in college.

6. Ask what's missing.

Suggestion: Think about advice or information you were given about college, marriage, parenthood, working, or some other aspect of life. What was left out that you wish you had been told?

From Thinking Tools to Writing

One student, Winston, used the "take something away" thinking tool to freewrite about life without his favorite fast food. Then he revised his freewriting to produce the following paragraph.

Adios, Amigo

I love having a twenty-four-hour Taco Bell only two blocks from my apartment. It makes mealtime fun and easy and saves me a lot of work. But last week I decided to try to get a different perspective on Taco Bell. Just to see what would happen, I decided not to eat there for seven days. What an eye-opener! I saved twenty dollars in less than a week. At this rate, I could cut way back on my part-time job. Although I hate to cook, there are plenty of simple, cheaper things I could eat in my apartment. Frozen dinners go on sale all the time. I could eat fruit and salads. I'd probably be healthier if I didn't go to Taco Bell so much. I also noticed I saved a lot of time. Driving to Taco Bell, standing in line, eating, and driving home take up more time than I thought. Those trips break up my study time, too. If I just went to the kitchen to eat, I'd get more studying done. I'm definitely going to cut back on my trips South of the Border.

Writing Assignment: Think and Write

Instructions: Develop one of the Discovery Activities you just completed into a paragraph. Work through all the steps of the writing process as you prepare your paragraph. Read your final draft to a group of students, and consider making additional revisions based on their suggestions.

Another Thinking Tool: "Journalist's Questions"

"Journalist's questions" are another thinking tool many writers find useful. Journalists are men and women who write about news for newspapers, magazines, radio, and television. To make sure their notes are organized and complete, they ask journalist's questions: Who? What? When? Why? Where? By asking themselves *who* is involved in a news story, *what* happened, *when*, and so on, journalists ensure that they don't overlook anything important.

The same questions can help you explore an event thoroughly, perhaps discovering something you hadn't noticed before. Often the result will be ideas and details you can include in your writing.

The procedure is simple. Write the subject you're going to explore at the top of a piece of paper. List the five words (who, what, when, where, why) along the left side, leaving large spaces between them. Put a question mark after each word. Now answer each "question" by writing words, phrases, or sentences that come to mind. If you run out of space, keep writing on the back or on another piece of paper. Don't try to be tidy or logical: Let your ideas flow.

The following worksheet was done by a student named Gail.

Who, What, When, Where, Why

Your topic: I loved working as a vet's assistant

Who? Me, Kala (receptionist), Peg (groomer), Andy (technician), Dr. Rogers, cats, dogs, exotic birds, iguanas, snakes, clients who love their pets

What? Cleaning cages, exercising animals, playing with them, helping Dr. Rogers, talking to clients, giving medicine, running errands

When? Last summer, five days a week, some weekend hours to take care of animals boarding or treated there

Where? Usually in the "back"—cages, surgery, treatment room. Also cleaned runs and exercise space outside.

Why? Money for college, work experience, love animals, Dr. Rogers an old friend—takes care of my cat Peachy and dog Bruno

Discovery Activity 6: Ask the "Journalist's Questions"

Instructions: Look again at the list of topics from your journal entries (pages 28–30). Choose a topic (it can be one you chose earlier, or a different one). Use the journalist's questions to generate ideas about the topic you've chosen.

WHO, WHAT, WHEN, WHERE, WHY

Your topic:

Who?

What?

When?

Where?

Why?

Writing Assignment: Who, What, When, Where, Why?

Instructions: Freewrite about the topic you explored with the journalist's questions. Then develop your freewriting into a paragraph. Share your final draft with a group of other students, and consider making additional revisions based on their suggestions.

The Seventh Thinking Tool: Plus, Minus, Interesting

Using the words "plus, minus, interesting" to develop lists of ideas is another helpful thinking tool. According to thinking expert Edward de Bono, these three words often stimulate new ideas that can be used in writing. An added benefit is that the "plus, minus, interesting" thinking tool can be used for both kinds of writing you'll be doing in college—personal and issue-centered. Sometimes, like Hattie, Jeff, and Patricia, you'll be writing about ideas related to your everyday life—college, family, friendship, work, church, vacations, and the like. At other times you'll be assigned to write about events and issues outside yourself, from such areas as history, current events, literature, and the sciences.

A student named José was assigned to write about his life as a college student. He decided to use the "plus, minus, interesting" strategy to explore a decision he was facing at the time: whether to keep his car or sell it and depend on public transportation.

To make his "plus, minus, interesting" sheet, José wrote his subject—owning the car—on top of a piece of paper. Then he put the three headings underneath—plus, minus, and interesting. They became the column headings for his three lists.

José listed positive features about owning the car in the "plus" column and negative features in the "minus" column. Everything else that came to mind was listed in the "interesting" column. Items in this list were useful later on, when he needed details about his car to make his writing more lively and personal. Here's what José's "plus, minus, interesting" sheet looked like:

Jose's "Plus, Minus, Interesting" Sheet

+	−	Interesting
—convenient— shopping, errands	—I don't plan shopping trips	—I can ask Glen to show me how to change the oil myself
—you can't take a date on a bus	—driving at night can be dangerous— 2 near accidents	—Amy might enjoy a bus ride to zoo or park— money saved can pay for a good restaurant meal
—good gas mileage	—cost of repairs, insurance	

After José finished this "plus, minus, interesting" sheet, he worked the ideas into this paragraph.

Car Convenience

Last year my parents helped me buy a used Toyota from a neighbor. I paid my share by working various jobs during the school year and summer vacation. I brought my Toyota to college with me, and it makes my life better. Still, I've decided to make some changes in my driving habits. I realize I have to cut back on the trips I make. Even though my car gets good mileage, I fill the gas tank too often. Yesterday I made two trips to the drug store because I forgot to pick up razor blades the first time. I'm also going to look for some ways to have fun that don't involve driving. Twice since college started, I've been in near-accidents with drunk drivers. Some dates could be an afternoon at the zoo, Frisbee in the park, or a free concert at the band shell downtown. They're only a few minutes away by bus, and I don't think Amy would mind. We could go out to dinner once in a while with the money saved. But I don't want to give up the car entirely. Driving relaxes me, and I don't want to start every date with a bus trip. Sometimes I absolutely have to make a quick trip to the store, and my friends appreciate it when I offer them a ride. Although I'm going to have to work next summer to pay for insurance and other expenses, having the car on campus is well worth it.

Discovering Ideas about a Current Issue

José again used the "plus, minus, interesting" thinking tool for a very different assignment: a paragraph about a current issue. He selected affirmative action as his topic, did some reading in the college library, and prepared a "plus, minus, interesting" sheet:

Affirmative Action: Plus, Minus, Interesting

+	−	Interesting
Helps correct injustices from the past	Quota hiring is unfair to majority candidates	Gen. Colin Powell was promoted through a military affirmative action program
Overcomes advantages of private schools, family wealth and personal contacts—makes equal playing field for hiring	Increases tension between mainstream citizens and minorities	Some minorities don't like ethnic labels
Diversity can be good for business and government	Possible hiring of unqualified candidates	"Equal opportunity" is different from preferences and quotas

Here is José's paragraph about affirmative action:

Opening the Door

If America is to continue to be a great country, it must be run on merit. People must be hired on the basis of their skills, knowledge, and experience. Hiring preferences and quotas are wrong. But there's still a place for affirmative action. In many cases, several qualified people have applied for a job. The person from a wealthy family may have an advantage because of private schooling, travel, and opportunities to meet influential people through relatives. Other applicants, just as qualified, may be overlooked because they grew up in more ordinary circumstances. They may have been the first in their families to graduate from college. Employers need to consider the benefits of hiring a diverse group of employees. "Equal opportunity" is tough in a society like ours, with very rich and very poor citizens. It's simple fairness to give every qualified person a chance at a job.

Collaborative Activity: Plus, Minus, Interesting

Instructions: The "plus, minus, interesting" thinking tool works especially well when a group is contributing ideas. Meet with a small group of other students and choose either an aspect of college life or a current issue to evaluate. The list below may be helpful in choosing a topic; feel free to choose another one if you wish. Then prepare a "plus, minus, interesting" sheet, as José did.

College life:

- Working while attending college
- Dorm life
- Living at home or with a roommate
- A belief or value
- Stress
- Freedom
- Connecting or breaking up with another person
- An authority figure in your life
- Your support system or lack of one

Current issues:

- Needle exchanges
- Adoption
- The drinking age
- Home schooling
- Mandatory AIDS testing
- Love on the Internet

- Law enforcement and youth
- Role models in the media

Writing Activity: Evaluate an Idea

Instructions: Develop the ideas from the previous activity into a paragraph. When you've finished, share what you've written with other group members.

SUMMARY

1. As a writer, it is up to you to decide what your ideas and experiences will *mean* to your readers.
2. Ideas for writing may be hidden in your unconscious mind. Being active by writing, drawing, reading, and talking can help you discover writing ideas hidden in your unconscious.
3. You should try a variety of Discovery Activities as you tackle your writing assignments in college.
4. Talking, clustering, and drawing can help you discover ideas without lengthy writing.
5. "Thinking Tools" can help you discover fresh ideas in familiar topics, memories, and experiences.

LOOKING AHEAD

Discovering ideas is an early step in the writing process. After you've begun to generate ideas for a writing task, you can start planning what you will write and how you will organize it. In Chapter Three, "Writing by Steps," you will learn more about the writing process.

CHAPTER THREE

Writing by Steps

Preview

Effective writers work in several steps, rather than trying to produce good writing all at once. It's important to know these five keys to successful writing:

a) Writing is a process.
b) Effective writing makes a point and develops it with related ideas and examples.
c) Good writing is the result of knowledge and practice.
d) Successful writers make a writing plan for each task.
e) Most successful writers share their work.

In this chapter you will follow the writing process as you write a college paragraph and an essay. You will practice using details and examples to "make meaning" for your readers.

Introducing the Writing Process

Many students mistakenly believe good writing should happen all at once. Because they expect instant success, they give up too quickly when a writing task doesn't seem to be going well for them. What they may not realize is that most writers have to struggle in the early stages of composing a piece of writing. Hattie, Jeff, and José—the students whose work you've already seen—allowed their writing to develop one step at a time. In this chapter you'll learn more about the writing process, and you'll be introduced to other keys to successful writing.

FIVE KEYS TO EFFECTIVE WRITING

1. *Writing is a process.* Good writing doesn't happen all at once. Successful writers work through several steps: discovering ideas, planning, writing one or more drafts, and fine-tuning what they've written. If you're patient enough to tackle a writing project one step at a time, you're likely to be pleased with the final results.

2. *Effective writing "makes meaning."* You'll feel confident if you remind yourself that your basic goal is simply to communicate an idea to your readers. Subjects to write about are all around you—and inside your head and heart as well.

3. *Good writing is the result of knowledge and practice.* You don't need talent or inspiration to write effectively. Like most subjects, writing is easier for some people than for others. But with practice and professional instruction, anyone can learn how to write well.

4. *Successful writers make a writing plan for each task.* Thoughtful planning makes your writing more effective and often saves time later on. It's helpful to ask questions like these before you start drafting an essay:

   What am I going to write about? (your topic)

   How will I tackle this writing task? (your plan)

   Who will read it? (your audience)

   What am I trying to accomplish? (your purpose)

5. *Most successful writers share their work.* Friends, family members, and other writers can encourage you by pointing out the best features of your writing. Feedback is important for another reason as well: Your readers can help you recognize any weak spots in your writing—usage errors and unclear ideas, for example. Even famous writers depend upon editors to give them feedback about their writing. Besides developing your writing skills, group sharing teaches cooperative strategies that you'll find useful again later on, in your career.

How to Work with a Writing Group

1. Have each paper read aloud without interruption. Listen attentively while group members are reading their essays.

2. When each student is finished reading, appreciate the essay: Describe any features you especially liked. Positive feedback helps writers develop confidence and focus on the strengths they've already developed.

3. Next, ask questions and share experiences. Make sure you understand what the writer was trying to say. Ask the writer to explain anything that is unclear. If the essay you just heard reminds you of an experience of your own, briefly share it with the group. Remember that writing is about life: The purpose of writing is to help people connect with one another through ideas and experiences.

4. Wait until everyone has had a chance to appreciate the essay before you suggest changes and corrections. Remember that it's up to each author to decide what changes, if any, will eventually go into the essay.

5. Practice courtesy. Listen thoughtfully to everyone's suggestions; don't insist that everyone agree. You can learn a great deal by taking the time to understand viewpoints different from your own. Remember too that sometimes there's no absolute "right" or

"wrong" in a discussion about writing. For example, writers often disagree about the choice of a particular word or the way a sentence is written. Respect differences of opinion.

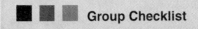

■ ■ ■ Group Checklist

Many students find it helpful to answer these questions about each essay in their writing group:

1. What did I like best about the essay?
2. Did the essay trigger any memories for me?
3. What questions do I have for the writer?
4. Can I suggest any changes that might improve the essay?

Collaborative Activity: The Keys to College Writing

Instructions: Meet with a small group of students to discuss the five principles you read on pages 46–47. Did any of these principles surprise you? Were any already familiar to you?

Writing Activity: Your Writing Experiences

Instructions: Freewrite "for your eyes only" about one of the statements below to explore writing experiences you've had in the past—or write a statement of your own. (Names in parentheses are the authors of the statements.) Begin by explaining what you think the statement means. Then draw from your memories and feelings to explain how your experiences match the statement you've chosen. Remember to write without stopping. Don't try to correct what you've written, and don't be afraid to repeat yourself. Feel free as you're writing.

1. "Miss Parklane would write three titles on the front board and then each student could choose the one he liked, either 'A Moral Decision,' or 'Types of Bells,' or 'Wintertime.' These had to be done in pen so we would learn to write without erasing." (Ken Macrorie)
2. "I am a writer perhaps because I am not a talker." (Gwendolyn Brooks)
3. "Writing really helps you heal yourself." (Alice Walker)
4. Writing well is harder than speaking well, but the benefits are worth the trouble.
5. It takes patience and effort to overcome negative experiences with writing in the past.
6. "Your words should be constructive, bring people together, not pull them apart." (Miriam Makeba)

■ ■ ■ **How to Discover Ideas**

- Writing (freewriting, writing in a journal, brainstorming)
- Clustering
- Drawing
- Talking
- Using "Thinking Tools":

  1. Take something away.
  2. Add something more.
  3. Put yourself into a situation you've read or heard about.
  4. Change one factor.
  5. Focus your attention on something that surprises you.
  6. Ask what's missing.
  7. Ask: Who? What? When? Where? Why?
  8. Make a "plus, minus, interesting" list.

A CLOSER LOOK AT THE WRITING PROCESS

Most writers work through several steps when they tackle a writing assignment: discovery, planning, drafting, revising, editing.

In the *discovery* step, early in the writing process, you should think about your audience and purpose, as well as work out a timeline for your writing project. When is the assignment due? How much time will you set aside for each step? Scheduling time for each task helps ensure that your final draft will be ready on time and you won't have to rush through any of the steps.

The next step is choosing a subject and deciding the point you want to make about it. This is a good time to experiment with the Discovery Activities in the box above.

Once the ideas have begun to flow, you're ready for *planning* your essay. Many students make a *planning cluster*—a variation of the clusters you did in Chapter Two. You'll learn more about this later. Others just write a simple list of ideas and examples. The method you choose is up to you provided you organize your thoughts before you start drafting.

The next writing step is *drafting*—writing your ideas in rough but complete sentences. Often this is a messy stage, with many crossouts and changes. Effective writers routinely produce two, three, or many more drafts. Allow yourself to make errors: You'll eliminate them later.

The "clean-up" step in the writing process is called *revising*. Here you evaluate and improve what you've written. Questions like these are often helpful: Are you satisfied with the way you organized your ideas? Are they interesting and well developed?

Editing is an important part of the revising step: You should carefully make corrections in spelling, punctuation, and usage, as well as rewrite sentences that seem awkward or unclear. Many successful writers check their work several times, looking for errors that they may have previously overlooked.

In the revising and editing steps, many writers also seek feedback from others. Reading your work aloud to a friend or family member can help you get in touch with its strengths and weaknesses. An idea that seems clear to you because you thought of it may puzzle a friend who's reading it for the first time. Hearing both positive and negative comments about your work can help you produce writing you're proud of.

Feedback is so beneficial that many writers include friends and family members throughout the writing process. Talking to others can help you discover ideas and arrange them. Many writers share their early drafts with friends: Their suggestions can make the writing process work more smoothly for you. Most important, feedback from supportive friends and family members can strengthen your skills and build your confidence.

Remember too that the writing process is a flexible one. Feel free to repeat steps and jump back and forth between them as needed. If you run out of ideas while you're drafting your essay, go back to the discovery step. And it's all right to change ideas and examples during the editing step. Make the writing process work for you.

▪ ▪ ▪ Successful Writers

Bonnie Friedman, author of *Writing Past Dark,* says, "Successful writers are not the ones who write the best sentences. They are the ones who keep writing. They are the ones who discover what is most important and strangest and most pleasurable in themselves, and keep believing in the value of their work, despite the difficulties."

Collaborative Activity: The Writing Process

Many students learn about the writing process for the first time when they arrive at college. You may find it helpful to talk about your past writing experiences.

Instructions: Meet with three or four other students to talk about how you prepared writing assignments before you came to college. Which steps in the writing process are familiar to you? Are any new to you?

A CLOSER LOOK AT PARAGRAPHS

Many college writing assignments are two, three, or more pages long. Occasionally, however, you may be given shorter writing tasks that are only one paragraph long: Essay questions on some tests are one example; one-paragraph homework assignments are another. Short writing tasks are also common in the workplace. For example, a manager may write an evaluation paragraph for each employee.

An example of each type of paragraph follows. In each paragraph the *topic sentence* (main point) has been underlined. The first is a student's response to an essay question in an American history course.

1. Instructions: The names of four African-American women appear below. Choose one woman and discuss her contributions to the Civil Rights movement in the United States.

Harriet Tubman   Sojourner Truth   Marian Anderson   Rosa Parks

Rosa Parks (born 1913) performed an act of courage that helped end racial segregation. On December 1, 1955, in Montgomery, Alabama, she was arrested for refusing to give up her seat on a bus to a white passenger. Parks was highly respected in the African-American community for her work with the NAACP. Her arrest was widely publicized. The NAACP demanded integrated buses. The city refused. As a result, the NAACP organized a bus boycott, with Dr. Martin Luther King Jr. and the Reverend Ralph Abernathy among its leaders. In 1956 the U.S. Supreme Court ended segregated buses. Rosa Parks was a heroine. But she endured many problems because of her courage. She lost her job and was often humiliated in public. Still she always acted honorably, and she modestly denied that she was anyone special. In 1988 the Reverend Jesse Jackson said, "All of us are on her shoulders."

The second paragraph was written by Lani, the student who did the drawing you saw in Chapter Two. In her writing class, Lani was assigned to write a single paragraph about a challenge she faced in college. Because paragraphs are usually short—less than fifteen sentences long—Lani chose a simple problem that she could cover effectively in a short piece of writing. Here is the result (her thesis statement is underlined).

Speaking Up

Although I was outgoing in high school, I've become shy since I came to college. To begin, I haven't made many friends here. I need to speak up more in college. Instead of introducing myself and joining conversations, I've been keeping to myself too much. Yesterday after my fitness class, three students were having fun talking about bowling. I could have walked over to join them, but I didn't. Talking to my professors is another problem. I'm too quiet in class, and professors don't even know who I am. Yesterday my English professor asked if anyone had read any poetry by Rita Dove. Instead of raising my hand, I kept quiet. My shyness keeps me from asking for help when I need it. I've been wasting a lot of time in the library and learning center because I'm afraid to ask questions. I want to use the laser printer for my biology report, but I'm embarrassed to ask how to set it up. Writing this paper has helped me get focused. Now all I have to do is start changing. Before I leave the Arts and Letters Building today, I'm going to introduce myself to three students.

The last example is an evaluation written by Ben Williams, a department supervisor in a retail store. He is evaluating Lacey, a part-time associate who sells shoes.

Lacey Clark's Evaluation

Lacey Clark is an effective sales associate. She is responsible, knowledgeable, and helpful. Lacey is always current about sales information and changes in our inventory. Many customers ask for her by name when they purchase shoes. Her outgoing personality is an asset to the department. Lacey needs improvement in only two areas. I'd like to see her spend less time in conversation with the other associates. I would also encourage her work with Robin Macy to learn how to set up floor displays. Because Lacey is attending college and doing well, she can look forward to a good future in sales and store management.

These examples illustrate three important features of paragraphs. First, most paragraphs have a topic sentence that states the subject of the paragraph and the point the writer is making. Writers often put the topic sentence at the beginning of the paragraph. But it may appear anywhere in the paragraph, and it can even be omitted altogether. Second, effective paragraphs have unity: Every idea and detail supports the topic sentence.

Most important, paragraphs have a limited scope because they are usually brief—often less than fifteen sentences long. When an instructor gives you a paragraph assignment, you need to choose a topic that is narrow enough to develop effectively. For example, "managing personal finances" is too broad: It could include credit cards, savings, income tax, budgeting, record keeping, and long-range planning. But you could write an essay explaining how you manage your finances, and each item on the list could be covered in a separate paragraph.

Exercise 1: Evaluating Topic Sentences

Instructions: Mark every effective topic sentence with a check. Write B in front of any that are too broad to be developed in a single paragraph.

_____ 1. The Alateen program helps troubled teenagers who live with alcoholic parents.

_____ 2. Alcoholism has devastating effects on families.

_____ 3. To protect themselves from date rape, single women should know these three guidelines.

_____ 4. College students should familiarize themselves with recent developments in technology.

_____ 5. A new computer program helped my father cut his tax bill in half last year.

_____ 6. Frequent sessions in the writing lab helped me earn a B in English last semester.

_____ 7. Even if you've never danced before, you can quickly learn line dancing.

_____ 8. Dancing is a beautiful art form.

_____ 9. Working out on Nautilus equipment helps me relieve some of the stress of college.

_____ 10. Being organized is important to me.

Collaborative Activity: Writing Topic Sentences

Instructions: Read the partial paragraphs below and devise a topic sentence for each. Then meet with a small group of students to compare and evaluate your topic sentences.

A) _____

Our human brains contain billions of brain cells—far more than we can ever use. Over a lifetime of learning, many of these brain cells gradually group together, line up, and organize themselves. While this process is going on, learning feels painful. When the unorganized parts of our brains are challenged by new mental tasks, we feel inadequate and start worrying that we're not as smart as everyone else. New ways of thinking always seem alien and difficult until our brains figure out ways to accomplish them. The process requires effort, courage, and patience. When the new pathways and storage areas are complete, we feel confident once again—until the next mental challenge plunges us into confusion and doubt, and the learning process begins again.

B) _____

Halloween parties give adults a needed break from their everyday responsibilities. The fun begins with the search for the perfect costume, and it lasts until the Halloween photos are picked up at the drugstore the first week in November. Furthermore, adults who celebrate Halloween can brighten the lives of many other people. Every October 31, nurses dressed up as vampires take blood samples in hospitals. Food-service workers in pumpkin costumes serve lunches in school cafeterias, and health aides disguised as scarecrows dance down the halls of nursing homes. As many grown-ups are discovering, Halloween is too much fun to be limited just to children.

INTRODUCING THE ESSAY

Essays consist of multiple paragraphs—usually at least three. An essay can include many paragraphs and be several pages long. The main point of an essay is called a *thesis statement.* Often it appears at the end of the first paragraph, but it can be placed anywhere in the essay. Everything in the essay must develop the thesis statement.

The ideas and examples in a college essay are grouped together in paragraphs. As you've already learned, it's a good idea to start each paragraph with a topic sentence that predicts what the paragraph is about.

The decision to write a single paragraph or several—even many—depends upon your purpose. Often an assignment will include specific instructions: For example, you might be asked to write a paragraph-long answer to a question on a test, or an instructor might ask for a five-paragraph essay. Professional writing too can vary in length. If you're preparing a routine evaluation of an employee you're supervising, a single paragraph might work well. A report about a business trip, on the other hand, might be several pages long.

This course will offer you many opportunities to write both single paragraphs and essays. The rest of this chapter follows a first-year student named Tony as he worked on his first college essay.

Here's a practical way to organize a college essay:

> Paragraph 1
> –Introduce your topic to get readers interested.
> –Provide background information about your topic.
> –Write your *thesis statement*—a sentence that tells readers the main point of your essay.

> Paragraph 2
> –Begin with a topic sentence that supports your thesis statement.
> –Use the rest of the paragraph to develop this idea with details and examples.

> Paragraph 3
> –Begin with another topic sentence that supports your thesis statement.
> –Use the rest of the paragraph to develop this idea with details and examples.

Write as many paragraphs as needed to develop your thesis statement. When you are ready to end the essay, write a concluding paragraph:

> Paragraph 3
> –Begin with another topic sentence that supports your thesis statement.
> –Use the rest of the paragraph to develop this idea with details and examples.

A STUDENT WRITES A COLLEGE ESSAY

Tony, a first-year college student, used the organizational pattern you just saw for an essay about family life. Because he comes from a large, close family, he found himself thinking about grandparents, cousins, aunts, and uncles as he planned his essay. He decided that the annual family reunion would be a good subject. Here is his freewriting:

Tony's Freewriting

My family is big and very close. My family is grandparents, aunts, uncles, cousins, plus my parents, me and my two sisters and brother. All of us have a reunion every year at a Bible camp about thirty miles away. We take over the whole camp for one night. On Saturday afternoon there's a picnic. We play games like softball and basketball. My Uncle Ralph plays better than my cousins and I do. He was a baseball star in high school. At night there's a talent show. On Sunday we have a religious service and another picnic. Everyone wears T-shirts, Marcus Family Reunion. We stay in cabins at the camp. I invited a girl I'm dating, Tarsha. She thought my family was amazing. She doesn't see her relatives much. She sings in a church choir and sang in our talent show. My aunts and grandmother hugged her. She didn't think she'd like spending a weekend with people she didn't know, so it was a big surprise. My cousins and I swapped stories about when we were kids. Summers we kids went from family to family, a week here and a week there. I got to know my cousins that way. I can talk to my cousins about family stuff that I wouldn't tell my friends.

Tony Writes His First Draft

After Tony reread his freewriting, he started to plan his essay. He decided that his main point (the *thesis statement* of his essay) would be the love his family has for one another. Although Tarsha wasn't a family member, he decided to keep her in the essay because his family had welcomed her so warmly. Seeing how they treated her during the reunion made him realize for the first time that his is a special family.

Then Tony planned his essay. He decided to write *chronologically*—in time order—starting with Saturday's picnic and ending with the sad good-byes on Sunday. He understood the importance of sticking to his purpose—describing the love in his family—so he omitted irrelevant details: the drive to the reunion, unpacking, cooking, changing clothes.

Tony decided to write five paragraphs: An introduction, three paragraphs about the events at the reunion, and a conclusion. He divided the weekend into three parts—picnic, family games, and talent show—and wrote a paragraph about each.

Before Tony began writing his first draft, he checked his essay plan to be sure that his ideas "made meaning." A college essay is very different from a list of events or facts: Every detail in an essay must be related to the writer's purpose. Tony carefully planned his essay to emphasize the point he wanted to communicate—that his family is a loving one.

Here is Tony's first draft. His thesis statement (main point) is underlined.

Bigger is Better

To me family is more than mother, father, two sisters, and a brother. I come from a large family that's very close. Every year we have a reunion at Bethany Bible Camp. We all wear T-shirts that say "Marcus Family Reunion." Even my grandmother wears hers. My girlfriend Tarsha went with me. Her family isn't close like mine is. This was the first time I realized how special my family is.

The reunion started on Saturday with a picnic. It took almost two hours to eat because we talked so much. My cousins and I grew up spending summers visiting each other. My aunts and uncles treat me like their own son. They're not afraid to tell me what they think.

My family loves to have special kinds of fun together. We always play softball and basketball at the reunion. Older people and younger people play together. My Uncle Ralph can pitch a baseball and run better than a teenager. My aunts remember

Tony's Essay Plan

Paragraph 1
–background about the reunion and his family members
– Thesis: This was the first time I realized how special my
family is.

Paragraph 2
–Saturday's picnic
–I spent time with my aunts, uncles, and cousins. We have
always been close.

Paragraph 3
–Fun and games on Saturday afternoon
–My family shows their love by teasing one another.

Paragraph 4
– The talent show
–I'm proud of Tarsha's singing.
–My family makes Tarsha feel like one of them.

Paragraph 5
– The reunion ends with a church service and picnic.
–Our faith unites us.
–I'm proud of my special family.

when he was a baseball star in high school and tease him about it. He pretends he's angry, but he loves it.

Saturday evening we celebrated our talents with a show. My family was lovely to Tarsha. She has a beautiful voice and sang in our talent show Saturday evening. She was amazed they wanted her to sing and applauded and cheered. Afterwards my grandmother and aunts hugged her.

My family is united by strong religious faith. On Sunday we had a church ser- vice. Then another picnic and it was time to leave. Tarsha was crying, and I felt sad. But also proud of my special and loving family.

Tony Writes His Final Draft

Tony shared his essay with a group of other students in his class, who thought he'd written an effective and interesting story. But they also had several questions about the reunion. To begin, they wanted to know more about some of Tony's family members. And several students thought this sentence in Tony's second paragraph needed more explanation: "They're not afraid to tell me what they think." Group members asked for examples of what his aunts and uncles had told him and how he had reacted. They also wanted to know how many people had come to the reunion and what the church service had been like. In addition, they smoothed out some awkward spots and helped correct two usage problems. Finally, they suggested more emphasis on Tarsha since Tony said she was supposed to be an important part of the essay.

When Tony was finished, his essay had grown from five to seven paragraphs:

Bigger is Better

I come from a large family that's very close. I live with my parents, my two sisters, and my brother. My father owns a hardware store, and my mother helps out there. Both my sisters, Tiffany and Cella, are in high school. My older brother John is a mechanic. But the Marcus family has a total of forty-two members. At our family reunion last month I realized for the first time how loving my family is.

Every year the family reunion reminds us that we are connected by both blood and love. We all arrive wearing T-shirts that say "Marcus Family Reunion." Even my grandmother wears one although she usually wears old-fashioned dresses with lace collars. The reunion began with hugs and lots of excitement. This year I really felt special about it because my girlfriend Tarsha was with me. She's a first-year college student just like I am. Everyone at the reunion tried to make her feel welcome. Later she told me she's sorry she doesn't have a big, close family like mine.

At the picnic we had so much to talk about that it took two hours just to eat. My cousins and I know each other well because we used to spend summers visiting each other. We laughed a lot and traded stories about when we were kids. One year we secretly wrote a silly song and planned a funny skit for the talent show at the reunion. The grownups almost fell off their chairs laughing. I was afraid Tarsha would feel left out, but she never did. She enjoyed the stories, and we all encouraged her to tell us about her own family memories.

I feel really special because my aunts and uncles treat me like their own son. They're not afraid to tell me what they think. My parents and I told them all about college and my business plans. They're sure I'm going to make it. Uncle Preston, who's a councilman, said he could help me meet some business people who might help me get my clothing store started. My aunts and uncles spent some time talking to Tarsha, and later they told me how much they liked her.

Having fun together makes me feel loved. My family loves to play softball and basketball. Everybody gets a turn playing, so we did a lot of laughing at mix-ups and mistakes. But some people in my family are fine athletes. My Uncle Ralph can pitch a baseball and run better than a teenager. My aunts remember when he was a baseball star in high school and tease him about it. He pretends he's angry, but he loves it.

Saturday night we celebrated our talents with a show. Tarsha has a beautiful voice, so she sang for us. She was amazed when everyone applauded and cheered.

Later my grandmother and aunts hugged her. She said nothing like that ever happens in her family.

My family is united by strong religious faith. The next morning we had a church service near the lake, with my Uncle Charles preaching. During the week he repairs appliances, but he's a part-time preacher on the weekends. We sang our favorite hymns and prayed together. I could tell that Tarsha was really moved by the service. Then there was another picnic, and we said good-bye until next year. I was sad when we left, and Tarsha looked like she wanted to cry. But I felt prouder than ever of my large and loving family.

Collaborative Activity: Discuss the Changes

Instructions: Meet with a small group of other students to discuss the changes in Tony's final draft. You may find it helpful to highlight the differences by marking them on his first and final drafts. Then, working as a group, list what you consider the three or four best changes Tony made as he revised his essay.

Writing Assignment: Step by Step to a College Essay

Instructions: Plan, draft, and revise an essay about some aspect of family life. The family story you wrote about in Chapter One may help you get started. It will also be helpful to try one or more of the Discovery Activities you practiced in Chapter Two. (They are listed in the box on page 49.)

Some tips for writing your essay:

- Remember to introduce family members to your readers: Give names, ages, occupations, and other helpful information. Include details and examples to make your family seem real to your readers.
- Make sure your information is understandable. Your readers may not understand that the "curling" your family enjoys is a popular ice sport in Canada or that you belong to a religious tradition that celebrates many sacred events in the home rather than in a public place of worship. It's always a good idea to ask someone unfamiliar with your subject—in this case, someone outside your family—to check your writing for clarity.
- Most important, strive to "make meaning" for your readers. Remember that good writing is much more than a list of details: It has a purpose and communicates meaning to readers. As you draft and revise your essay, make sure you have focused on a single, significant idea about your family.

Collaborative Activity: Share What You've Written

Instructions: Follow Tony's example by meeting with a small group of other students to share your essay about your family. Note any suggestions offered by other group members, and consider including them in a revision of your essay. To help guide your discussion, here again is the Group Checklist from page 48:

■ ■ ■ **Group Checklist**

1. What did I like best about the essay?
2. Did the essay trigger any memories for me?
3. What questions do I have for the writer?
4. Can I suggest any changes that might improve the essay?

Collaborative Activity: Review What You've Learned

Instructions: On your own, list four or five of the most important ideas about writing you've learned while working on this chapter. Then share your list with a small group of other students, taking notes on your discussion. What similarities and differences did you notice? Did any new ideas occur to you during your conversation?

SUMMARY

1. Good writing develops one step at a time, rather than all at once.
2. The steps in the writing process include discovering ideas, planning what you will write, making one or more drafts, revising, and editing.
3. Effective writing "makes meaning" by communicating an idea to readers.
4. Sharing and feedback are important to writers.

LOOKING AHEAD

The most important factor in your writing is you—the experiences, feelings, ideas, and beliefs that you share with your readers. In this chapter you wrote a college essay and developed it with ideas and examples. In Chapter Four, "Seeing through a Writer's Eyes," you will practice using description to communicate your ideas.

Seeing Through a Writer's Eyes (Descriptive Writing)

Preview

You are the most important factor in your writing. Your experiences, feelings, and beliefs help shape the ideas you share with your readers. Using imagination, memory, and other mental powers, writers "see" the world in special ways that go beyond physical eyesight. Descriptive writing involves communicating your impressions and feelings to readers. "Brainstorming" is an effective discovery tool that can be done on your own or with others.

HOW DOES A WRITER SEE?

For a writer, "seeing" involves much more than swiveling the eyes to look around. Writers can see even without physical eyesight (like John Milton and Helen Keller, both visually impaired) by observing, reacting, probing, and interpreting these experiences for their readers. In the search for writing topics and ideas, writers rely on all five senses: sight, sound, touch, taste, smell. Even an impersonal writing task—a business report, research paper, or newspaper story—is shaped by the writer's perceptions and impressions. Even if two newspaper reporters cover the same story, they will notice and emphasize different details. Those differences make each piece of writing unique. To put it differently, a "writer's eyes" are "thinking eyes."

Most people can learn to "see" more accurately, thoroughly, and thoughtfully. Have you ever returned from a weekend at a friend's home with new discoveries about your family? Your absence gave you a different perspective: You are "seeing" your family differently. Perhaps you suddenly realized how special they are. Or you might have realized for the first time how much your family has in common with other families. Such experiences provide ideas you can share with others in your writing.

Any kind of change—travel, marriage, divorce, the passage of time—can provide writing topics by helping you take a fresh look at places and events. Novelist Ernest Hemingway said he couldn't write about Michigan until he had lived in Paris. Although you may never have been to Paris, you have probably had many experiences that can help you develop a "writer's eyes." A move to a different town, school, or job may have given you new insights. New relationships offer more possibilities for writing—and you can undoubtedly think of others.

Seeing with the Eyes of an Outsider

You don't always have to remove yourself from a situation to discover writing ideas. By looking through the "eyes" of an outsider, you can make your perceptions fresh and interesting. What surprises or intrigues you? When the first McDonald's opened in Moscow, Russians waited in line for hours to get inside. What impressions would you have if you'd never seen a fast-food restaurant before? What details would interest you? Would you be skeptical about this new type of business, or impressed by its ingenuity? Questions like these can help you see McDonald's, your home, or your college campus—or another familiar setting— through a writer's "eyes."

Your present college life may seem quite ordinary to you because you experience it every day and you've probably spent years in school already. But your daily routine may fascinate someone who's still dreaming of going to college. Your special circumstances might also make intriguing reading for someone whose life is different from yours. Are you the first person in your family to go to college, a student returning after a long break from school, or an international student? Are you heading for a long-dreamed-of career, or are you just beginning to discover life's possibilities? These experiences—and others like them—are worth exploring on paper.

Seeing and Thinking

For writers, seeing is closely related to the mental processes of imagining, remembering, and thinking. Ordinary items become interesting when you explain how special they are to you. A red scrap of printed cardboard turns out to be the ticket stub from a memorable concert; pink and white beads strung on a bit of elastic are the wristband your baby wore in the hospital. Writers constantly face the challenge of digging into experiences like these, exploring their significance, and putting their discoveries into words for others to read. That concert may have been the first time you felt a sense of belonging with new college friends; the elastic wristband may awaken memories of your baby's first feeding in the hospital.

To discover your own "writer's eyes," visit a place that is new to you and get in touch with its atmosphere—a mood, feeling or idea from a particular place. For example, walk into the lobby of a hospital or nursing home. Do you find this place comforting, cold, professional, or frenzied? What details created that impression? Did you see a wilting plant, hear an unanswered telephone ringing, watch a smiling couple and their toddler wave good-bye to nurses and physicians?

INTRODUCING BRAINSTORMING

The following activity invites you to use your "writer's eyes" to view an unfamiliar place. You'll also be trying a new discovery activity—"brainstorming." Like freewriting, brainstorming is writing "for your eyes only." But instead of trying to write complete thoughts and complete sentences, you make a list of words and phrases. Many students especially like "brainstorming" because they find listing easier than writing sentences.

Brainstorming has another advantage as well: It works well with a partner or group, since it's easy for others to add items to the list. The brainstorming list below was done by a student named Alice for an essay about her dining room table. Alice is a single mother of two children. She plans to major in business management; right now she's taking courses in English, biology, and algebra.

■ ■ ■ **Alice's Brainstorming List**

messy

elementary algebra book

biology book

map of Sinclair Nature Reserve

looseleaf notebook

two issues of Business Week
   (*I subscribed and said I'd read every issue and clip and file the articles. I did read some articles in one issue.*)

newspaper articles about ecology

biology folder

phone bill

light bill

cable bill

English book

dictionary

letter from Sandy

Discovery Activity: Make a Visit

Instructions: Drop into an unfamiliar place, look around carefully, and get in touch with its atmosphere. After you leave (or while you're sitting there, if that's comfortable for you), brainstorm "for your eyes only" about what you've seen and felt. Include as many details as you can; don't cross anything out, and don't try to write a finished essay. If you wish, take another person with you and "brainstorm" your list together.

Discovery Activity: Explore a Familiar Place

Instructions: Make another brainstorming list, but about a place that's familiar to you—as Alice did. Try to see the place you've chosen through the "eyes of an outsider." It may be helpful to have another person brainstorming with you.

■ ■ ■ **A Writer Looks at Life**

Here's how novelist Joseph Conrad described his mission as a writer: "My task which I am trying to achieve is, by the power of the written word, to make you hear, to make you feel—it is, before all, to make you *see*. That—and no more, and it is everything."

READING TO WRITE: BALLET DREAMS

Before you begin reading this selection, spend a few minutes freewriting in the space below about something you desire so much that you would tolerate a great deal of inconvenience or discomfort in order to get it.

Your freewriting:

The "Ballet Dreams" selection you're about to read is an example of *descriptive* writing. Ballerina Suzanne Farrell uses her "writer's eyes" to help her readers see the studio apartment where she lived when she first moved to New York City. At that time, Farrell and her sister Bev were in their teens. Bev was studying music, and Suzanne had won a scholarship to the School of American Ballet. The two girls lived with their mother, who had divorced their father, left Cincinnati, and set out for New York to make her daughters' dreams come true. Mark up this selection as you read, and write down any questions that come to mind.

Vocabulary:

Horn & Hardart Automat	(noun) cafeteria offering food in vending machines
dreary	(adjective) depressing
oppressive	(adjective) difficult to bear
enthralled	(adjective) spellbound

The Ansonia
adapted from Holding on to the Air *by Suzanne Farrell*

We needed a place to live, but we couldn't afford much. Acquaintances in the Cincinnati arts community had told Mother about the Ansonia, a large prewar apartment hotel on Broadway and 73rd Street. It was famous for housing musicians, opera singers, and other theatrical people, and now it seemed that we qualified. Many of the apartments were huge and spacious, with views over Broadway—but not ours.

We had a one-year lease on a one-room studio on the sixteenth floor, and after the trundle bed and Bev's second-hand baby grand piano were installed, there was very little room for us. There were two small window seats, but we kept the blinds drawn because we faced over the courtyard directly into other apartment windows. There was a little closet in one corner where we installed our hot plate, but we weren't supposed to cook because of the lack of ventilation. More often than not we ate at the Horn & Hardart Automat across the street.

Mother had saved only enough money for the security payment and the first month's rent, so she immediately enrolled with a nursing agency that provided her with a steady stream of jobs as a private-duty nurse. She worked, as she always had, at night so that she could be home for Bev and me during the day. This was also practical, since the bed slept only two; she used it during the day, and because the curtain was drawn we had to do our homework by candlelight. Even with the scholarships—Bev got one to the Manhattan School of Music and attended the High School of Performing Arts, which was free— there was very little cash, and Mother often worked twenty-hour shifts, arriving home completely exhausted.

The bathroom had a bathtub, but the toilet often didn't work, so we used the one at the Automat. We decided to paint the room what we thought would be a wonderful sky blue, but given the total lack of natural light, it was dreary and oppressive. None of these inconveniences bothered me, however; my home was not at the Ansonia. It was ten blocks uptown. Classes at the School of American Ballet began the first week of September, and I was immediately enthralled.

Responding to What You Have Read

1. Would you like to live in the studio apartment that housed Suzanne Farrell, her mother and her sister? Why or why not?
2. How did Suzanne feel about the apartment? Why?
3. What did you learn about Suzanne as you read this selection? About her mother and Bev?
4. What ordinary furnishings did Suzanne include in her description? Why did she include them?
5. The studio apartment was "home"—an ordinary, everyday place—to the three women. What seemed unusual or intriguing?
6. Suzanne saw the furnishings in the apartment with a "writer's eyes." List the items she mentioned; then explain how each one helps readers understand the kind of life she, Bev, and their mother were living.
7. In what ways were Suzanne, Bev, and their mother different from a typical family?
8. What was Suzanne's purpose in describing the apartment?

WRITING A DESCRIPTIVE ESSAY

Because all of us are unique and special, the places where we spend our time are special, too. Later in this chapter you will write an essay describing a place that's important to you. Begin by choosing a place to write about. If possible, go there to view it with your "writer's eyes."

If that is impossible, spend some quiet time imagining that you're there. Talking to friends or family members who remember your special place can be helpful; photos, postcards, and letters may also help you get in touch with your memories of your special place.

Discovery Activity: See through a Writer's Eyes

Instructions: Look at a place that reflects your individuality, such as your room, car, desk, bureau, locker, or closet. List the items that express something about you, your personality, interests, and values. Then freewrite about the person—you—revealed in this setting.

A STUDENT WRITES A DESCRIPTIVE ESSAY

Alice, the student you met earlier, decided to describe her dining room table because it reflected the changes in her life since she began college. Her "writer's eyes" helped her take a fresh look at the items piled there: books, folders, bills, and letters. You saw Alice's brainstorm list earlier, on page 62. After Alice had reread her list a few times, she spent some time thinking about what these items signified about the new kind of life she was living. Then she brainstormed a second time, jotting down ideas about her lifestyle. Here is her second brainstorming list:

■ ■ ■ **Alice's Second List**

we used to eat dinner on the dining room table
now I just throw the mail on the table
drive Elaine to Girl Scouts
drive Danny to hockey practice
classes, studying
no place to hide stuff
I need the desktop for studying
messy life
happy to be in school
busy
getting confident
looking forward to becoming a business manager

At this point Alice felt confident that she could write a college essay about the dining room table. She began by freewriting, using her brainstorming lists to supply ideas.

Alice's Freewriting

I'm going to try to write about the dining room table. It looks pretty messy. Like my life. We stopped eating on it. We eat in the kitchen. I don't have time put things away and cook dinner and take Elaine to Girl Scouts, etc. I run in the house and throw down the mail on the table. Look at it later. I bet the table will work.

Elementary algebra book, biology book, biology folder, map of Sinclair Nature Reserve the class is going there in two weeks. Maybe I'll take Elaine and Danny sometime. English book, dictionary. Phone bill, light bill, cable bill, letter from Sandy. Loose-leaf, newspaper articles about ecology. Two issues of *Business Week*. I subscribed and said I'd read every issue and clip and file the articles. I'm majoring in business. I did read some articles in one issue. I should put this stuff away. Mom got after me about it. Put stuff in the desk drawers. Neat and organized. No time. Clear the table instead of writing about it. No. I need the desk for writing. No place to hide all this stuff.

What does the table say about me? Messy life. Many things are new. I'm busy and excited about college. I've changed. I don't care about the mess. I never thought I could do anything on my own. Now I think I'm going to be a successful business manager.

Alice Organizes Her Ideas

Alice thought her ideas might work well in a college essay: She could "make meaning" by showing how the table reflected her own changing life. In the past it had been used only for meals; now it displayed assorted items related to her busy college schedule.

First Alice worked on a sentence that stated the main point of her essay. After some experimentation, she decided she liked this one: *When I look at my dining room table, I can see how much college has changed my life.* It became the main point of her essay—the *thesis statement*.

Then Alice decided to put her ideas into three groups, each of which would become a paragraph. The first paragraph would describe the table's contents. The second paragraph would tell about her hectic life—children, day-to-day tasks, college assignments. The final paragraph would describe her feelings. She could accept the mess because college was a good place to be.

Alice Drafts Her Essay

Following her instructor's directions, Alice began writing her first "draft"—a first attempt at her college essay. Alice organized her ideas and wrote in complete sentences. But she didn't try to write elaborate sentences, and she didn't correct mistakes. Her instructor had told the class that writers feel an emotional lift after they write a complete first draft. Alice experienced that lift after she wrote this:

Alice's First Draft

I'm going to write about my dining room table. It's full of college stuff. We don't eat on it anymore. My table has an elementary algebra book, a biology book, a biology folder, a nature map, my English book, my dictionary, the phone bill, light bill, cable bill, letter from Sandy, my looseleaf notebook and newspaper articles about ecology. Anything I'm doing ends up on the table. There's a page of math problems. When I look at the dining room table, I can see how much college has changed my life.

My son is eleven. My daughter is nine. I used to tell them I was going to clear the table so we could eat there again. But I don't have time. I shop and run errands. Elaine goes to Girl Scouts. Danny plays hockey. My mother came to visit and said to use the desk. Maybe I should, but I don't have time to move everything. I could pile stuff on the desktop, but I do my assignments there.

I think I like the table this way. I always know where to find my college things. I used to try to be a perfect mother, and we ate a nice meal in the dining room every night. Now I'm thinking about a business career. Before I didn't think I could do anything on my own. We decided we like eating at the kitchen table. Of course I'll have to clear the table for Thanksgiving dinner. But Elaine said we should go to a restaurant. I like that idea.

Alice Revises Her Essay

After she'd completed her first draft, Alice rewrote it. She substituted a more interesting first sentence, corrected a few usage errors and rearranged some ideas. In addition, she added more details in several places.

Here is Alice's revision. Her thesis statement (main point) is underlined.

The Table

We haven't eaten at the dining room table since the semester started. In the past the only thing I saw when I walked by was a bowl of fruit or bouquet of flowers. But here's what's on the table today: my elementary algebra book, a biology book, a biology folder, a nature map, my English book, my dictionary, the phone bill, light bill, cable bill, a letter from Sandy, my looseleaf notebook and newspaper articles about ecology. Anything I'm doing ends up on the table. I just saw a page of math problems there. When I look at my dining room table, I can see how much college has changed my life.

My son Danny is eleven, and my daughter Elaine is nine. I used to tell them I was going to clear the table so we could eat there again. But I don't have time. I shop and run errands and drive the kids to Girl Scouts and hockey. My mother came to visit and said to use the desk instead. Maybe I should, but I don't have time to move everything. I could pile stuff on the desktop, but I do my assignments there.

I like the table this way. I always know where to find my college things. More important, the table reminds me that my values have changed. I used to try to be a perfect mother, and we ate a nice meal in the dining room every night. I didn't think I could have a career of my own. Now I'm excited about becoming a business manager. The children enjoy my new life and often remind me that I don't have to be a perfect housekeeper. Luckily we like eating at the kitchen table. Of course I'll have to clear the table for Thanksgiving dinner. But Elaine said we should go to a restaurant. I second the motion.

Alice Completes Her Final Draft

Finally Alice read her essay aloud to students from her class, who gave her feedback and encouragement. The group enjoyed her essay, thought of a title, and suggested a few changes. They wanted Alice to expand the end of the essay to include more about her feelings. They also asked her to "introduce" her two children early in the first paragraph, instead of waiting until the middle of the essay. Here is Alice's final draft, with the thesis statement underlined:

No Dishes, Please

We haven't eaten in the dining room since the semester started. In the past the only thing I saw when I walked by was a bowl of fruit or bouquet of flowers. But now I eat in the kitchen with my daughter Elaine, who's nine, and my son Danny, who's eleven. My college books are piled up on the dining room table, along with library books, a looseleaf binder, several colored folders, and some newspaper articles I'm saving. Anything I'm doing for college classes is likely to land on the table. I just looked and saw a page of math problems and a map of the nature reserve where my biology class is meeting. And the daily mail usually sits there until I sort through it. When I look at my dining room table, I can see how much college has changed my life.

I used to set the table every evening to eat dinner with my two children. But when I enrolled in college, the table became messy, and we started eating in the kitchen. For a week or so I kept promising to clear the dining room table so we could go back to eating dinner there. Then more things kept piling up. I'm always rushing to drive the children somewhere or get my errands done. I have a desk, but I don't have time to sort things and put them in the drawers. And I need the desktop clear because I do assignments there.

Actually I like the table this way. I always know where to find the phone bill or the latest biology handout. The kitchen table is a cozy place for the three of us to eat.

More important, the dining room table reminds me that my values have changed. I used to try to be a perfect mother, and we ate a nice meal in the dining room every night. I didn't think I could have a career of my own. Now I'm excited about becoming a business manager. Danny asked if I would clear the table for Thanksgiving dinner. Elaine said we should go to a restaurant instead. I like that idea. Messiness doesn't bother me anymore. I'm a college student at last.

Writing Assignment: From Discovery to an Essay

Instructions: Develop your Discovery Activity from page 65 into a college essay. Like Alice, you should write your paper in several steps—planning, drafting, revising, and editing. The information on the following pages will help you complete each step successfully.

A Closer Look at the Writing Process

1. *Plan your essay.* Reread the Discovery Activity (or Activities) you've already done. Circle anything you plan to include in your essay. Make notes and additions, using arrows and circles if you wish. Don't worry if you have only a few bits and pieces for your essay. You can discover more ideas by trying these activities:

   ■ Talk to a friend or family member about the place or experience you've chosen. Even if the person is unfamiliar with your subject, talking can stimulate ideas. Plan to take notes during your conversation.

   ■ Look at pictures, postcards, letters, home movies, or videos related to the subject you've chosen.

   ■ Use your "writer's eyes," as Alice did, to discover interesting details and fresh ideas in familiar surroundings.

   ■ Draw a sketch or diagram to sharpen your memory and make details more vivid. Even a simple picture, for your eyes only, can trigger ideas.

   ■ Think about your subject while you're walking the dog, folding laundry, or washing your car.

2. *Write a rough draft.* Look at your planning sheet (or sheets, if you've done several) and group related ideas together. Select a starting point—the idea that seems most important to you—and write a sentence about it. Continue writing, putting ideas into sentence form. Don't stop to make corrections: Your goal here is to write a complete essay, no matter how rough it seems. You'll be making improvements later, as Alice did.

   If you find it hard to organize your ideas, follow Alice's example by listing them in short word groups before you attempt any complete sentences. If additional ideas occur to you while you're writing, use arrows and circles to insert them. This rough draft is for your eyes only: Neatness doesn't count—and it can actually work against you by slowing the discovery of useful ideas. And don't stop with one rough draft if you'd like to write another one—or several.

3. *Revise and edit.* Your goal here is to look for ways to improve your rough draft. Can you move, delete, add, or develop any ideas? Clarify any points that might confuse your readers. Remember that you're writing about ideas and experiences that are uniquely yours: Readers have to rely on your information. Mark up your rough draft freely with crossouts, arrows, circles, and corrections. Then go on to editing: Rewrite any awkward sentences, and use the dictionary to check any words that might be misspelled.

Suggestions for Writing Your Essay

1. *Write your introduction.* Your first sentence should introduce your subject and involve your readers. Here's an effective opening sentence from a reading selection later in this chapter:

   You see things vacationing on a motorcycle in a way that is completely different from any other. (Robert Pirsig)

You can also plunge into your subject, making readers feel that they're sharing the experience with you, as Suzanne Farrell did:

> We needed a place to live, but we couldn't afford much.

Avoid vague, lifeless announcements, like these:

> I'm going to write about the place where I lived when I moved to Florida. WEAK

Don't tell readers what you're going to do: Simply do it. Here's a better introductory sentence:

> When I was six, I lived in a tiny house next to a lake and orange grove in Florida. *BETTER*

Notice that Alice's first sentence immediately places you in her dining room—and her life: "We haven't eaten in the dining room since the semester started." Finally, "introduce" any important people who appear in your essay, as Tony did when he wrote about the family reunion.

2. *Organize your paragraphs.* Paragraph breaks are important because they make your writing easier for readers to understand. In a well-written essay, each paragraph should focus on one idea. Start thinking about paragraphs before you write your first draft. Listing your ideas and arranging them in groups, as Alice did, can be helpful.

   Evaluate your paragraphs when you revise your essay, making sure that each centers on one idea. The selection by Suzanne Farrell contains four paragraphs: two about the studio apartment, one about her mother's hardships, and a final one about Suzanne's feelings while she lived at the Ansonia. Follow her example by ensuring that every paragraph in your essay has a single focus.

3. *Share your writing experience.* Your essay is the product of your individual history, personality, knowledge, and values. But you can still benefit from the input of family members, friends, and other students. Professional writers rely on feedback from editors. Follow their example by reading your essay to others and listening thoughtfully to their comments, as Alice did. In addition to the guidelines for group discussions on page 59, you may find the questions in the box on page 71 helpful.

Freewriting Activity: How Does the Writing Process Feel to You?

Instructions: Now that you've composed a college essay, you know how the writing process feels. This assignment may have been fun, frustrating, difficult, or rewarding—or a combination of feelings. Choose one of the statements below (authors' names are in parentheses), or write a statement of your own. Then freewrite about how your writing experiences feel to you.

1. A writer uses what experience he or she has. (John Irving)
2. Each one of us is the custodian of one first class story, the story of his own life. (Stephen Leacock)
3. I'm never really alone when I'm writing, because I enjoy imagining how my readers will react to what I've written.

■ ■ ■ **Questions for Your Writing Audience**

What did you find interesting in this essay?

What did you especially like about this essay?

What ideas or memories did it trigger?

What questions do you have about it?

What might be improved?

What needs to be more clear?

What doesn't seem to fit?

What awkward spots need rewriting?

Does each paragraph fully develop a single idea?

What other comments or suggestions do you have?

4. It's a big challenge to make the ordinary details of my life interesting enough for others to read.

READING TO WRITE: A WRITER'S "EYES"

Both of the following selections invite you to learn more about how writers see. They're followed by questions and suggestions for freewriting. As before, mark up the selections, and write down any questions that come to mind.

Before you read the first selection, freewrite about a walk, bicycle ride, or motorcycle ride you remember. What did you see and experience that you would have missed if you'd been looking through an automobile window?

Vocabulary:

hinterland   (noun) remote area

On the Road
from Zen and the Art of Motorcycle Maintenance *by Robert M. Pirsig*

In this selection, author Robert M. Pirsig describes the roads he travels on his motorcycle. Notice that Pirsig describes not only what he sees, but also how the motorcycle ride *feels* to him. He "makes meaning" by *thinking* about the sights around him, rather than simply listing what he sees.

You see things vacationing on a motorcycle in a way that is completely different from any other. In a car you're always in a compartment, and because you're used to it you don't realize that through the car window everything you see is just more TV. You're a passive observer and it is all moving by you boringly in a frame.

On a cycle the frame is gone. You're completely in contact with it all. You're *in* the scene, not just watching it anymore, and the sense of presence is overwhelming. The concrete whizzing by five inches below your foot is the real thing, the same stuff you walk on, it's right there, so blurred you can't focus on it, yet you can put your foot down and touch it anytime, and the whole thing, the whole experience, is never removed from immediate consciousness. . . .

Twisting hilly roads are long in terms of seconds but are much more enjoyable on a cycle where you bank into the turns and don't get swung from side to side in any compartment. Roads with little traffic are more enjoyable, as well as safer. Roads free of drive-ins and billboards are better, roads where groves and meadows and orchards and lawns come almost to the shoulder, where kids wave to you when you ride by, where people look up from their porches to see who it is, where when you stop to ask directions or information, the answer tends to be longer than you want rather than short, where people ask where you're from and how long you've been riding.

It was some years ago that my wife and I and our friends first began to catch on to these roads. . . . I've wondered why it took us so long to catch on. We saw it and yet we didn't see it. Or rather we were trained *not* to see it. Conned, perhaps, into thinking that the real action was metropolitan and all this was just boring hinterland. It was a puzzling thing. The truth knocks on the door and you say, "Go away, I'm looking for the truth," and so it goes away. Puzzling.

Responding to What You Have Read

1. People ride motorcycles for a variety of reasons. List as many as you can.
2. What is different about Pirsig's reasons for enjoying his motorcycle?
3. Explain these statements: "On a cycle the frame is gone." "We saw it and yet we didn't see it."
4. Pirsig prefers twisting, hilly roads. What does he see, feel and think about as he travels these roads?
5. What was Pirsig's purpose in writing this selection?
6. If you've ever ridden on a motorcycle or a similar machine that allows you to be close to the road (such as a bicycle or motorized scooter), freewrite about the experience.

Freewriting Activity: On the Road

Instructions: Recall a time when you were traveling and felt close to the road—on a motorcycle, motorbike, bicycle, or your own feet. How was the experience different from riding in a car?

Discovery Activities: Seeing and Not Seeing

Instructions: Complete one of these activities in preparation for the writing assignment on page 74.

1. Brainstorm or freewrite about an experience of your own when you "saw it" and yet "didn't see it"—in other words, when it took you a while to realize the significance of an experience.

2. Brainstorm or freewrite about the "real action" in life. Where do you think it can be found? Why? Have you looked for it—or do you plan to do so? How?

READING TO WRITE: SPIRES AND TOWERS

Before you begin reading the next selection, freewrite about your first visit to your college campus. What did you see and feel?

Your freewriting:

In this selection, British scholar C. S. Lewis recalls his first impressions of Oxford University, where he had won a scholarship to study English literature. As Lewis stepped off the train, he looked into the distance for a glimpse of the university, which was famous for its beautiful buildings. Notice how Lewis uses his "writer's eyes" and "makes meaning" as he describes his walk from the railway station.

Vocabulary:

sallied   (verb) set out for a destination

agog   (adjective) eager, excited

spire   (noun) a slender, pointed tower

mean   (adjective) inferior

fabled   (adjective) made famous in legends and stories

Spires and Towers
from Surprised by Joy by C. S. Lewis

I had made no arrangements about quarters and, having no more luggage than I could carry in my hand, I sallied out of the railway station on foot to find either a lodging house or a cheap hotel; all agog for "dreaming spires" and "last enchantments." My first disappointment at what I saw could be dealt with. Towns always show their worst face to the railway.

But as I walked on and on I became more bewildered. Could this succession of mean shops really be Oxford? But I still went on, always expecting the next turn to reveal the beauties, and reflecting that it was a much larger town than I had been led to suppose.

Only when it became obvious that there was very little town left ahead of me, that I was, in fact, getting to open country, did I turn around and look. There, behind me, far away, never more beautiful since, was the fabled cluster of spires and towers. I had come out of the station on the wrong side.

Responding to What You Have Read

1. What did Lewis see on his first walk through Oxford? List the sights in order.
2. Would the selection have been more interesting if Lewis had seen "the fabled cluster of spires and towers" as soon as he left the train station? Why or why not?
3. Did Lewis's mistake spoil or enhance his first impression of Oxford?
4. What was Lewis's purpose—what did he want readers to "see" when they read this selection?

Writing Assignment: Use Your "Writer's Eyes"

Instructions: Choose one of the Discovery Activities for "On the Road" or "Spires and Towers" to develop into a college essay. Follow the steps described on pages 69–70 to plan your essay, write one or more drafts, and revise and edit what you've written. Do additional freewriting if necessary; discussing your ideas and memories may also be helpful. When your final draft is completed, read it to a small group of other students in your writing class. Consider using their suggestions to make further improvements in your essay.

SUMMARY

1. Writers' "eyes" are thoughtful "eyes": Successful writers develop the ability to perceive their surroundings thoroughly, accurately, and thoughtfully.
2. In descriptive writing, you communicate the specialness of a particular place, thing, or experience to your readers.
3. "Brainstorming" is an effective discovery tool that can be done on your own or with others.

LOOKING AHEAD

In Chapter Five, "Writing with a Plan and a Purpose," you will learn how to make a *writing plan.* This chapter will introduce you to four concepts important to your success as a writer: *purpose, audience, unity,* and *coherence.*

Writing with a Plan and a Purpose

Preview

It's a good idea to make a writing plan at the beginning of a writing task. You should identify your purpose and think about your audience before you begin drafting an essay. College writing requires unity—*organizing your ideas and examples around a central point—and* coherence—*logical organization.*

THE IMPORTANCE OF A WRITING PLAN

After using your "writer's eyes" to discover ideas and experiences for a writing task, you need to plan your organization and development. Successful people usually begin a new project with a plan. Successful writers agree that thoughtful planning simplifies writing tasks. Working in small steps, with a clear idea of what to do next, is much easier than staring at a blank piece of paper, fearfully wondering how to begin.

The following checklist for college writing can help you tackle your writing assignments. As you work through this chapter, you'll learn more about the items on this list.

College Writing Plan Checklist

1. I've been assigned to write an essay about:
2. The required length is:
3. The essay is due on:
4. Special instructions include:
5. I plan to write about:
6. My essay will be read by:
7. Before I start my first draft, I need to:
8. Before I hand in my final draft, I need to:
9. My deadline for completing my first draft is:
10. My deadline for completing my final draft is:

Filling Out the Checklist

Begin by filling in as many spaces as you can: special instructions, due date, length. If your instructor and other students in your class will be reading your essay, enter that information in your plan. Write down your topic if you know what it will be—and any subjects you've thought about:

> I think I'm going to choose a special place from my trip to Washington, D.C. with the senior class.
>
> I'm looking for a family memory that shows how much we enjoy outdoor activities together.
>
> I'm going to write about a room in my house that I fixed up for *me*—either the kitchen or den.

Item 7, which asks how you plan to begin, is a good place to list your favorite Discovery Activities. You may also decide to talk to your instructor during office hours, reread your notes, or visit the writing lab. Other activities for item 7 include writing a thesis statement (a sentence stating the main point of your essay) and listing the points you'll be making in your essay.

Item 8 asks you to list the final tasks you'll be completing before handing in your essay. These might include:

- Reading and discussing your essay with a friend, family member, or peer editing group
- Evaluating and revising ideas and examples
- Checking sentences for clarity and appropriate word choices

In this final stage you'll also edit what you've written, correcting usage mistakes that may have crept into your writing. Editing tasks might include:

- using a dictionary or spellchecker to correct misspelled words
- referring to the usage chapters in this book to check commas, periods, semicolons, and apostrophes
- asking a friend to help check over what you've written
- making a clean, corrected final copy for your instructor

Items 9 and 10 ask you to set deadlines for your first and final drafts. Time limits are good motivators. If you—like many writers—find it hard to tackle a writing assignment, a deadline for your completed first draft may help you get started. Setting the deadline ahead of time ensures that you won't have to rush through the revision and editing stages of writing.

WRITING WITH A PURPOSE

Establishing your *purpose* is an important step while you're planning a writing task. In college writing, your instructor usually defines the purpose for you. In the previous chapter you used your "writer's eyes" to write descriptively. Other college assignments may require persuasive writing—trying to convince readers to share your opinion about an issue. For example, you might write a research paper about a current issue that you feel strongly about, such as health care or crime. College assignments also may require informative writing—transmitting useful information to your readers. You might recount the early years of the Civil Rights movement or explain the process of photosynthesis in plants.

So far you've been reading about public writing. But writing can also be "for your eyes only." You can write in a diary or journal to express private feelings or record in a personal way the events in your life. Writing can also be a learning tool. Taking notes in class is a useful memory aid, and writing what you know about a subject from memory is a good way to review for a test. The act of writing strengthens your memory, and you can see just how much you really know about a subject.

Collaborative Activity: What is Your Purpose?

Instructions: Meet with a small group of other students to discuss the following imaginary writing tasks. Working together, write a sentence or two explaining the goals of each task. Be as creative as you wish. (You are not required to perform these tasks.)

1. You're taking a night class. The lighting near your building is very poor, and you feel unsafe walking across the campus. You are going to write a letter about the problem to the campus newspaper.
2. You're taking a biology course. Your instructor asks you to visit a zoo in your city and to write a report about what you saw there.
3. Your family is compiling a memory book as a surprise for your grandparents on their fiftieth wedding anniversary. Each family member, including you, has been asked to write a letter to be placed in the book.
4. An essay test in a government course requires you to discuss three major events in the history of the Civil Rights movement.
5. You're involved in student government on your campus. At a meeting to plan your fall activities, you volunteer to write a letter inviting a U.S. senator from your state to speak at a "Know Your Leaders" breakfast.
6. You've just had a serious argument with a friend who's been close to you since junior high. You pour out your feelings in a diary.
7. You're majoring in nursing and hoping to work with infants after you graduate. You write a research paper about medical services for newborns in your county.
8. You are a youth counselor in a community recreational center. You're on a committee that's writing a plan for a Career Day for the teenagers at your center.

WRITING FOR AN AUDIENCE

When you're writing, your "audience" includes anyone who will read your work. Most writing is either private—"for your eyes only"—or public—intended to be read by others. Private writing—keeping a diary, for example—is a good way to record memories and explore feelings. You can be as honest as you wish on paper, and no one will ever know what you're thinking.

Writing for others demands that you think about the effect your words and ideas will have on your readers. Whether you're writing a love letter, a college essay, or a business report, you must ensure that what you've written is appropriate for its intended audience. A letter to your mother won't sound like a business letter or a romantic love letter; an essay convincing high school seniors to vote may be quite different from one directed to middle-aged citizens.

The audience for college writing is usually your professor, along with other students who may be reading what you have written. As you prepare your assignments for this course, keep these readers in mind. "Well, this guy sure turned out to be a jerk" is too casual for a college essay; "My date treated me badly" works better. Correct spelling and punctuation will be equally important to your audience.

You also need to consider what your readers know—and don't know—about your subject. If you're describing your success at rebuilding an automobile engine, you may have to explain the automotive terms you're using. Your professor may not be familiar with your favorite musical groups, and fellow students may not recognize the financial terms you learned while working as a bank teller.

Make sure you respect your readers' intelligence and experience. When you were younger, you may have been irritated by adults who spoke to you as if you had little intelligence. The same problems sometimes creep into college writing. Don't assume that women have no interests outside of home and family, or that all men are crude and insensitive, or that all foreigners are ignorant of American customs.

One important benefit of college is exposure to people with widely differing backgrounds and viewpoints. Your writing should show tolerance and respect for others who may be different from you. Racial, religious, and sexual putdowns do not belong in college writing. Be aware also of the image of yourself that you are presenting. Sometimes students are so eager to entertain their readers that they exaggerate negative qualities in themselves. A college essay shouldn't glorify irresponsibility or cruelty: Don't try to amuse readers with stories about reckless driving, mistreated pets, or insensitive practical jokes.

Collaborative Activity: Private and Public Writing

Instructions: Meet with a small group of other students to list reasons for writing "for your eyes only." Then list reasons for writing to a larger audience. Finally, list as many differences as you can between the two types of writing.

READING TO WRITE: PARENTS AS ROLE MODELS

The two readings that follow illustrate the difference between writing "for your eyes only" and writing for others to read. Both selections make the same point—that parents should be good role models—but in different ways.

The first is from a teenager's diary. Anne Frank, who died in a Nazi concentration camp in 1945, spent two years during World War II with her family hiding from the Nazis in an attic. Her private diary often records the tensions and arguments that arose during those two difficult years: One example appears below. The second selection is from *Parent Effectiveness Training*, a book for parents that has been read by thousands of people. The author, Dr. Thomas Gordon, is a physician who has advised many patients about their family problems.

Before you begin reading, spend a few minutes freewriting a response to this question: What are some good teaching techniques that parents can use with their children?

Your freewriting:

Instructions: As you read the following two selections, mark them up and write down any questions that come to mind.

1. from *The Diary of Anne Frank:*

   Nothing, I repeat, nothing about me is right; my general appearance, my character, my manners are discussed from A to Z. I'm expected (by order) to simply swallow all the harsh words and shouts in silence and I am not used to this. In fact, I can't! I'm not going to take all these insults lying down, I'll show them that Anne Frank wasn't born yesterday. Then they'll be surprised and perhaps they'll keep their mouths shut when I let them see that I am going to start educating them. I'm simply amazed again and again over their awful manners. . . .

2. from *P.E.T. Parent Effectiveness Training,* by Thomas Gordon, M.D.

   Parents are continuously modeling for their offspring—demonstrating by their actions, even louder than by their words, what they value or believe. Parents *can* teach their values by actually living them. If they want their children to value honesty, parents must daily demonstrate their own honesty. If they want their children to value generosity, they must behave generously. This is the best way, perhaps the *only* way, for parents to "teach" children their values. "Do as I say, not as I do" is not an effective approach in teaching kids their parents' values. "Do as I *do*," however, may have a high probability of modifying or influencing a child.

Responding to What You Have Read

1. What was Anne's purpose, and who was her audience?
2. What is Dr. Gordon's purpose, and who is his audience?
3. Suppose you didn't know that the first reading was from a teenager's diary. Would you be able to tell that the author was writing for herself, rather than for others? Use examples from the reading to explain your answer.
4. Suppose you didn't know that the second reading came from a published book. Would you be able to tell that the author was a professional writer? Use examples from the reading to explain your answer.

Writing Activity: Your Ideas about Parents

Instructions: Write a paragraph about good or bad parental teaching that you've observed or experienced. Before you begin, decide whether you prefer to write for yourself or for a larger audience. If you are going to write for others, decide on your main point before you begin your first draft. If you are writing "for your eyes only," let the ideas flow freely as you write.

Collaborative Activity: Talk about Writing

Instructions: Meet with a small group of other students to discuss the previous Writing Activity. How did your decision (writing for yourself or a larger audience) affect what you wrote? What choices did you make about vocabulary, arranging your ideas, and usage? You may also share what you wrote about parents in the previous Writing Activity if you wish to do so.

INTRODUCING UNITY

Unlike private writing, college essays require *unity:* Everything must support your main point (*thesis statement*). To write about your family's love for music, you might describe the baby grand piano in your living room, the family room shelves filled with compact discs and audio cassettes, the musical evenings when everyone picks up an instrument or sings. But you must omit everything nonmusical, no matter how interesting it seems: your brother's award-winning tennis skills, your parents' fascination with the game of bridge, the funny things your little sister does in restaurants.

Strongly focused writing doesn't come naturally to most writers. Before you begin your first draft, reread your freewriting and circle everything that supports your main point; cross out everything else. Then list the ideas and examples you plan to include in your first draft.

Do this evaluation again after each draft. Seek feedback from others to determine whether you've made a strong point and supported it sufficiently. Ask friends or family members to listen to what you've written, and ask them three questions: What main point do you think I'm trying to make in this essay? Did I make it successfully? Should I delete anything that doesn't support my main point?

Exercise 1: Look for Unity

Instructions: Ideas for three essays appear below. Put a check in front of each idea that matches the main point of the essay (thesis statement). Put an X in front of each idea that does not fit into the essay.

A. Thesis statement: I'm cutting back on my TV viewing.

_____ Last semester I spent two or three hours a day in front of the TV.

_____ I wasted time that I could have put to better use.

_____ Sometimes I even sat through shows I didn't like.

_____ My biology professor encourages the class to watch *"Nova"* to learn more about science.

_____ Two months ago I cut back my viewing to seven hours a week.

_____ Now I watch only shows and movies that really interest me.

_____ When I lived at home, I enjoyed watching the news and discussing current events with my parents.

_____ Last night I watched a new comedy show, just to see what I was missing.

_____ Ted Danson is one of my favorite performers.

_____ The jokes weren't very funny, and the commercials were annoying.

_____ I've found better ways to spend my spare time.

B. Thesis statement: I don't enjoy going to the movies anymore.

_____ I used to go to a movie almost every weekend, but it's been two months since I've been to one.

_____ One problem is the price of refreshments.

_____ Drinks and candy cost three times what I'd have to pay anywhere else.

_____ The expense really adds up when I take a date and pay for her refreshments.

_____ The woman I'm dating now doesn't enjoy movies much.

_____ The movies aren't as good as they used to be.

_____ It's been years since I saw a movie that excited me the way *Star Wars* did when I was growing up.

_____ Ever since I saw that movie, I've been interested in science fiction.

_____ Moviegoers' rudeness bothers me more than anything else.

_____ I like to rent a video and take it home so that I don't have to watch it all at once.

_____ Several times I've had to change my seat because people near me were talking so loudly.

_____ Going to a movie used to be a great, inexpensive pastime, and I wish that could happen again.

INTRODUCING COHERENCE

Another feature of good college writing is *coherence*—organizing your ideas logically so readers can follow them. The selection you read earlier from Anne Frank's diary does not have coherence because Anne was writing only for herself. There was no need to organize her thoughts logically; she didn't even record the argument that triggered the angry words she recorded in her diary.

Dr. Gordon's selection, however, does have coherence. Writing for educated readers, he makes his point clearly—"Parents *can* teach their values by actually living them"—and then follows it with an explanation: "If they want their children to value honesty, parents must daily demonstrate their own honesty. If they want their children to value generosity, they must behave generously."

Grouping related ideas is one effective way to organize them. You can also use a *time sequence* to organize your ideas, tracing the beginning, middle, and end of an event or series of events. Tony used a time sequence in his essay about the family reunion: His essay began when his family arrived for the reunion on Saturday morning, and it ended when everyone left on Sunday afternoon.

Introducing Transition Words

Transition words are special words that act as signals, helping you put your ideas in order and making your writing easier for readers to understand. Tony used the transition words *later* and *then* to help organize his essay about the family reunion:

> Later she told me she's sorry she doesn't have a big, close family like mine.
>
> Then we played softball and basketball.

Transitions have two important purposes. First, by linking ideas together, they make writing smoother and more logical. Second, by providing clues about what's coming next, they make ideas easier to read. For example, "but," "however," and "although" are useful when you're contrasting two things that are different.

To see for yourself how useful transitions are, read the following paragraphs. The first has transitions; the second doesn't. Notice that the second paragraph is choppy and disjointed and ideas are abrupt.

Not Fair (transitions are underlined)

Life is easy for my little sister and brother. When I was in elementary school, I had to do homework right after dinner and be in bed by eight-thirty. My parents drilled me on saying "Sir" and "Ma'am" to older people because they thought I would learn respect that way. If I didn't have homework, I had to spend at least an hour a day on chores. But my parents have softened during the past ten years. Sally and Charlie call adults by their first names, stay up until ten, and finish their homework at the breakfast table or on the school bus. Although my parents keep saying they need more help around the house, Sally and Charlie do very little. <u>Worst of all,</u> Mom and Dad laugh <u>when</u> I complain about my awful childhood. It just isn't fair.

Not Fair (without transitions)

Life is easy for my little sister and brother. I was in elementary school. I had to do homework right after dinner and be in bed by eight-thirty. My parents drilled me on saying "Sir" and "Ma'am" to older people. They thought I would learn respect that way. Sometimes I didn't have homework. I had to spend at least an hour a day on chores. My parents have softened during the past ten years. Sally and Charlie call adults by their first names, stay up until ten, and finish their homework at the breakfast table or on the school bus. My parents keep saying they need more help around the house. Sally and Charlie do very little. Mom and Dad laugh. I complain about my awful childhood. It just isn't fair.

Later in this course you will be introduced to lists of transitions that perform special functions (Chapters Six, Seven, Nine, Ten, Eleven, and Twelve).

The box below includes two lists of transition words and phrases that you may wish to start using right away.

■ ■ ■ **Useful Transitions**

To develop ideas: also, next, in addition, another, including, but, however, although, for example, for instance, such as, if, by contrast, therefore, because, as a result.

To organize a series of events: to begin, first, second, third, last, most important, recently, finally, when, while, during, before, after, since, then, later.

Exercise 2: Organize Ideas Logically

Instructions: Ideas and examples for two paragraphs appear below. They are out of order. Number the sentences to show how they can be arranged logically.

A. The Chinese New Year

_____ Then neighbors, aunts, and uncles gave us children "lucky money" in red envelopes.

_____ The dragon dances were the most fun of all, especially for us children.

_____ Those gifts of money represented good fortune and happiness.

_____ We laughed to see the "dragon" having so much fun.

_____ Although the noise frightened me when I was small, later I learned to enjoy the awesome display.

_____ Relatives, neighbors, and friends gathered for a festive celebration.

_____ At midnight the whole neighborhood lit up with fireworks.

_____ When I lived in China, I loved celebrating the Chinese New Year.

_____ Every year I start wishing I could enjoy another of those celebrations.

B. How Not to Get a Job

_____ Next time I'll be more prepared.

_____ My worst mistake was not being prepared for the interview.

_____ The interviewer, Mrs. Wilkins, sent me home for my Social Security card.

_____ I'll never repeat the mistakes I made the first time I applied for a job.

_____ Next, I didn't know my Social Security number.

_____ I finally blurted out, "For money."

_____ First, I forgot to bring a pen with me and had to borrow one to fill out the application.

_____ When Mrs. Wilkins asked why I wanted the job, I couldn't think of an answer.

Exercise 3: Evaluate Paragraphs for Unity and Coherence

Instructions: Two paragraphs appear below. Cross out or move any ideas that are out of place.

Making Friends with My Watch

After a semester of college, I've learned the importance of being punctual. When college started, I thought I could come and go whenever I wanted. As a result, I was late four or five times a week. I had a lateness problem in high school, too. One day a professor complained that I was disrupting the class by coming in late. This semester I haven't been late once. I was terribly embarrassed when the professor singled me out, and I resolved to change. Soon I learned there are advantages to arriving a little early. I can get settled and talk to other students for a few minutes. I've learned a lot that way and made two new friends. My life is less stressful because I don't rush around anymore. Best of all, I'm on good terms with all my professors.

Poorer but Wiser

I learned an important lesson the hard way when I was robbed at an automatic teller machine two months ago. Just before I went to bed one night, I realized I was meeting a friend for lunch the next day and didn't have any cash. I always look forward to talking to Jenny because I trust her more than anyone else I know. I wouldn't have time the next morning to stop at an ATM. I got dressed, hopped in my car, and drove to an ATM machine outside my bank. I also needed money for groceries for the weekend. Suddenly two teenagers came around the corner of the bank, grabbed my money, and ran off down the street. I called the police from a pay phone, but I knew I wouldn't get my money back. I was so terrified that I didn't sleep at all that night. The next day I was tired and distracted during all my classes. Usually I concentrate and get a lot out of going to class. Now I plan ahead to avoid last-minute trips to ATM, and I don't go out alone at night. I still tremble when I think about what happened that night at the bank.

READING TO WRITE: CAREER CHOICES

In the following selection, newspaper columnist Sydney J. Harris offers advice about career choices. Before you begin reading, freewrite answers to these two questions:

1. What factors are you considering as you plan for the future?
2. What kind of career do you think you would enjoy?

After you have read this selection, mark it up and write down any questions you have.

Vocabulary:

implacable (adjective) impossible to defeat
aptitude (noun) talent
drudgery (noun) boring, hard work

Advice for Career Seekers
from Clearing the Ground *by Sydney J. Harris*

The only advice I ever give to young people who come to me for career counseling consists of ten one-syllable words: "Find out what you do best, and stick with it."

No failure in life is as final or implacable as the failure to find out what you do best. For there is at least one worthy thing that we can do better than most people—and whatever this aptitude or ability may be, it is the thing we should be doing.

Also, in a certain sense, this activity must come naturally and easily. This does not mean that hard work and long practice may be avoided, but it does mean that the work will be as much a pleasure as a chore, and that practice will seem more than simply drudgery. By finding out what you do best, and by being the best you can at it, you will achieve a satisfaction that falls to too few.

Responding to What You Have Read

1. In your own words, state what Harris believes about success and failure.
2. Harris believes "there is at least one worthy thing that we can do better than most people." Do you agree or disagree? Why?
3. List the "worthy things" that you can do as well or better than most people.
4. Look at your list from the previous item. What careers might these abilities and aptitudes lead to?

Freewriting Activity: Careers, Real and Imaginary

Instructions: Freewrite about either suggestion below.

1. Freewrite about a career that interests you. You need not be seriously committed to this career. Your freewriting might explore these ideas: what appeals to you about the career, what a typical day might be like, your special interest in the career.
2. Invent an imaginary career that you might like, such as a tour guide on the moon, a time traveler, or an inventor of new life forms. Freewrite about what your career might be like and your reasons for finding it interesting.

Writing Assignment: A Career for You

Instructions: Write an essay about a career—real or imaginary—that you think would be perfect for you. (You need not to be seriously comitted to the career.) The freewriting you just completed may help you get started; the Discovery Activities from Chapter Two may also be helpful. Begin by filling out the Writing Plan Checklist on page 75. During the revising and editing steps, work with a group of other students to make necessary changes in your essay.

Freewriting Activity: Your Writing Preferences

Instructions: Choose one of the statements about the writing process listed below. Write a few sentences explaining why you agree or disagree with the statement.

1. Discovery is my favorite part of the writing process. I enjoy exploring and playing with ideas, and I don't have to worry about a grade.
2. The best part of writing for me is the first draft. I like to watch a piece of writing develop right in front of my eyes, and I don't bother fixing anything until I'm ready to revise.
3. Revising is my favorite part of the writing process. Once I have a complete draft in front of me, fixing it up seems easy.

WRITING A SUMMARY

A summary is a condensed, objective report about a reading selection. Summaries are always shorter than the original selection, and they must exclude the reader's opinion. As you practice writing summaries, you will increase your awareness of the importance of a writer's purpose. You'll also be developing an important academic and professional skill. Here are the steps for writing an effective summary of a reading selection:

How to Write a Summary

1. Read the selection at least twice to ensure that you understand it. More readings may be necessary. Use the dictionary to look up any words you don't understand.
2. Determine the writer's main point (the *thesis statement*). Asking these questions can help: What was the writer's purpose? What clues are in the title of the selection? Re-

member that the main point may appear in the middle or the end of the selection. It can even be implied rather than stated directly.

3. Determine the writer's supporting ideas. Remember that writers organize their ideas in groups. Ask yourself what point a group of details, descriptions, and examples is making.

4. Now you're ready to draft your summary. Begin with a sentence stating the title and author of the selection. Then write the author's main point. Follow up with a sentence about each of the supporting ideas. Omit details, descriptions, and examples, and don't state your own opinion.

5. Check your summary for coherence. Do the supporting ideas match the author's purpose and main point? If so, your summary is probably accurate. If not, reread the selection and begin again.

6. Proofread and edit your summary; read it to a friend or family member and ask for feedback.

A Student Writes a Summary

A student named Maggie wrote this summary of the excerpt from Thomas Gordon's *P.E.T. Parent Effectiveness Training* on page 79–80:

Parents as Teachers

In *P.E.T. Parent Effectiveness Training,* Thomas Gordon advises parents to teach their children through example. Telling children how to behave does not work well, especially if the parents set a poor example. When parents are good role models, children imitate them and develop good values.

Notice that Maggie met all the requirements for an effective summary. What she wrote is short and objective. She did not state her own opinion about Dr. Gordon's ideas, and she focused only on his main point about parental models, omitting his examples of generosity and honesty.

Writing Assignment: Summarize a Reading Selection

Instructions: Write a brief summary (three or four sentences long) of the Sydney J. Harris reading selection on page 85.

SUMMARY

1. A writing plan can help you manage your time and complete a writing task successfully.

2. Private writing—"for your eyes only"—is less demanding than the public writing required in college and professional life.

3. Both college and professional writing require *unity* and *coherence*.

LOOKING AHEAD

Chapter Six, "Organizing Your Essay," will offer more information about putting an essay together. You'll practice evaluating thesis statements, and you'll learn how a "cluster wheel" can help you plan an essay.

Organizing Your Essay

Preview

Before you begin your first draft, choose your main point—your thesis state-ment—and decide how you will develop it. A "cluster wheel" is an excellent tool for organizing ideas in an essay. A college essay may be descriptive, informative, or persuasive.

HOW TO WRITE AN EFFECTIVE THESIS STATEMENT

A thesis statement is a sentence that states the main point you want to make in your essay. Usually it appears in the introductory paragraph, but it can be placed elsewhere or even omitted.

Here are the introductory paragraphs from two essays you read earlier, with the thesis statements underlined.

From Alice's essay in Chapter Four:

We haven't eaten in the dining room since the semester started. In the past the only thing I saw when I walked by was a bowl of fruit or bouquet of flowers. But now I eat in the kitchen with my daughter Elaine, who's nine, and my son Danny, who's eleven. My college books are piled up on the dining room table, along with library books, a looseleaf binder, several colored folders and some newspaper articles I'm saving. Anything I'm doing for college classes is likely to land on the table. I just looked and saw a page of math problems and a map of the nature reserve where my biology class is meeting. And the daily mail usually sits there until I sort through it. <u>When I look at my dining room table, I can see how much college has changed my life.</u>

From Tony's essay in Chapter Three:

I come from a large family that's very close. I live with my parents, my two sisters, and my brother. My father owns a hardware store, and my mother helps out there. Both my sisters, Tiffany and Cella, are in high school. My older brother John is a mechanic. But the Marcus family has a total of forty-two members. <u>At our family re-union last month I realized for the first time how loving my family is.</u>

Your thesis statement serves two important functions. First, it helps you focus your ideas. If your Discovery Activities generated a great deal of material, your thesis statement will help you decide which ideas and examples to include in your essay, and which to omit. Every detail in your essay should support your main point. When you follow this principle, you ensure that your essay has unity.

Second, your thesis statement helps readers grasp the main point you're trying to make. By organizing your ideas around your thesis statement so that readers can understand how they relate to one another, you ensure that your essay is coherent.

FOCUSING YOUR THESIS

1. Limit your thesis to a single point you can make effectively in your essay.

   If your thesis is too broad, readers may notice your omissions and decide that you don't know much about the topic. For example, no essay could possibly explain how to rear a child. Successful parents must think about a wide range of psychological, developmental, health, nutritional, spiritual, and social issues—far too many for one essay. You could, however, write about a particular issue. Any of these thesis statements might work in a college essay:

   Both toddlers and their parents are likely to enjoy playing these simple games. EFFECTIVE THESIS STATEMENT

   If you want to earn your teenager's respect, make sure your information about illegal drugs and alcohol is accurate and timely. EFFECTIVE THESIS STATEMENT

   Here's another thesis that needs a sharper focus:
   My college classes are difficult. WEAK

   This version is better:
   Now that I'm in college, my old study habits don't work. BETTER

   If you are overwhelmed with ideas during a Discovery Activity, you probably need to narrow your topic. Chances are you wrote a "discovery" draft that needs drastic changes before it becomes a finished essay. Sometimes a subject is so interesting that a long, rambling draft is the result. If you suspect that you're trying to cover too much in your essay, seek feedback from your instructor or writing group, or visit the writing lab on your campus.

2. Make sure your thesis statement is clear and specific.

   A thesis statement that's too general can confuse readers, as this one does:

   I need a new attitude. VAGUE

"A new attitude" can have many meanings. Readers don't know whether you need to be more cooperative, self-confident, or ambitious—or to change in some other way. And they don't know whether you're referring to college, a paying job, or family life. Here's a better version:

I need to cooperate more with the other students in my math study group. BETTER

Your thesis should clearly tell readers what your essay is about. For example, don't state that you're involved in or dealing with a situation: Those words and phrases are too vague. It's better to write that you're struggling to solve or overcome a specific problem. In the sentence pair below, notice that the second thesis has a clearer focus than the first one:

Right now I'm dealing with a difficult situation. VAGUE

I'm struggling to keep my grades up while working overtime to help train a new manager at work. BETTER

In a thesis statement, avoid neutral words like *change, affect* and *influence* that aren't clearly positive or negative. In the following sentence pairs, notice that the second thesis is more specific and more interesting:

Beki should change her eating habits. VAGUE

Beki should eat more healthful foods. BETTER

In high school, my friend Chuck was an important influence on me. UNCLEAR

In high school, my friend Chuck helped me set my future goals. BETTER

Secondhand smoke can affect your health. UNCLEAR

Secondhand smoke can harm your health. BETTER

My political beliefs have changed since I started college. WEAK

My political views have become more liberal since I started college. STRONGER

Living in a college dorm is different from living at home. WEAK

I'm glad I decided to live in the college dorm this year. STRONGER

We need to alter the way our student government works. WEAK

College administration needs more input from student government. STRONGER

3. Make sure you'll have enough ideas and examples to develop your thesis.

If you have trouble generating ideas during your Discovery Activities, you've probably chosen a topic that's too narrow. For example, it's not a good idea to write about a part-time job that you barely remember. But don't give up too quickly if you start having trouble finding development. Trying additional Discovery Activities can be helpful. Research can also help: Photo albums and old letters may stimulate ideas, and you can ask a friend or family member to help you recall details about past experiences.

Be careful not to confuse a fact with a thesis statement. If a sentence merely states information, it can't be developed into an essay. In the following pairs, the first sentence is a fact and too narrow to be the subject of an essay; the second can be supported with additional ideas and examples.

I plan to wash my car this month. FACT—TOO NARROW

I've decided to take better care of my car. BETTER

Every Saturday I call my parents in Pittsburgh. FACT—TOO NARROW

Staying close to my parents is important to me while I'm away at college. BETTER

Peppermint Patty in the Peanuts comic strip often falls asleep in class. FACT—TOO NARROW

College students and comic-strip characters often share the same problems. BETTER

Cigarettes were once advertised as an aid to healthful living. FACT—TOO NARROW

Americans have been slow to recognize the dangers of smoking. BETTER

4. Avoid ideas that are too obvious.

Most people already know that love is wonderful, families are important, and hard work is essential to success. Challenge your readers by making a point they aren't expecting. In the following sentence pairs, the first thesis statement is too general; the second is better.

Child abuse is wrong. TOO OBVIOUS

Many parents are unsure of the difference between discipline and abuse. BETTER

Divorce has many effects. TOO OBVIOUS

Divorce can bring painful changes to a child's life. BETTER

Relationships between the sexes are complicated. TOO OBVIOUS

Asking a for a date can be awkward. BETTER

My Introduction to Sociology course is interesting. TOO BROAD

My Introduction to Sociology course has shown me new ways to think about communities. BETTER

5. Make sure your thesis statement emphasizes only one idea.

Avoid confusing your readers with a thesis statement that combines two points, like this:

My goal is to make the dean's list and earn a promotion in my job at the sporting-goods store. CONFUSING—TWO IDEAS

I plan to make the dean's list this term. BETTER

Similarly, avoid contradictory words and phrases that might weaken your thesis:

Mr. Betz is my favorite English teacher although I don't like his political views. WEAK

This version is better:

Mr. Betz is my favorite English teacher. BETTER

Here's another contradictory thesis statement:

I'm saving money for a ski trip in November, but I may need to use the money for car repairs. WEAK

This version is more effective:

I'm saving money for a ski trip in November. BETTER

Collaborative Activity: Evaluate Thesis Statements

Instructions: Meet with a small group of students to discuss the following thesis statements. Place a check in front of any that are effective. If a statement is a fact rather than a thesis statement, write F. If it is too broad, write B.

_____ 1. Many college students work.

_____ 2. A minimum-wage job can teach students important skills they don't learn in college.

_____ 3. I'm working at my parents' real-estate business.

_____ 4. I'm gaining valuable experience by working at my parents' real-estate business.

_____ 5. More students should get involved in work-study programs.

_____ 6. The hockey coach has developed a new strategy for winning games this year.

_____ 7. I spend twenty hours a week taking care of my house and children.

_____ 8. Bob, a student in my algebra class, works part-time to buy accessories for his Mustang.

_____ 9. The college students on TV are different from real college students.

_____ 10. When I come home from work at nine o'clock, I'm too exhausted to study.

_____ 11. I wish I'd done more to prepare for college.

_____ 12. Since the football season began, the cheerleading squad has had to deal with a problem.

_____ 13. I plan to major in French.

_____ 14. French is important to my career choice as an international lawyer.

_____ 15. Many college students aren't sure about their future plans.

Collaborative Activity: More Practice with Thesis Statements

Instructions: Meet with a small group of students to discuss the following thesis statements. Place a check in front of any that are effective. If a statement is a fact rather than a thesis, write F. If it is too broad, write B.

_____ 1. Ecology courses help students become more sensitive to the environment.

_____ 2. The environment is in serious trouble.

_____ 3. Brazilian peppers and cajeput trees are overtaking parts of the Everglades.

_____ 4. Juvenile crime is increasing.

_____ 5. Thirty-five juvenile offenders toured the local correctional facility last summer.

_____ 6. A tour of a correctional facility can convince juvenile offenders to become law-abiding citizens.

_____ 7. After I graduate, I'll either attend law school or spend a year working in my mother's wholesale business.

_____ 8. Now that I'm on my own, I'm not eating as healthfully as I used to.

_____ 9. Habitat for Humanity built four homes in our town last year.

_____ 10. I became less judgmental about poverty when I worked on a Habitat for Humanity project.

CLARIFY YOUR VIEWPOINT

An effective thesis statement does more than simply establish the scope of an essay: It makes an assertion by communicating the writer's attitude or opinion. In most essays, you should make this assertion early, in the first or second paragraph. Don't save your opinion for the conclusion of your essay: If you do, your convictions will sound like an afterthought, weakening your whole essay.

Avoid weak introductory phrases like "There is" and "There are" in a thesis statement. When possible, rewrite the thesis to state your point of view clearly. Study these examples:

There are two kinds of students in my French class. WEAK

The best students in my French class are the ones who aren't afraid of making mistakes. STRONGER

There is a reason why I decided to major in chemistry. WEAK

I'm majoring in chemistry because I hope to help discover new cures for diseases someday. STRONGER

Exercise 1: Look for Assertions

Instructions: Read the thesis statements below. Underline the words that express an attitude. If a thesis does not express an attitude, mark it with an X.

_____ 1. College life is different from what I expected.

_____ 2. Hurricanes cause extensive damage.

_____ 3. Our county needs stricter building codes to prevent possible hurricane damage.

_____ 4. Joining a chemistry study group has worked out well for me this semester.

_____ 5. My sleeping habits have changed since I moved into the dorm.

_____ 6. I dislike living with a roommate although sometimes I'm glad she's there for me to talk to.

_____ 7. My parents' divorce last year affected my college plans.

_____ 8. By attending college while rearing my children, I'm enjoying the best of two worlds.

_____ 9. Although I've always done poorly in math, my algebra teacher is helping me develop confidence in my math skills.

_____ 10. My part-time job is affecting my study habits.

Exercise 2: Effective Thesis Statements

Instructions: Put a check in front of any thesis statement that effectively asserts the writer's attitude. Rewrite the others so that they express an opinion or viewpoint about the subject.

_____   1. My taste in clothing is more sophisticated now that I'm attending college.

_____   2. The Board of Regents has proposed a tuition increase for next year.

_____   3. I stopped meditating because after six months I wasn't experiencing any benefits.

_____   4. Students risk their lives when they attend parties without a designated driver.

_____   5. There are many women who are rearing small children while working for a degree.

_____   6. National news programs cover religious issues poorly.

_____   7. College has much to offer.

_____   8. There have been several changes in the way I manage my time since I came to college.

_____   9. Joining a math study group has raised my math grades from D's to B's.

_____ 10. There are three ways to prepare for a science test.

Writing Activity: Write a Thesis Statement

Instructions: Prepare to write an essay about college life by choosing a topic from the list below. Begin by filling out as much of the College Writing Plan (which appears below) as you can. (Your instructor will supply the completion date, length, and other requirements.) Use one or more of the Discovery Activities you've already learned to explore your topic in preparation for writing. Then write a thesis statement that asserts your viewpoint about your subject. You might write, for example, "I've had a hard time sticking to my budget since I came to college."

Suggested Topics: An important reason for coming to college; your family's role in your college plans; your biggest surprise since you started college; your biggest challenge since you started college; your best experience in college.

■ ■ ■ How to Discover Ideas

- Writing (freewriting, writing in a journal, brainstorming)
- Clustering
- Drawing
- Talking
- Using "thinking tools":
  - Take something away.
  - Add something more.
  - Put yourself into a situation you've read or heard about.
  - Change one factor.
  - Focus your attention on something that surprises you.
  - Ask what's missing.
  - Ask: Who? What? When? Where? Why?
  - Make a "plus, minus, interesting" list.

■ ■ ■ **College Writing Plan**
1. I've been assigned to write an essay about:
2. The required length is:
3. The essay is due on:
4. Special instructions include:
5. I plan to write about:
6. My essay will be read by:
7. Before I start my first draft, I need to:
8. Before I hand in my final draft, I need to:
9. My deadline for completing my first draft is:
10. My deadline for completing my final draft is:

USING THE CLUSTER WHEEL FOR PLANNING

As you've already seen, a good essay always begins with a plan. The clustering activity you practiced in Chapter Two can help you make a plan for developing your thesis statement into an essay. You're about to see how Patricia, a student you met in Chapter Two, wrote a thesis statement and shaped her ideas about victims into the first draft of an essay.

Patricia's First Cluster

After Patricia had finished her cluster, she spent some time thinking about the ideas she had used. She decided the essay would be more interesting if she included other friends. After some thought, she wrote this thesis statement: I wish some of my friends would stop feeling sorry for themselves. Patricia then made a second cluster, called a cluster wheel, that included her friends Chuck, Leo, and Linda.

Patricia's Second Cluster

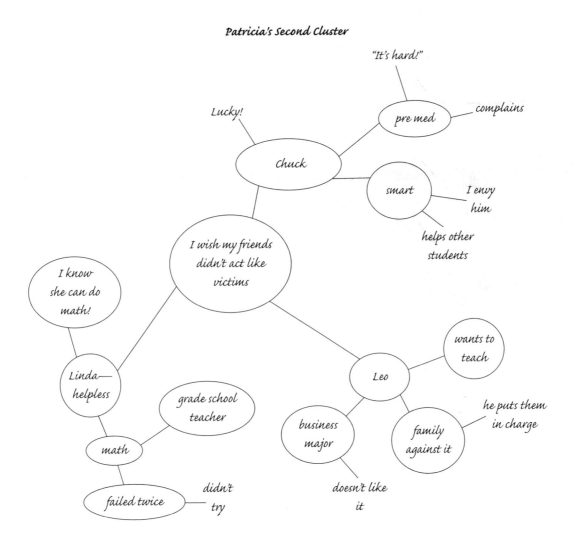

When this revised cluster was finished, Patricia knew she had an effective essay plan. Each circle eventually became a paragraph in her essay.

Patricia's next step was writing a topic sentence about each circle: one about Chuck, another about Leo, and still another about Linda. Later, when Patricia drafted her essay, she put a topic sentence at the beginning of each paragraph.

Patricia now had a plan that looked like this:

> ■ ■ ■ **Patricia's Essay Plan**
>
> I wish some of my friends would stop feeling sorry for themselves. THESIS STATEMENT
> Chuck doesn't take responsibility for changing his college major. TOPIC SENTENCE
> Leo exaggerates how hard college is for him. TOPIC SENTENCE
> Linda is a smart person who acts like she's helpless. TOPIC SENTENCE

Many writers call this kind of plan an outline, and they use it as a guide when they draft an essay.

Patricia Drafts Her Essay

Patricia then went on to the drafting step, expanding each small circle (supporting idea) into a complete paragraph. Because Patricia was writing a first draft, she didn't worry about errors and awkward spots. Here is the first draft she wrote, with her thesis statement in bold type and both thesis and topic sentences underlined.

Victims

When I was little, my mother started working on my attitude. She didn't let me feel sorry for myself when things went wrong. She would always ask me, "Who's in charge of your feelings?" I was too young to understand what she meant. But now I do. **I wish some of my friends would stop feeling sorry for themselves.** They do a lot of blaming. They don't put themselves in charge of their lives.

Chuck doesn't take responsibility for changing his college major. He wanted to be a teacher. His family kept complaining about it, so he switched to business. Now he doesn't enjoy his business courses. He blames his family. But he's the one who made the decision. He's an adult and he has to earn his own living. He should listen to himself, not his family.

Leo exaggerates how hard college is for him. He's an A student, and he wants to become a doctor. He's brilliant and helps other students with their math and science homework. But he complains because his premed courses are very hard. He's lucky to be so gifted, and I wish he appreciated that.

Linda is a smart person who acts like she's helpless. She failed math twice and may have to drop out of college. She won't ask for extra help because she believes she's hopeless. I've gone shopping with her and seen her do math in her head. But in class she refuses to try. She thinks she's bad in math because in elementary school a teacher told her she can't do it.

I talk to my friends about their attitudes. Some change but some don't. I wish people had a mother like mine who taught them that they were in charge.

In Chapter Seven you will learn more about developing your essay plan into a draft, as Patricia did.

Jeff Uses a Cluster Wheel

You can create a cluster wheel to plan your essay even if you started with a different discovery activity. Jeff, the student who wrote about his mother's enrollment in college, began with the journal entry you read in Chapter Two:

I was angry today when I had to do a load of clothes and fix my own dinner in the microwave. But now I feel better. I went to the Athletic Stop before Mom came home. I didn't have to tell her where I was going. She hasn't bugged me about my room lately!

Here is the cluster wheel he used to plan his essay:

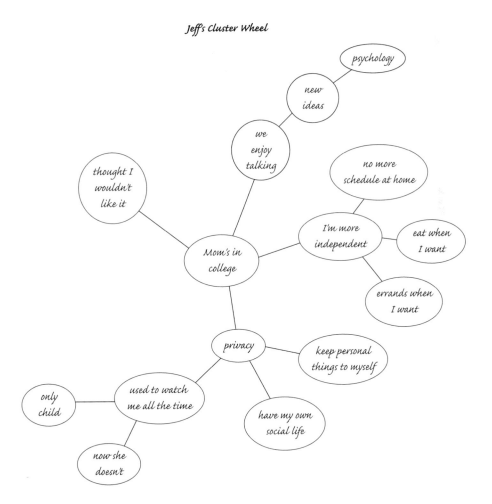

Jeff's Cluster Wheel

And here is Jeff's essay plan:

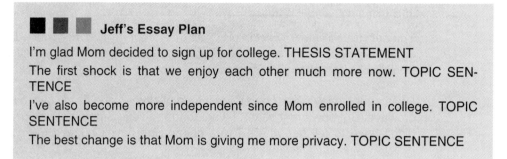

■ ■ ■ Jeff's Essay Plan

I'm glad Mom decided to sign up for college. THESIS STATEMENT

The first shock is that we enjoy each other much more now. TOPIC SEN-TENCE

I've also become more independent since Mom enrolled in college. TOPIC SENTENCE

The best change is that Mom is giving me more privacy. TOPIC SENTENCE

Exercise 3: Practice Making Planning Clusters

Instructions: Three partial planning clusters appear below. Add at least one new idea to each cluster, and circle it. Then draw lines to add details to the circles. Be as creative as you wish.

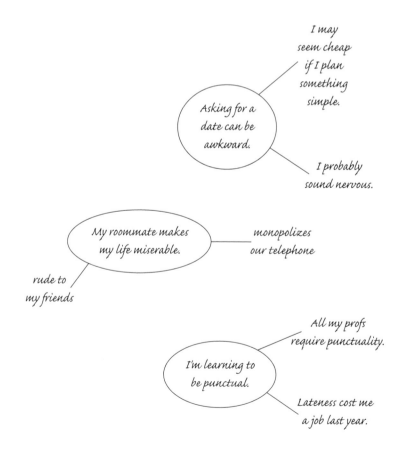

Evaluating Cluster Wheels

Because your cluster wheel will eventually become a fully developed essay, it must be consistent. Since your goal is to organize your ideas rather than discover them, you must make decisions about what to discard and what to keep. Anything that doesn't match your thesis statement should be crossed out and omitted.

This cluster wheel, for example, contains two ideas that don't match the thesis statement:

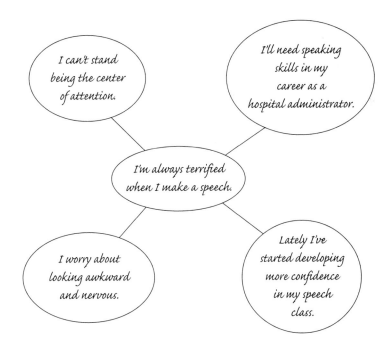

The ideas that don't work are "I'll need speaking skills as a hospital administrator" and "Lately, I've started developing confidence." Neither statement explains how or why the writer is terrified of public speaking.

Also make sure your supporting ideas (the smaller circles) are general enough to become supporting paragraphs in your essay. Each supporting idea will become a topic sentence when you draft your essay. Don't confuse these supporting ideas with examples—the specific facts and incidents that make your paragraphs vivid and interesting.

In the next cluster wheel, one supporting idea—"In speech class yesterday everybody saw my red face and shaking hands" is actually an example of looking awkward and nervous.

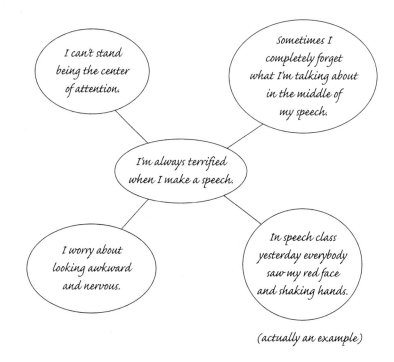

(actually an example)

The cluster needs a completely different idea to complete the essay plan. Here's a better one: "Students say I talk too fast."

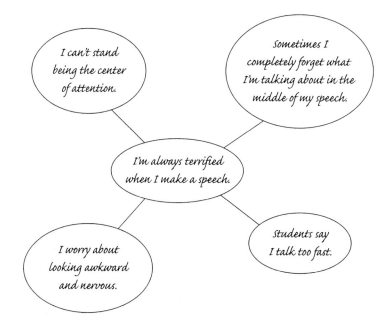

Exercise 4: Evaluate Cluster Wheels

Instructions: The two cluster wheels below need to be more consistent. Make any changes needed, and be as creative as you wish.

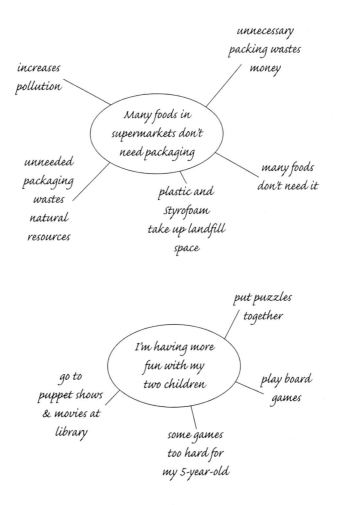

Exercise 5: Make a Cluster Wheel

Instructions: Make a cluster wheel for two of these thesis statements. Then write an essay plan—a thesis statement and several topic sentences. Be as creative as you wish.

a) The clothes I wore in high school are too juvenile for college.
b) Every weekend I discover that I'm short of money.
c) College dances are great places to make friends.
d) My working experience has been valuable.

Exercise 6: More Practice with Essay Plans

Instructions: Complete each thesis statement below. Then write an essay plan for each one by adding at least two supporting ideas. Be as creative as you wish.

    a) I wish my family would _____.

    b) I wish I could spend some time with _____, a special person I knew when I was growing up.

    c) I'd like to learn more about_____.

Exercise 7: Evaluate Plans

Instructions: Two thesis statements and supporting ideas appear below. Evaluate each group of ideas, and cross out any that don't help develop the topic sentence.

    A) Thesis Statement: I'm perfectly content to watch professional football games on television rather than in the stands.

    Ideas:

- I don't envy the fans shivering in the stadium while I'm warm and comfortable at home.
- I like the instant replays on TV.
- Fans in the stadium get to see the halftime show and other things that TV viewers miss.
- If the game gets out of hand, I look for something more interesting on another channel.
- I save a lot of money by watching the games at home.
- I'm thrifty with money and paid cash for an excellent secondhand computer last year.
- I'm more interested in baseball than football.

    B) Thesis Statement: I'm glad my father introduced me to the joys of gardening.

    Ideas:

- I developed good work habits and a sense of responsibility by taking care of my garden.
- I learned a lot about geography when my father told me where my plants had come from.
- He's a good teacher who often helped me with high school math and English.
- I remember special times when he told me stories about plant explorers.
- Some died from diseases and accidents while collecting plants in remote places.
- I've heard similar stories about missionaries and other travelers.
- Learning about plant processes has helped me in my science classes.

ORGANIZING AN ESSAY WITH A PURPOSE

In Chapter Five, you learned that thinking about your purpose in writing is an important step in planning an essay. You saw that a college essay may have a descriptive, informative, or persuasive purpose. Now you're ready to learn how the purpose of an essay affects its organization.

A descriptive essay aims to create a particular impression, feeling or mental picture: a place where you lived as a child, a challenge you're facing in college, or the special features of a car. Personal essays—those you write about yourself—are often descriptive. All the student essays you've read so far in this book are descriptive. Alice's essay in Chapter Four, for example, describes both her dining room table and her life; Tony described his family reunion in Chapter Three.

An informative essay shares knowledge; unlike the personal essays you read earlier, it usually deals with a subject that affects many people. You might inform readers about cooking methods, the most common types of computer criminals, or the reasons for your career choice. Here is an informative essay that explains how schools are protecting young people from violence. Notice that the thesis statement (underlined and in bold type in the first paragraph) states the purpose of the entire essay. Each paragraph has a topic sentence (also underlined) to introduce the information that is presented there.

How Schools Are Preventing Violence

Studies show that one-fourth of teenage deaths are caused by gunshot wounds. Youthful violence is spreading from poor, inner-city neighborhoods to wealthy suburban areas. In 1999, both students and a teacher were killed when two suburban teenagers went on a killing rampage in Columbine High School in Colorado. Across the country, guns and knives have ended the lives of thousands of children and teenagers. Many others suffer serious injuries such as stabbing wounds, paralysis and brain damage. Prison sentences prevent many students from completing their education and finding jobs. **Fortunately, many neighborhood schools are helping protect young people from violence.**

First, many schools are improving their security practices. In 1990, Congress made it a felony to bring a gun within one thousand feet of any school. Many schools use metal detectors to keep weapons out of the building; security guards patrol hallways, and police officers are available to deal with problems before they get out of hand.

Second, some school officials are cooperating with local efforts to reduce violence. In Chicago and New York, school buildings are used for social services, clinics, and recreation programs that benefit the whole neighborhood. School personnel have met with law-enforcement officers, ministers and social workers to bring improvements to the community.

Most important, some schools are teaching teenagers how to avoid violence. The Reverend Jesse Jackson has visited high schools to teach students the difference between "snitching" and self-defense in potentially violent situations. Some schools are teaching skills that reduce violence. Family life and parenting classes can teach young people how to reduce stress, anger and violence at home.

Although these changes are happening slowly, they are bringing hope to many young people. As more schools adopt these procedures, more young people can find a safe haven from the violence of modern life. The neighborhood schools we see every day can be lifesavers to young people at risk.

A persuasive essay also contains information, but its purpose is convincing readers to share your opinion—for example, to support a particular position or behave in a particular way. You might urge readers to donate money to public broadcasting, support low-interest student loans, or vote for gun control legislation. The following essay, like the one you just read, is about violence and schools. But this essay has a persuasive purpose: convincing readers that schools need to be more involved in solving the problem of youthful violence. Often forceful words like "must" and "should" appear throughout a persuasive essay, indicating that readers are being asked to change their thinking and behavior. Notice how these words are used in the thesis statement (underlined and bold type) and topic sentences (underlined) of this persuasive essay:

Schools against Violence

Studies show that one-fourth of teenage deaths are caused by gunshot wounds. Youthful violence is spreading from poor, inner-city neighborhoods to wealthy suburban areas. In 1999, both students and a teacher were killed when two suburban teenagers went on a killing rampage in Columbine High School in Colorado. Guns and knives have ended the lives of thousands of children and teenagers. Many others suffer serious injuries such as stabbing wounds, paralysis and brain damage. Prison sentences prevent many students from completing their education and finding jobs. **Neighborhood schools must do more to protect young people from the rising tide of violence.**

First, more schools should offer young people a haven from the dangers of violent neighborhoods. In 1990, Congress made it a felony to bring a gun within one thousand feet of any school. Many schools use metal detectors to keep weapons out of the building; security guards patrol hallways, and police officers are available to deal with problems before they get out of hand. More school districts should consider adopting such measures. In addition, schools could schedule extended office hours with a nurse and security officer present. Teenagers from troubled relationships could find shelter from abusive family members and violent friends. Since students are required by law to spend much of their time in school, security practices can save many young lives.

Second, schools should cooperate with local efforts to reduce violence. School buildings are underused during vacations, evenings, and weekends. This space could be used for social services, clinics, and recreation programs that benefit the whole neighborhood. School personnel could meet with their neighbors, act as role models, and take an active role in the community.

Most important, schools can teach teenagers how to avoid violence. The Reverend Jesse Jackson has visited high schools to teach students the difference between "snitching" and self-defense in potentially violent situations. Principals, teachers, and other staff members could follow his example. Some schools are already teaching skills that reduce violence.

Making these changes may be difficult at first. These suggestions may disturb people who think that schools should concern themselves only with academic subjects. Administrators, staff, and faculty may have trouble getting used to their new roles, and neighborhoods may be slow to change their expectations of their local school. But these changes are vital to children and teenagers who live in violent areas.

Exercise 8: Make Cluster Wheels

Instructions: Make cluster wheels for the two essays you just read.

■ ■ ■ **Useful Transitions for Persuasive Writing**

Consequently, furthermore, but, however, even better, as a result, most important, worst of all, best of all, therefore, because, since, also, another, in addition, moreover

Overlapping Purposes

Despite their differences, all three purposes often overlap. A persuasive essay arguing against hunting might also be informative (offering facts about hunting accidents) and descriptive (explaining how injured animals suffer). An informative essay about computer technology might describe a group of programmers, the computers they use, and the tasks they perform; a descriptive essay about your dream car might include information about expected mileage, engine size, decor, safety features and anti-theft controls. The assignments in Part Two of this text will offer suggestions for writing descriptive, informative and persuasive essays. Page 83 in Chapter Five lists transition words that can be useful in these essays.

Exercise 9: Label Paragraphs

Instructions: Label the following paragraphs descriptive, informative or persuasive.

A) A Fitness Bargain

You can achieve fitness without joining an expensive health club. Don't be fooled into thinking that you need high-tech equipment to reshape your body. Discount stores sell weights, jump ropes, and exercise mats. You can monitor your heart rate by taking your own pulse instead of depending on an electronic cardiograph. Why pay money to a personal trainer when you can listen to an expert for free on a TV exercise show?

When you add up the savings—not to mention the gasoline and time you spend driving back and forth to a gym—it just doesn't make sense to exercise anywhere but at home.

B) Interview Insights

My older sister, a job counselor for a government agency, has some valuable advice about applying for a job. Be prepared to fill out the application form accurately. The night before, write out the names, addresses and telephone numbers of your references and previous employers. Know exactly when you held each job, and make a few notes about your responsibilities. She suggests using a pocket dictionary or electronic speller to doublecheck everything you write on the application. Next, look and act like a person you'd want to hire. Appropriate clothing is important; so are courtesy and enthusiasm. When it's your turn for questions, ask what qualities the interviewer looks for in evaluating employees. Be enthusiastic about the job, and thank the interviewer for meeting with you. By following these suggestions, you'll have an excellent chance of being offered the job.

C) Money and a Smile

Banks have become friendlier since I was younger. Carpeting has replaced the marble floors, and tellers don't work in cages anymore. It's been years since I've seen one of those green eyeshades many tellers used to wear. Bank employees seem younger now, and they're usually smiling. My credit union (it's not even called a bank) gives away hot popcorn every Friday, and there are always free balloons for my grandchildren. Video cameras and electronic alarms have replaced the armed guards I found so frightening as a child. Since banks depend on people like me to stay in business, I'm glad they're trying hard to make me feel welcome.

Collaborative Activity: Label Thesis Statements

Instructions: Meet with a small group of students to label the following thesis statements descriptive, informative, or persuasive.

_____ 1. New technology is offering solutions to the problem of overcrowded prisons.

_____ 2. Because of recent legal changes, judges are imposing longer sentences on criminals.

_____ 3. American businesses should stop trying to dictate Japanese economic policies.

_____ 4. Many American landscapes feature beautiful plants that are native to Japan.

_____ 5. Japanese business practices emphasize employee decision-making and quality control.

_____ 6. Many colleges still aren't providing equal athletic facilities for women.

_____ 7. The YMCA downtown has superb exercise facilities for active families.

_____ 8. Steroids give unfair advantages to athletes who use them.

_____ 9. Modern medicine is discovering the benefits of ancient herbal remedies.

_____ 10. Physicians should rely more on natural substances to treat illnesses.

_____ 11. A dude ranch is an ideal vacation spot for a family that enjoys the outdoors.

_____ 12. The United States can maintain a high level of national security with a decreased defense budget.

_____ 13. Women in the military services are enjoying expanded opportunities for promotion and education.

_____ 14. After five years in the Air Force, Marilyn is glad she signed up for a military career.

_____ 15. It's important to know how to evaluate information sources on the Internet.

SUMMARY

1. A thesis statement tells readers the main point you will make in your essay.
2. A "cluster wheel" can help you organize your ideas and plan the paragraphs in an essay.
3. Essays are made up of paragraphs—brief units of writing that develop one idea.
4. A college essay may be descriptive, informative, or persuasive.

LOOKING AHEAD

After you've planned the essay you want to write, the next step is to write a draft. In this step, you develop your ideas in sentences. Completeness, not perfection, is your goal: When your first draft is finished, no matter how flawed it is, you can start focusing on details. In Chapter Seven, you will learn more about drafting an essay.

CHAPTER SEVEN

Drafting Your Essay

Preview

Most writing projects go through several early, imperfect versions called drafts. The introduction to an essay has three purposes: stimulating your readers' interest, providing background information, and stating your point of view. The body of your essay consists of one or more paragraphs that develop your thesis statement. The conclusion of your essay reinforces your main point and signals to your readers that your essay is finished.

INTRODUCING THE DRAFTING STEP

In the previous chapter, you learned how to plan an essay. Now you're ready for a close look at the drafting step, in which you expand your essay plan into complete sentences. Early drafts are usually messy, "for your eyes only," just as Discovery Activities are. But it's a good idea to share early versions of an essay with friends or family members. Many successful writers get helpful ideas by asking for feedback about their early drafts.

THE PARTS OF AN ESSAY

Most college essays consist of an introduction, body, and conclusion; each part may be one or more paragraphs long. The *introduction* serves three functions: stimulating your readers' interest, providing background information, and stating your main point (your thesis statement). Next is the *body*—one or more paragraphs that develop your thesis statement. The *conclusion* appears at the end of the essay: It signals to readers that you have completed your writing task.

You don't have to draft your essay in this order. Writers sometimes work on the end of an essay before they write the beginning. Or they may outline their main ideas before perfecting the thesis statement. And it's all right to jump back and forth between the steps. For example, you may decide to write and edit a sentence during a Discovery Activity, and you may need to brainstorm new ideas while you're revising.

Only one rule applies to drafting: Write quickly and imperfectly. Novelist Tony Hillerman advises, "Don't spend much time on it. You're going to have to rewrite it." Introductory paragraphs and conclusions are particularly challenging for many writers. Draft them quickly, and plan to revise them carefully later, if necessary. (Specific suggestions for introductions and conclusions appear later in this chapter.) And ignore problems with spelling and usage until you're ready to revise and edit your work. There's a psychological advantage to completing your essay once, even if you're dissatisfied with it: You can always go back and improve it, as professional writers do.

■ ■ ■   **Overcoming Writer's Block**

All writers, including professionals, sometimes experience a problem called "writer's block"—difficulty tackling a writing task. Author Gloria Steinem says, "Writers are notorious for using any reason to keep from working: overresearching, retyping, going to meetings, waxing the floors—anything." Waiting until you're "in the mood" can be disastrous: What if "the mood" never comes?
   Here are a few suggestions for overcoming "writer's block":

1. Freewrite about your negative feelings. You may decide that the obstacles holding you back aren't so frightening after all. And once the words start flowing on paper, you may feel like getting started on your assignment.
2. Talk to a friend about your topic. Have a pen and paper in front of you for jotting down any ideas that appear during your conversation. Even if you don't think of any new material for your essay, talking is a good warmup for writing.
3. Try a Discovery Activity that doesn't require much writing, such as clustering or drawing.
4. Allow yourself to write a weak first draft. Put down anything you can think of just to get started.
5. Give yourself an energy boost by imagining the results of your efforts: a high grade, an encouraging note from your professor, warm praise from friends. Picture yourself in class, proudly reading your final draft to your editing group. Return to the picture often; it will encourage you to write.
6. Accept yourself. Don't force yourself to be creative or clever. Strive to communicate honestly and intelligently with your readers, and good writing will result. Trust your own sense of what's interesting and important.

WRITING THE INTRODUCTION TO YOUR ESSAY

Donald Murray, an English professor and Pulitzer-Prize winning author, says he sometimes experiments with fifty introductions before finding one he likes. Many times a writer may keep revising an introduction long after the rest of an essay is finished. This intense effort is necessary because an introduction is the hardest-working part of an essay. It has to introduce your subject, state your viewpoint, catch your readers' interest, and convince them you have something worthwhile to say.

TIPS FOR WRITING AN EFFECTIVE INTRODUCTION

1. Quickly let your audience know what you're writing about. Avoid slow-moving introductions like these:

    A person who had an important effect on my life was my grandmother. WEAK

    The place I enjoy visiting most is Sagamore Hill, Theodore Roosevelt's home on Long Island. WEAK

    The next two introductions get to the point more quickly:

    My grandmother taught me the importance of courage. BETTER

    I have always loved visiting Sagamore Hill, the Long Island home of Theodore Roosevelt. BETTER

2. Give your readers enough information to understand what you're writing about. Did you win a championship, lose a job, grieve over a loss, or suffer an injustice? Use the journalist's questions to check your introduction for completeness: who, what, when, where, and why.

3. Offer definitions and explanations to readers who might be unfamiliar with your subject. If you've worked for a fast-food restaurant, you know what "openers" and "closers" do—but your audience might not. Someone who doesn't enjoy hockey may not know that a "hat trick" involves scoring three goals in one game.

4. Include vivid, specific details to make your introduction lively and interesting. The following introductory paragraph is dull because it lacks specific details:

    My next-door neighbor taught me many things. His name is John Avery, and he's a manager in a department store. He visits my family all the time. Thanks to him, I'm a better person today. I plan to be successful like him. He's made a big difference in my life. WEAK

    Lively details make the following version more interesting:

    When I was in junior high, a wonderful man named John Avery bought the tiny frame house next door. We soon learned he was a manager in a store downtown. Because he had no relatives nearby, he began visiting us frequently. Sitting on our front porch in the evenings, he spoke of college, books, concerts, and distant places. More than anyone else, he encouraged me to take pride in myself and to set goals for the future. I owe a great deal to John Avery. BETTER

5. Avoid beginning an essay with a commonplace idea. Don't bore readers with dull observations that they are likely to have heard before. Compare the following sentence pairs:

    Love is important. WEAK

    It's easier to talk about love than to put it into action every day. BETTER

    Many people have been helpful to me during my life. WEAK

    I'll always be grateful to Mrs. Holcomb, a guidance counselor who helped me enroll in college. BETTER

6. Make sure your introduction is unified around a single topic. The following introduction is ineffective because readers have to wait too long to discover the subject of the essay:

> I used to be terribly afraid of police officers. My mother says I always hid behind her when I saw an officer. The fears stayed with me until I met Officer Rodriguez, who did magic tricks for the kids in my neighborhood. Now that I'm a nursing student, I'm trying to show children in the hospital that I care about them too. A red clown's nose is a vital part of my nursing equipment. WEAK INTRODUCTION

The following introduction is more effective because it immediately focuses on nursing:

> A red clown's nose is a vital part of my nursing equipment. I go to the hospital once or twice a week as part of my nursing program, and the clown's nose is always in my pocket. When I meet a frightened child, I put it on and do my clown act. If a child seems bored or lonely, I pop it onto his nose and ask him to amuse me. It works like magic. With the help of my clown's nose, I'm bringing love to the children in the hospital. BETTER

7. Don't call attention to your writing process. Avoid weak statements like these:

> I'm going to write an essay about homelessness. WEAK
> I had trouble thinking of an idea for this essay. WEAK

Instead of telling readers about your difficulties, find a way to stimulate their interest in your subject. Here is an effective introductory paragraph about homelessness:

> Homelessness is no longer limited to the very poor. Many working families have no savings to protect them against financial emergencies. A layoff, pay cut, or illness today could mean homelessness tomorrow. EFFECTIVE INTRODUCTION

And here is an effective introduction to an essay about America's role in human rights:

> Although Americans agree that human rights are important, we disagree about ways to protect them overseas. Should American soldiers be involved? Should we end trade when a country violates human rights? What about payments to foreign governments? We seem to ask the same questions every time there's a human-rights crisis. EFFECTIVE INTRODUCTION

STRATEGIES FOR WRITING EFFECTIVE INTRODUCTIONS

1. Ask a question that stimulates readers' interest, as in this introductory paragraph:

> What's due tomorrow? I frantically asked myself that question every evening during my first two weeks in college. I hadn't been to school in ten years, and I had forgotten how to tackle assignments. Lately I've been doing much better. My goal is to complete every assignment on time for the rest of this semester.

Here's another effective introduction:

> Would you be in favor of a process that safely converts a gallon of water into an energy source as powerful as three hundred gallons of gasoline? The process is called nuclear fusion, and scientists all over the world are exploring its possibilities.

Remember that a question is an introductory device, not a thesis statement. You must still tell readers the main idea of your essay, as these examples show:

> My goal is to complete every assignment on time for the rest of this semester. THESIS STATEMENT
>
> The process is called nuclear fusion, and scientists all over the world are exploring its possibilities. THESIS STATEMENT

2. State a fact that will arouse readers' curiosity.

> Experts say that many American students are under-prepared for college math and science courses. After a month of college chemistry, I strongly agree. I'm finding it difficult to understand my text, perform the experiments, and follow the lectures. And I'm not the only one. At least half the class seems to be struggling along with me.

3. Tell a story that makes an important point, as in this essay about drunk driving:

> Mark, my best friend from high school, believed that he could drive safely no matter how much alcohol he'd had. Last July 4 he tried to talk me into joining him for a full round of parties. My parents wouldn't let me go, and their decision may have saved my life. Later I found that Mark had been driving from party to party with a six-pack of beer on the passenger seat. At one a.m. he died in an alcohol-related accident. Since then I've learned that drunk driving is the number-one killer of teenagers like Mark.

4. Begin with a strong statement, as in this introduction to an essay about a student's decision to enroll in college:

> I want to be more than a wife and mother. For ten years I've devoted myself to my husband and two children. My family is a loving one, and I'm glad I was able to give them so much of my time and energy. But now it's time to pay attention to my own needs. My goal is to become a registered nurse.

Here's an effective opening paragraph for an essay about domestic violence:

> Women face their greatest dangers at home, not in the street. Domestic violence is the leading cause of injuries to women. Half of all rapes and murders are committed by someone the woman knows. It might be a friend, family member, husband, ex-husband, or former lover. Because these crimes are "all in the family," sometimes the justice system fails to view them seriously. Our nation needs to show more concern for female crime victims.

Exercise 1: Effective Introductions

Instructions: Place a check in front of each effective introductory sentence.

_____ 1. I spent a long time thinking about my teenage years before I started writing this essay.

_____ 2. Although I've been in love many times, no experience was like my first romance.

_____ 3. Teenagers often feel confused and insecure.

_____ 4. Voting is both a duty and a privilege for every citizen.

_____ 5. High schools should do a better job of preparing students to become voters.

_____ 6. How effectively did your parents prepare you for the responsibilities of citizenship?

_____ 7. Careful planning is essential for a successful semester.

_____ 8. It was my first day at college, and I was scared.

_____ 9. As of last Friday, I no longer own a Doberman pinscher.

_____ 10. When my family decided to visit Hawaii, all of us helped plan our trip.

_____ 11. It's hard for me to find the words to describe that unforgettable vacation.

_____ 12. I looked out the window of the plane at the bluest water I'd ever seen.

Writing Assignment: Plan Your Introduction

Instructions: Write an introductory paragraph (or paragraphs) for your essay about college life. Check your introduction to make sure it meets the guidelines on pages 111–114. Then meet with a small group of students to discuss your introductions.

WRITING THE BODY OF YOUR ESSAY

The paragraphs that develop your thesis statement are called the *body* of an essay. As you saw in Chapter Six, the small circles on your cluster wheel become body paragraphs in your essay. Here is a cluster wheel done by a student named Kent:

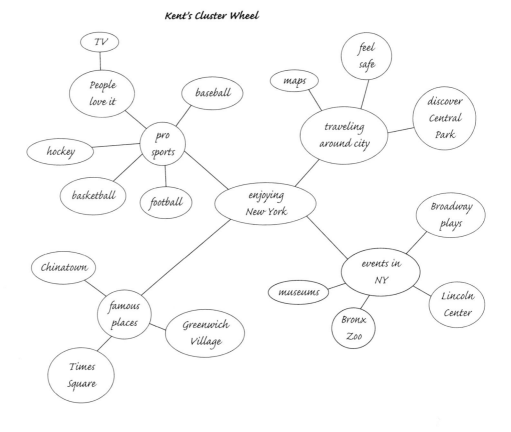

Kent's Cluster Wheel

And here is Kent's essay plan:

■ ■ ■ **Kent's Essay Plan**

Although I've been here only five months, I'm having a wonderful time in New York. THESIS STATEMENT

It didn't take long for me to feel confident traveling around the city. TOPIC SENTENCE

After I stopped being afraid of New York, I started having a great time here. TOPIC SENTENCE

Besides having new cultural experiences, I've become hooked on professional sports for the first time. TOPIC SENTENCE

What I enjoy most is exploring the famous areas that make New York special. TOPIC SENTENCE

Right now I'm looking forward to a visit from my parents, who are coming here during spring break. TOPIC SENTENCE

This is Kent's essay. His thesis statement is in bold type; both his thesis statement and topic sentences are underlined.

Enjoying the Big Apple

I had mixed feelings when I stepped off the plane in New York last September. My parents, who grew up in New York, assured me I'd love going to college in the city. But at first it seemed very big and frightening to me. What about crime? How would I cope with the subways and buses? Could I afford to do the neat things my parents always talked about, like going to plays and concerts? Luckily it didn't take long for the city to win me over. College friends who grew up here have taught me a lot. **Although I've been here only five months, I'm having a wonderful time in New York.**

It didn't take long for me to feel confident traveling around the city. I carry maps everywhere I go, and I ask for help when I need it. I worried about crime until I noticed that New Yorkers hardly ever think about it. My friend Bob laughed when I told him I was frightened of Central Park. He said it's like a big playground for New Yorkers, and he was right. Now it's one of my favorite places.

After I stopped being afraid of New York, I started having a great time here. Some Broadway plays have discount tickets, and there are good shows for even lower prices outside the theater district. The Student Services Office has a long list of events that students can afford. Last semester friends and I went to a concert at Lincoln Center, two plays, the Bronx Zoo, and five or six museums.

Besides having new cultural experiences, I've become hooked on professional sports for the first time. New Yorkers love sports, and it's hard to resist their excitement. Everywhere I go, radios and TV sets are tuned to baseball, hockey, basketball, or football games. New Yorkers have turned out to be much friendlier than I expected. Just mention sports, and everybody starts talking.

What I enjoy most is exploring the famous areas that make New York special. Chinatown, Times Square, and Greenwich Village are wonderful to visit. Bob and I often take our dates to unusual places we've heard about. Afterwards we look for a coffee house where we can sit for hours and talk about what we've seen.

Right now I'm looking forward to a visit from my parents, who are coming here during spring break. Although they remember the city well, it's changed since they lived here. I'm excited about taking them to my favorite places. And I don't mind a bit admitting that they were right. I very quickly fell in love with this wonderful city.

Here is Kent's essay once more, with arrows to show how his topic sentences are related to his thesis:

Enjoying the Big Apple

I had mixed feelings when I stepped off the plane in New York last September. My parents, who grew up in New York, assured me I'd love going to college in the city. But at first it seemed very big and frightening to me. What about crime? How would I cope with the subways and buses? Could I afford to do the neat things my parents always talked about, like going to plays and concerts? Luckily it didn't take long for the city to win me over. College friends who grew up here have taught me a lot. **Although I've been here only five months, I'm having a wonderful time in New York.**

It didn't take long for me to feel confident traveling around the city. I carry maps everywhere I go, and I ask for help when I need it. I worried about crime until I noticed that New Yorkers hardly ever think about it. My friend Bob laughed when I told him I was frightened of Central Park. He said it's like a big playground for New Yorkers, and he was right. Now it's one of my favorite places.

After I stopped being afraid of New York, I started having a great time here. Some Broadway plays have discount tickets, and there are good shows for even lower prices outside the theater district. The Student Services Office has a long list of events that students can afford. Last semester friends and I went to a concert at Lincoln Center, two plays, the Bronx Zoo, and five or six museums.

Besides having new cultural experiences, I've become hooked on professional sports for the first time. New Yorkers love sports, and it's hard to resist their excitement. Everywhere I go, radios and TV sets are tuned to baseball, hockey, basketball, or football games. New Yorkers have turned out to be much friendlier than I expected. Just mention sports, and everybody starts talking.

What I enjoy most is exploring the famous areas that make New York special. Chinatown, Time Square, and Greenwich Village are wonderful to visit. Bob and I often take our dates to unusual places we've heard about. Afterwards we look for a coffee house where we can sit for hours and talk about what we've seen.

Right now I'm looking forward to a visit from my parents, who are coming here during spring break. Although they remember the city well, it's changed since they lived here. I'm excited about taking them to my favorite places. And I don't mind a bit admitting that they were right. I very quickly fell in love with this wonderful city.

Exercise 2: Analyze an Essay

Instructions: A student essay appears below. Underline and label the thesis statement and topic sentences. Use arrows, as on this page, to show how the thesis statement and topic sentences are related to one another and to the paragraphs.

From Spud to Sparkle

I've spent the last five years of my life doing very little. I hated high school so much that I vowed never to go to school again. Because my parents liked having me at home with them, I didn't need much money for living expenses. I found a job working at a hardware store. The owners are wonderful to work for, and I quickly learned enough about hardware to do a good job. Most of my free time was spent in front of my parents' television set. All went well until Sally, my girlfriend, began accusing me of being a couch potato. After months of arguments, I began to see that she was right. It was time to do something with my life.

The first thing I did was to join Toastmasters, a club that helps people learn to speak in public. I enjoy talking to people in the store, so I thought Toastmaster training would help me develop more confidence and qualify for a better job. The results have been even better than I expected. My family and the people at the store have noticed a positive change in me.

Soon after I joined Toastmasters, my new friends there persuaded me to enroll in college. They said I was smart enough to succeed, even though I had some doubts. I'm gradually completing the requirements for a major in business administration. Some day I'll be running a business instead of standing behind a cash register.

The change I've enjoyed the most was signing up for dance lessons. Sally and I want to get married next year, and we think it's important to have fun together in our free time. I used to be pretty awesome on the dance floor in high school, even though I didn't really know what I was doing. After only a few lessons, I'm really enjoying the studio dance parties, and we've made several new friends.

My free time now finds me working on a Toastmasters speech, writing an English essay, or practicing my mambo steps. Even Sally says that I've begun to sparkle in public. I'm glad I decided to quit my career as a couch potato.

Writing Assignment: Draft Your Supporting Paragraphs

Instructions: Using your essay plan as a guide, develop your topic sentences into body paragraphs for your essay about college life. If you don't think you have enough material, try additional Discovery Activities. If you're still having difficulty, discuss your essay with someone who may be able to help—your instructor, another student, a staff member in the learning center. When you are finished, share what you have written with a small group of other students.

Learning More about Transition Words

As you saw in Chapter Five, *transitions* are words that help readers understand the connections between ideas in an essay. Transitions make your writing more *coherent* by helping readers see how one idea follows another. Kent used transitions effectively in his essay about New York. Here are several examples, with the transitions underlined:

My parents, who grew up in New York, assured me I'd love going to college in the city. <u>But</u> at first it seemed very big and frightening to me.

My friend Bob laughed when I told him I was frightened of Central Park. He said it's like a big playground for New Yorkers, <u>and</u> he was right. <u>Now</u> it's one of my favorite places.

Emphatic Order

"Enjoying the Big Apple" is written in *emphatic* order. Kent gradually built up to the high point of his essay—the fun of exploring places like Chinatown, Times Square, and Greenwich Village:

<u>After</u> I stopped being afraid of New York, I started having a great time here. TOPIC SENTENCE

<u>Besides</u> having new cultural experiences, I've become hooked on professional sports for the first time. TOPIC SENTENCE

<u>What I enjoy most</u> is exploring the famous areas that make New York special. TOPIC SENTENCE

Two essays you read earlier in this book use emphatic order. Here are Hattie's topic sentences from her essay "A Better Future" in Chapter One, with the transitions underlined. Hattie's most important reason for attending college appears last:

My hard work makes college possible for me. TOPIC SENTENCE

<u>Another</u> benefit of working hard is that my future opportunities will be good. TOPIC SENTENCE

<u>Best of all,</u> I'm setting a good example for my sisters Delonda and Keshia. TOPIC SENTENCE

Alice, in Chapter Four, used the phrase "more important" to emphasize her most significant point about her dining room table:

<u>More important,</u> the dining room table reminds me that my values have changed. EMPHATIC ORDER

Transitions are helpful when you're writing an essay in emphatic order. Phrases like "at first" or "to begin" can introduce your first supporting idea; "second," "better," or "worse" can signal your next idea; "worst," "happiest," or "most of all" signal your final and most important point.

Remember that emphatic order is only one of many ways to organize an essay. In Chapter Three, Tony used time order (also called "chronological order") to write about his family reunion. In Part Two of this book you'll explore several other ways to organize ideas.

■ ■ ■ **Transition Words for Emphatic Order**

- first, to begin, one, initially, primary, in the beginning, at first, basically
- second, another, also, furthermore, in addition, even worse, even better, more, next
- most of all, ultimately, most, best, worst, chief, leading, prime, foremost

Note that "last" and "finally" are usually *not* good choices to introduce your most significant point because they signal completion, not importance. They give readers the impression that you're winding up your essay rather than launching a new point that is the most powerful supporting idea in your essay. "Most of all," "most important," "best of all," or a similar phrase may be a better choice.

Exercise 3: Recognize Transitions

Instructions: Reread "From Spud to Sparkle" on page 119, underlining all the transitions. Write **C** above transitions that draw connections between two ideas; write **TS** above transitions that introduce topic sentences in the essay.

Exercise 4: Learn More About Transitions

Instructions: Several thesis statements and topic sentences appear below. Write additional topic sentences to support each thesis statement. Arrange the topic sentences in emphatic order, using a transition to begin each one.

A) College students who are interested in dating should know about these ways of meeting new people. THESIS STATEMENT
First are computer dating services, which use technology to match up compatible people. TOPIC SENTENCE

_____

_____ TOPIC SENTENCE

_____

_____ TOPIC SENTENCE

_____

_____ TOPIC SENTENCE

B) Single women who enjoy dating can protect themselves by following these guidelines. THESIS STATEMENT

First, listen for verbal clues that your date is aggressive or has little respect for women. TOPIC SENTENCE

_____

_____ TOPIC SENTENCE

_____

_____ TOPIC SENTENCE

_____

_____ TOPIC SENTENCE

C) College students enjoy many freedoms denied to high school students. THESIS STATEMENT

One privilege that college students enjoy is unsupervised free time. TOPIC SENTENCE

_____

_____ TOPIC SENTENCE

_____

_____ TOPIC SENTENCE

_____

_____ TOPIC SENTENCE

Writing Assignment: Add Transitions

Instructions: Reread the draft of your essay about college life (page 119), adding transitions to connect ideas and introduce your topic sentences.

WRITING WITH EXAMPLES (EXEMPLIFICATION)

Anna Quindlen, a Pulitzer-Prize winning columnist, believes that details are the key to effective writing. She says, "If you want to write what the world is about, you have to write details. . . . You can write about war, love, jealousy, hate. It's tempting to stack up all the seven deadly sins and to write about them. But real life is in the dishes. Real life is pushing strollers up the street, folding T-shirts, the alarm clock going off early and you dropping into bed exhausted every night. That's real life."

Quindlen is talking about _exemplification_—developing ideas through specific examples. Generous use of examples can enhance your writing in several ways. First, it gives your ideas clarity. A concept that's new to your readers, or difficult for them to understand, becomes much easier when you develop it with an example.

In an article in the *New York Times* about a scientific discovery, botanist Carrick Chambers used an example to explain why scientists were so excited about finding a grove of trees of an ancient type long thought to be extinct. According to Chambers, the discovery was "the equivalent of finding a small dinosaur still alive on Earth."

In the *Lakeland Ledger,* journalist Sean Loughlin used specific examples to help his readers understand the importance of the national debt:

> But the accumulated years of red ink spending—the debt—climbs ever higher. And a far more alarming trend persists: Each year a larger percentage of the country's total economic output is consumed by interest payments on the debt. That means there's less money available for new projects or programs, such as worker retraining, education, road and bridge repair, or even defense. The country is paying for its past, not its future.

In the next paragraph, notice how author Catherine Crier employed an example to explain the legal terms "circumstantial evidence" and "direct evidence":

> Basically, direct evidence is eyewitness testimony—someone testifying about what he or she saw. Circumstantial evidence is something that can be determined from all the circumstances surrounding the event. If you stood in a storm and saw and felt rain, that is direct evidence that it rained. If you were indoors and never looked out a window, but heard the sound of rain on the roof, then later walked outside to see water on the ground and dripping from trees, you could reasonably conclude it had just rained. This is circumstantial evidence. It is just as acceptable as direct evidence.

Another important advantage of examples is the individuality they bring to your writing. Human beings are united by untold numbers of shared experiences. Everyone in your college or university was at one time a newcomer to the school. Sharing your doubts and dreams about coming to the campus for the first time can help you feel closer to other students. At the same time, however, you are an individual whose feelings and experiences are unique to you. Getting in touch with the things that are important to you creates what is often called a writer's "voice"—awareness that you are a unique individual. Anna Quindlen explains, "the only thing that makes writing good is giving it our voice, our own personality. Writing is always an act of faith in your own character."

The following paragraph is an excerpt from an essay by a student named Rusty about his frustrations with the custody arrangements he'd made with his ex-wife. Similar problems are experienced by hundreds of thousands of parents who see their children only on alternate weekends. Notice how Rusty sets himself apart by describing his special concerns about his two sons:

> Not having daily influence upon Zeth's and Cameron's lives is an affliction. The weekend visits are proof of that. What happened to the manners I taught them? "Please" and "thank you" seem to have disappeared from their vocabularies. Why must they always use the word "ain't," even though I taught them otherwise? And the back talking is a flagrant display of disrespect, thought they're too young to understand but not too young to be corrected. One weekend every other week just isn't enough to

make an impression on them. Oh sure, they retain it until I have to take them back to their mother. But then on the next weekend visit the whole process starts over.

Writing Effective Examples

Skillful writers use many types of examples to develop their ideas. As you read the following list, think about your own favorite ways to support a point when you're writing or talking. Which are the most comfortable for you to use? Which would you like to use more often than you do now?

1. *Stories:* Also called "narratives," stories are one of the most effective ways to communicate an idea. Religious leaders from many traditions have long used stories—often called parables—as teaching tools. Parents often tell stories about their own growing years in hopes of impressing a point upon their children. In Chapter Three, Tony used a story effectively to show how loving his family is:

   > My family was lovely to Tarsha. She has a beautiful voice and sang in our talent show Saturday evening. She was amazed they wanted her to sing and applauded and cheered. Afterwards my grandmother and aunts hugged her.

2. *Lists:* Using your "writer's eyes" to make a list of details can make your writing engaging and vivid. Here are two excerpts from a *New York Times Magazine* article about a woman who's comparing her life before and after marriage and childbirth.

   > [Single life] When I was 24 I went to Europe for a year carrying one compact duffel that fit comfortably under an airline seat. In this bag I had packed a few interchangeable pieces of mostly black clothing, along with a blank journal and an elastic clothesline that could be stretched across any room. I wore my only pair of shoes—brown loafers.

   > [After marriage and motherhood] The night before our departure I surveyed the items I had spread out to pack. There were the portable crib and stroller; a box containing diapers, canned food, juice boxes and shelf-stable milk; a bag filled with toys and stuffed animals, and a suitcase containing at least two changes of clothes a day for the baby, with some extra cool-weather gear thrown in in case nature turned unpredictable.

   These details reinforce the new direction author Suzanne Matson's life has taken. She concludes that she likes the change—"toting, piece by awkward piece, my family's movable nest."

3. *Quotations from authorities:* Testimony from experts shows that you've researched your subject and your information is sound. In an article called "How to Find Your First Job," author Lyric Wallwork Winik reinforces advice about job hunting with a statement from an expert:

   > It helps to be focused. "There are two kinds of graduates," said Marilyn Moats Kennedy, a career counselor based in Chicago. "Those who know what they want to do and those who don't."

4. *Statistics:* Reliable statistics can add interest and credibility to your writing. In this excerpt from a newspaper editorial, statistics reinforce the main point—that many homeless people deserve help, not criticism:

> The homeless are apt to be victims of crime (41 percent). Many are veterans (33 percent). Homeless women tend to have at least one minor child living with them (65 percent).

Effective examples can help you write paragraphs with *closure*—a feeling that they have reached their highest point or a natural finish. The last sentence in the paragraph from Tony's essay has "closure" because it both finishes his story and reinforces his point about his loving family: "Afterwards my grandmother and aunt hugged her."

The following paragraph—from an article published by the International Palm Society—uses a list to create closure. Notice that author Mark Wuschke saves the most extreme item in his list for last. (The Latin words are scientific names of palm species.)

> Palms demonstrate an amazing ability to survive harsh conditions in nature. I've seen photographs of Trachycarpus fortunei lumbering under snow in the foothills of the Himalayas, and of Medemia argun roasting in the heat and drought of the Sudan Desert. The most extreme treatment nature can offer—fire—spells doom for most life forms, yet there are palms that can survive even this.

In this paragraph from an article about high schools, college student Jessica deCourcy Hinds uses a quotation both to reinforce her point and bring closure to her paragraph:

> Adults can be unsympathetic when kids complain about having to learn the boring basics. But it's all a matter of timing. One enlightened adult, Leon Botstein, president of Bard College, puts it this way: "When you teach someone baseball, they get invested in knowing what the rules are because they have enjoyed the act of hitting and catching. You don't sit them down and teach them the rule book."

Exercise 5: Look for Effective Examples

Instructions: Look in books, magazines, newspapers, or other published works for paragraphs with effective examples. Find at least one example of a story, a list, a quotation from an authority, and a statistic. Make a photocopy of each paragraph and highlight the sentence or sentences that serve as effective examples. Meet with a small group of other students to compare and discuss your selections.

Exercise 6: Look for Effective Paragraphs

Instructions: Find at least four examples of effective paragraphs in books, magazines, newspapers, or other published writings. Make a photocopy of each paragraph and highlight the sentence or sentences that create a sense of closure or climax. Meet with a small group of other students to compare and dicuss your selections.

Writing Assignment: Choose Effective Examples

Instructions: Look for opportunities to add examples to your essay about college life. Reread each paragraph of the body of your essay, and consider whether a story, list, quotation, or statistic could be added. Experiment with several types of examples; then meet with a small group of other students to discuss what you have written.

WRITING A CONCLUSION

Your concluding paragraph is your last opportunity to make a strong impact on your readers. It's worth investing extra time and thought to make a powerful final impression. Your conclusion should reinforce the main point you made in your essay. Never write a conclusion that contradicts or weakens your thesis statement. Writers sometimes use a conclusion to restate their thesis and summarize their main supporting ideas.

The guidelines you learned for opening paragraphs will also help you write an effective conclusion. Avoid statements that are too obvious, like this one: "My essay has attempted to prove that homelessness is a serious problem in our city." Avoid apologies, such as "I wish I could have covered this subject more thoroughly" or "I know I'm not an expert, but here's my opinion anyway." And don't stray from your main subject: Avoid introducing a new idea in your conclusion. Most important, don't hold back your opinion until the end of your essay. Readers should discover your viewpoint early, and it should shape the entire essay. Do leave your readers with a stimulating idea, fact or story.

STRATEGIES FOR CONCLUDING AN ESSAY

1. Describe a course of action. Here's the final paragraph of a student's essay about homelessness:

    > Job security is the best solution to homelessness. We must encourage legislators to fund new programs for vocational training. High school courses in math and English should emphasize career skills. Lessons that are taught and learned today can provide decent housing in the future.

2. Make a prediction. Here's an effective concluding paragraph from a student's essay about overpopulation:

    > The world's population doubled between 1950 and 1990, and it will double again in 2100 if present trends continue. Those numbers mean that more starvation and pollution lie ahead. We must act now to slow this growth.

And this is the conclusion to a student essay about college friendship:

> College life offers a rare opportunity to create deep friendships. For the next four years I'll be seeing my favorite people almost every day, in class and

out. It's worth investing extra time and energy in my relationships now. The friends I make on campus will be an important part of my life for years to come.

3. Tell a story. Here's how a student concluded an essay about his struggle to become physically fit:

> Yesterday I was almost late for class because the Science Building's parking lot was full. I parked near the Media Center, raced down the sidewalk to the Science Building, and bounded up the stairs. Jerry, my lab partner, said, "That was quite a performance. Are you training for the marathon?" I realized that I wasn't out of breath, and my heart wasn't pounding. My fitness program is paying off already. I'm a fitness convert.

Exercise 7: Evaluate Conclusions

Instructions: Put a check in front of each effective concluding statement.

_____ 1. Although I'm probably not qualified to tell our legislators how to run their prison system, I do think they should consider the points I've just made.

_____ 2. If professional teams continue moving to new cities every few years, football will soon lose the fans that have supported it so faithfully in the past.

_____ 3. Now that I've discussed the arguments for and against school vouchers, let me tell you what I think.

_____ 4. To avoid graduating with a mountain of consumer debt, students should avoid using credit cards until after college.

_____ 5. Remember that the day-to-day choices you make about how you spend your time will determine whether you achieve your career goals in the future.

Writing Assignment: Conclude Your Essay

Instructions: Write a conclusion to your essay about college life; then share what you have written with a small group of other students.

READING TO WRITE: EVALUATE YOUR SOCIETY

Michael Ventura is a social critic who frequently writes essays for the *Los Angeles Times*. In the following excerpt he evaluates "The Health of the Nation" as he perceives it. Before you begin reading, freewrite your ideas and impressions about the following areas of American life:

physical health

mental health

security

recreation

values

Vocabulary:

dysfunctional   (adjective) not operating properly
albeit   (conjunction) although

"The Health of the Nation"
Adapted from Letters at 3 A.M. *by Michael Ventura*

We can't seem to see what's in front of our eyes. When asked, as a people, to describe ourselves, we give dysfunctional answers, answers that are contradictory and/or don't correspond to reality. On the first day of the 1990s, the *Los Angeles Times* published the results of a nationwide poll in which it reported that "only 5 percent of Americans consider themselves to be in poor health"—despite massive data to the contrary; 89 percent claim to be "satisfied" with "the way your life is going," although 25 percent "feel unsafe walking alone at night in their own neighborhoods," while half of us keep a gun in our homes, and "one in 10 reported that they or a member of their household has been the victim of a serious crime *in the past year*" (my italics). One in ten Americans has considered suicide; 47 percent claim to be satisfied with the "national situation," yet 65 percent are dissatisfied with the nation's "moral values"; 87 percent are satisfied with their communities, although it's practically impossible for a middle-income American child to go to a first-rate high school, and although these same pollees overwhelmingly "regard crime as 'the single most urgent problem facing this country today.'" And if 87 percent are satisfied with their communities, why do so many of us feel we need a gun?

During the eighties, as reported in *USA Today,* handguns alone killed more than 75,000 Americans. That's half again as many as died in Vietnam. Dig it: in ten years of a shooting war, fewer Americans got shot dead than during ten years of "peace" in their own country. Yet 89 percent claim to be satisfied.

This poll describes, albeit unintentionally, a dysfunctional population—a population incapable of connecting the dots. People who can't describe themselves can't change. (At least not consciously.) All of which may be connected to the scariest statistic of all, parroted proudly by Walter Cronkite on a recent special celebrating the fiftieth year of television: "In this country we do more TV watching a day than anything else except sleep."

Take that in. As a people, we watch television more than we work, more than we play, more than we talk, more than we walk, more than we do *anything* except sleep. Watching television and sleeping constitute the bulk of our collective life.

What is such a people loyal to? What can such a people believe in? What can such a people contribute? Is it so surprising that these are the unhealthiest people in the developed world?

Responding to What You Have Read

1. What strategies did Ventura employ to develop his ideas?
2. How does Ventura define "health"?
3. What is Ventura's main point?
4. What questions did the *Los Angeles Times* ask in its poll?
5. How would you have answered those questions?
6. Ventura asks four general questions in the last paragraph of this selection. How would you answer them?

Writing Assignment: The Health of the Country

Instructions: Write an essay evaluating the health of the United States as you see it. Use several types of examples to develop your ideas: a story, a quotation from an authority, a statistic, a list.

READING TO WRITE: WHY DO WE SMOKE?

William Everett Bailey is an anti-smoking activist. The following selection is an excerpt from the Preface to his book *The Invisible Drug,* which explores the health hazards of tobacco. Before you begin reading, complete the following activity:

1. What experience have you and those close to you had with cigarettes?
2. Where do you usually encounter cigarette advertising? What impressions has it given you about cigarettes?
3. Why do you suppose that cigarettes are legal in the United States, while some other harmful substances are not?
4. What questions do you have about American attitudes and practices about smoking tobacco?

Vocabulary:

jeopardized	(verb) endangered
unimpeded	(adjective) unstopped
besiege	(verb) attack repeatedly
subconscious	(noun) part of the brain that thinks without our awareness
plethora	(noun) great quantity
vulnerable	(adjective) at risk
culling	(noun) selecting for destruction

Thinking about Cigarettes
from The Invisible Drug *by William Everett Bailey*

About the time my fourth family member died, the second one from lung cancer, my research had formed an unpleasant picture in my mind. The tobacco issue is an ugly story of the worst public health disaster in American history. The public's health has been seriously and negligently jeopardized. American smokers are dying at an unbelievable rate, 0.2% of the U.S. population every year. The daily body count is enough to fill three jumbo jets. A new view of the issue is necessary to fully realize the magnitude of this tragedy because most do not have it in proper perspective.

Why is it that a defective product, a dangerous poison, continues to be promoted and sold? The tobacco industry has invaded the government and manipulates it to protect their business at the expense of the citizens whom the government is dutifully bound to protect. There is no democracy where tobacco is concerned. Today nonsmokers outnumber smokers three to one. Yet, since the Surgeon General's Report in 1964, when smoking was announced to be the cause of cancer, heart attacks and premature death, Congress has voted down almost every major tobacco control legislation. Small steps have been taken, but little has been done to stop the unnecessary deaths and human suffering which continue unimpeded at the rate of one every 72 seconds.

Taking poisons and dying a slow painful death is not normal. Why then is smoking so socially acceptable? The tobacco industry, like the government, has a tight grip on the minds of most Americans. They spend $24 for every man, woman and child in the United States annually to "brainwash" us into believing smoking is a normal part of life. They bombard us with a plethora of very effective advertising associating smoking with good health, fun, popularity, independent life styles, and individual's rights. Billboards, magazine advertising, movies, and ads at sporting events constantly besiege the subconscious telling us that smoking is a normal part of life. The industry calls it "friendly familiarity," and that has been one goal of tobacco advertising that has been very successful. So we shrug it off and say let the smoker smoke, they know it's bad for them. We also say that secondhand smoke doesn't bother us.

Tobacco advertising has been successful in another arena. The tobacco messages start getting through to children before they learn to read. After years of constant repetition, and at the vulnerable age of ten to 12, 25% start smoking. For the most part, tobacco advertising works only on children; therefore it must be designed to attract the one audience it is most effective in reaching. Yet this systematic culling of the American kid, killing one of every three that starts smoking, goes unnoticed by most people.

Responding to What You Have Read

1. What strategies did William Everett Bailey use to develop his ideas?
2. What is his main point?
3. Bailey's book *The Invisible Drug* was published in 1996. What changes in policies about tobacco have taken place since then?
4. What questions did Bailey ask about tobacco? How do they compare to the questions you wrote on page 129?

Writing Assignment: Harmful Substances

Instructions: Write an essay about tobacco or another harmful substance whose effects you have witnessed in yourself or others. Use as many types of development as you can: stories, quotations from authorities, statistics, lists.

SUMMARY

1. Successful writing projects usually go through several drafts.
2. An effective essay has a well-planned introduction, body, and conclusion.
3. Writers use a variety of strategies to begin and end their essays.

LOOKING AHEAD

Once you've produced a draft of an essay, no matter how flawed it is, the hardest part of the writing process is over. Chapter Eight, "Revising Your Essay," introduces a variety of strategies to help you transform a draft into an effective, finished essay.

CHAPTER EIGHT

Revising Your Essay

Preview

During the revising step of the writing process, you evaluate and improve the organization and content of an essay. As you revise, consider whether changes are needed to make your writing appropriate for your audience and purpose. Feedback from others is invaluable when you're revising. Proofreading—correcting spelling, sentence structure, punctuation, and other usage errors—should be delayed until you're satisfied with the organization and ideas in your essay.

WHY REVISE?

If you're familiar with computers, you know that "bugs"—unexpected problems—appear even in programs carefully designed by experts. Writing often has "bugs" too: No matter how carefully you draft an essay, problems may appear. Sentences and paragraphs may need rewriting, ideas and examples may have to be deleted or added, and reorganization may be necessary. Even professional writers with years of experience must revise their work extensively.

Revising is an evaluative process: You reread what you've written, discard anything that dissatisfies you, and experiment with improvements. (A related process—editing to make sentences more effective and eliminate usage errors—is covered in Part Three, Editing Skills.) Careful revision can improve an essay in two ways. First, it helps you showcase your ability to organize, express, and explore ideas. Second, it strengthens the connection between you and your readers.

For many writers, revision is a continuous process. Even while they're organizing and drafting, they may cross out words and substitute different ones. Although it's all right to make a few minor changes while you're drafting an essay, don't let yourself be completely sidetracked by punctuation, spelling, and other usage issues. You'll have time to make those changes later. It's a waste of time to correct sentences that you may change drastically while you're reorganizing your essay. Proofreading (making minor editing changes) should be delayed until you're satisfied with the overall structure of your essay. Trying to produce a perfect draft all at once can be frustrating and discouraging.

Premature proofreading is one problem that student writers face. Another is reluctance to rework their early drafts. Some students feel that once is enough: What they've written seems fine, and they wonder why they should bother redoing it. And sometimes they've used up their energy on the first draft and don't want to start writing again. Here are five reasons why it's important to revise your work, even if you're tempted to leave it alone:

1. *You may need to state your message more powerfully.* E. B. White, author of *The Elements of Style*, warned: "When you say something, make sure you have said it. The chances of your having said it are only fair." Everyday conversations often miss the mark, and writers struggle with the same problem. Ask friends for feedback about what you've written. If they miss the point of your essay, don't blame them: The difficulties probably lie in your essay. Get busy revising.

2. *You may have written a warm-up or discovery draft rather than a final draft.* Writing feels good when you're excited about your topic and ideas are flowing. But your writing may not be ready for an audience yet: You're still generating in the discovery stage. Don't underestimate the value of this "discovery" or "warm-up" writing. It brings freshness and vitality to your ideas. But this spontaneous writing needs revision before it's ready for your readers.

3. *You'll make a better impression on your readers.* Awkward sentences, inexact ideas, wrong word choices, and organizational problems are bad for a writer's image. Thorough revising eliminates these problems.

4. *You'll add polish and professionalism to your writing.* As you revise, you can transform choppy writing into sophisticated sentence patterns. You can replace too-simple language with mature word choices. Examples and explanations can be strengthened so that your essay is more interesting and enjoyable to read and makes your point more powerfully.

5. *What you have written may not be appropriate for your audience.* Even superb writing may be useless if it isn't right for your readers. If your audience doesn't understand your vocabulary, examples, or ideas, they'll miss the point you're trying to make. The opposite problem can be equally damaging: Your essay may be full of obvious ideas that bore your readers. Thoughtful revision can help you avoid these problems.

■ ■ ■ **The Right Word**

Eli Wiesel, a Holocaust survivor who has written many books, has described his own long search for the right words to write about his experiences: "I was afraid that what I wanted to say, I would not be able to say. . . . The words, I feared, did not exist."

Collaborative Exercise: List Ideas about Revising

Instructions: Read the following excerpts, in which successful writers share their ideas about revising their work. Then, working with a small group of other students, list the most important points these writers have made.

1. Stephen W. Hawking, author of *A Brief History of Time*, recalled, "I have had suggestions of how to improve the book from a large number of people who have seen preliminary versions. In particular, Peter Guzzardi, my editor at Bantam Books, sent me pages and pages of comments and queries about points he felt that I had not explained properly. I must admit that I was rather irritated when I received his great list of things to be changed, but he was quite right. I'm sure that it is a better book as a result of his keeping my nose to the grindstone."

2. In his book *Feeling Good*, psychiatrist David Burns described how he revised a chapter about procrastinating:

    > The first draft of this chapter was overwritten, clumsy, and stale. It was so long and boring that a true procrastinator would never even have the fortitude to read it. The task of revising it seemed to me like trying to go swimming with concrete shoes. When the day I had scheduled for revising it came, I had to push myself to sit down and get started. My motivation was about 1 percent, and my urge to avoid the task was 99 percent. What a hideous chore!
    >
    > After I got involved in the task, I became highly motivated, and the job seems easy now. Writing became fun after all!

3. Susan Sontag, author of *Against Interpretation* and many other books, explains, "I don't write easily or rapidly. My first draft usually has only a few elements worth keeping. I have to find out what those are and build from them and throw out what doesn't work, or what simply is not alive."

4. Author Alex Haley once showed a manuscript page from his best-seller *Roots,* heavily marked with green ink corrections, to a friend and said, "Some of those chapters I rewrote fifteen times, twenty times, twenty-five times. I wanted it to be right."

5. American humorist Mark Twain declared, "The difference between the right word and the almost right word is the difference between lightning and the lightning bug."

6. An interview with novelist Ernest Hemingway contains this exchange:

    HEMINGWAY: I rewrote the ending of *A Farewell to Arms*, the last page of it, thirty-nine times before I was satisfied with it.
    INTERVIEWER: Was there some technical problem there? What was it that had stumped you?
    HEMINGWAY: Getting the words right.

SUGGESTIONS FOR REVISING YOUR ESSAY

1. *Evaluate your thesis statement.* Does your thesis statement appear in the first paragraph of your essay? Although you can place it elsewhere, or omit it completely, the first paragraph usually works best. (Many writers make it the final sentence in the introductory paragraph.) By promptly telling readers what your paper is about, you help them understand the development of your ideas.

2. *Check your essay for unity.* Everything in your essay should be unified around a single purpose—supporting (developing, explaining, and clarifying) your thesis. Delete any unrelated ideas that distract readers or weaken your main point. If parts of your essay seem off the subject, it may need major reorganization. As mentioned on page 133, you may have written a "discovery" or "warm-up" draft instead of a well-organized essay. Consider asking your instructor for guidance, or visit the writing lab on your campus for additional help.

   The following paragraph is part of an early draft written by a student named Janice. Notice that the sentences about bowling weaken her main point—her appreciation for her father:

   > My father has always set aside time to spend with me. Once or twice a month he plans a movie, an evening of miniature golf, or a shopping trip for us. Last week our favorite miniature golf range was closed for remodeling, so we went bowling. It wasn't as much fun as miniature golf because neither of us is good at bowling. The bowling alley was so noisy that we couldn't talk the way we usually do. But most of the time I enjoy telling him about my social life, friendships, and future plans. WEAK PARAGRAPH

   The revised paragraph below is more unified because every detail explains why Janice enjoys her father's company:

   > My father has always set aside time to spend with me. Once or twice a month he plans a movie, an evening of miniature golf, or a shopping trip for us. Besides having fun, we feel close to each other. I like to hear him rave about a new dress I've bought, and he thinks I have great taste in neckties. He teases me about the romantic films I like, and I pretend to complain about his science fiction movies. Our conversation moves easily from clothing and movie stars to social events, friendships, and future plans. None of my friends enjoy such a close relationship with their fathers. UNIFIED PARAGRAPH

3. *Look for coherence.* Make sure you've arranged your supporting ideas and examples logically. It's a good practice to begin a paragraph with a topic sentence (usually a supporting idea) so readers can follow your thinking easily. Group related ideas together, and aim for continuity. Make each paragraph a solid unit with an effective concluding sentence. Avoid tagging an extra idea or example at the end of a paragraph. Notice the strong final sentence in Janice's paragraph about her father:

   > None of my friends enjoy such a close relationship with their fathers. EFFECTIVE FINAL SENTENCE

   But the following paragraph lacks coherence because the word "also" makes the final sentence an afterthought rather than a continuation of the previous idea.

   > Coach Pyle taught me the value of teamwork. I wanted to be a basketball star and do all the scoring on the court myself. It was hard for me to pass the ball to another player and let him take the shot. Coach Pyle convinced me that I needed

to be part of a winning team, not a spectacular lone player. He also showed me that I could trust other players to give me many opportunities to score points.

Here's a more coherent revision of the same paragraph:

Coach Pyle taught me the value of teamwork. I wanted to be a basketball star and do all the scoring on the court myself. It was hard for me to pass the ball to another player and let him take the shot. Coach Pyle told me I needed to be part of a winning team, not a spectacular lone player. I learned to trust other players to give me opportunities to score points. After a year with Coach Pyle, I had a much better attitude towards my teammates.

4. *Strive to make your essay interesting.* Make sure you have supported your thesis statement with powerful ideas and interesting examples that will make a strong impression on your audience. Avoid obvious facts and commonplace details. If you're having trouble developing your thesis, spend a few minutes generating new ideas through lateral thinking. Choose a Discovery Activity you haven't already tried: It may produce a great deal of supporting material. Then select the best ideas and examples for your essay.

Here's an example of weak development in a student's essay about his father:

Most important, Dad always provided whatever we needed. My sister Polly and I always had clean, nice clothes for school. Dad worked hard to make sure that our family had food and a comfortable house to live in. Mom has often said that he has taken good care of us.

Providing shelter, food, and clothing is a basic responsibility of fatherhood. This student failed to explain what makes his father special. Janice's paragraph, which you read earlier, is a more effective tribute: It mentions miniature golf, movies, shopping trips, fun, and closeness. Janice avoided obvious statements about fatherhood, preferring to explore the unusual features of their relationship.

5. *Evaluate your ideas for clarity.* Effective writing is clear, helping readers grasp every point. But two difficulties may prevent readers from understanding what you've written.

First, there may not be sufficient background information—a frequent problem in papers about current issues. For example, your readers are sure to recognize major American political figures, but they may not know the names of prime ministers from other countries. Explain any words, names, and terminology that might confuse your readers. Parentheses, as well as *who* or *which* clauses, are useful for inserting information into a sentence.

Congress may remove some restrictions from the Hatch Act, which limits political activities for civil servants. EXAMPLE

Wayne Gretzky, one of the greatest of all hockey players, retired in 1999. EXAMPLE

Watson angrily denounced the Dragons' management for their decision to put him on waivers (canceling the contract he had signed with the team). EXAMPLE

A second problem is that readers may have difficulty following your reasoning. Sometimes adding a word or two can make your ideas more clear and emphatic to your audience. As you read the sentence pairs below, notice that the second version in each pair is more clear and emphatic because words like "mistakenly," "should," and "unfortunately" clarify the writer's position:

> Many government officials hope to control crime by building new prisons. VAGUE
>
> Many government officials mistakenly hope to control crime by building new prisons. CLEAR
>
> The School Board wants students to have access to all the books on the list, but parents want the right to control their children's reading. VAGUE
>
> The School Board wants students to have access to all the books on the list, but parents should have the right to control their children's reading. CLEAR
>
> Fuel efficiency isn't a major concern in most car purchases. VAGUE
>
> Unfortunately, fuel efficiency isn't a major concern in most car purchases. CLEAR

Choose words that clearly and specifically convey your meaning. Conductor Andre Previn once interrupted an orchestra rehearsal to tell the horn player, "I think that passage requires a more heroic approach, perhaps a little more accentuation, a greater assertiveness. . . ." The horn player asked, "You mean you want it louder, Mr. Previn?" While the rest of the orchestra laughed, Previn thought for a moment—and realized that loudness really was what he wanted. Avoid roundabout explanations: Keep working on your sentences until they clearly state what you want readers to know.

6. *Verify the accuracy of what you've written.* Check your information before you submit your paper. Confirm the spelling of all proper names; make sure all facts are accurate and current. *Catherine* can also be spelled *Katherine* or *Katharine*; *England* is not the same as the *United Kingdom*; the *Soviet Union* ceased to exist in 1991. If you're doubtful about a fact, ask a librarian for help. Never tell a professor that your paper might contain some errors: Instead check all your facts and make any corrections needed *before* you hand in your final draft.

Exercise 1: Learn More about Revision

Instructions: In the previous chapter you read an early version of an essay about victims by a student named Patricia. Here is her early draft again, followed by her final version. As you read and compare them, mark the changes she made. Using the checklist on page 138, try to find a reason for each change. Place the appropriate numbers (1–9) from the checklist on the changes you've marked.

Victims

When I was little, my mother started working on my attitude. She didn't let me feel sorry for myself when things went wrong. She would always ask me, "Who's in charge of your feelings?" I was too young to understand what she meant. But now I

■ ■ ■ **Revision Checklist**

Page numbers in parentheses direct you to more information.

- Does your title catch readers' interest?
- Will readers find your essay interesting as soon as they begin reading? (111–114)
- Does your thesis appear early in your essay? (110)
- Is your thesis a complete statement (not a question)?
- Does it accurately assert your point of view? (94)
- Do you need to add ideas and examples to develop your thesis? (123–125)
- Is each paragraph unified around a single idea? (135)
- Does every sentence support (explain or develop) your thesis? (135)
- Are all your ideas in logical order? (135)
- Did you use transition words to help readers understand the flow of ideas? (119–120)
- Will readers understand your vocabulary, examples, and ideas? (136–137)
- Will your audience find your ideas fresh and interesting? (136)
- Will readers feel that you have treated them fairly and respectfully? (78)
- Do the ideas in your conclusion match the rest of the essay? (125)
- Does the conclusion signal to readers that your essay is finished? (125)
- Did you fulfill the purpose of your essay? (125)
- Do you need to delete or add ideas, examples, or information? (135)

do. I wish some of my friends would stop feeling sorry for themselves. They do a lot of blaming. They don't put themselves in charge of their lives.

Chuck doesn't take responsibility for changing his college major. He wanted to be a teacher. His family kept complaining about it, so he switched to business. Now he doesn't enjoy his business courses. He blames his family. But he's the one who made the decision. He's an adult, and he has to earn his own living. He should listen to himself, not his family.

Leo exaggerates how hard college is for him. He's an A student, and he wants to become a doctor. He's brilliant and helps other students with their math and science homework. But he complains because his premed courses are very hard. He's lucky to be so gifted, and I wish he appreciated that.

Linda is a smart person who acts like she's helpless. She failed math twice and may have to drop out of college. She won't ask for extra help because she believes she's hopeless. I've gone shopping with her and seen her do math in her head. But in class she refuses to try. She thinks she's bad in math because in elementary school a teacher told her she can't do it.

I talk to my friends about their attitudes. Some change, but some don't. I wish people had a mother like mine who taught them that they were in charge.

Here is Patricia's final draft:

Victims

When I was about five years old, I suffered a big disappointment. My favorite aunt got sick and had to miss a trip to the circus with my parents and me. Although the three of us went anyway, I missed my aunt. The circus wasn't much fun, and I was very angry. I remember hearing my frustrated mother ask, "Who's in charge of your feelings?"

I was too young then to understand that I could have decided to have fun even though my aunt wasn't there. But since then my mother has asked that question many times, and it's helped me take responsibility for my life. Lately I've been noticing how many people never learned that important lesson. Instead of putting themselves in control, they choose to act like victims.

First, some of my friends don't take responsibility for the choices they've made. They whine about being pressured into important decisions, even when they had the final say. Chuck got tired of hearing his family complain about his plans for a teaching career, so he switched to business. But his family didn't make the decision—he did. I wish he'd stop blaming them for his career change.

I've also known people who exaggerate the obstacles they're facing. Leo is an A student who hopes to be accepted into medical school. He's so brilliant that he's always helping other students with their math and science homework. But he complains endlessly about all the difficult courses he'll have to pass to become a doctor. He doesn't appreciate how gifted and fortunate he is.

Most annoying are the people who won't help themselves. Linda has failed math twice and may have to drop out of college. She won't ask for extra help because she believes she's hopeless at math. I've gone shopping with her and seen her perform complicated calculations in her head. But in class she refuses to try. An elementary school teacher convinced Linda that she couldn't do math, so Linda stopped trying.

I've been able to talk a few friends out of their victim attitudes, but I've known others who refuse to change. I wish more people would get in touch with their power to take charge of their lives. They could do for others what my mother did for me— serve as guides and role models in the art of responsible living.

Collaborative Activity: Discuss Patricia's Revision

Instructions: Meet with a small group of other students to compare and discuss the changes you had marked on Patricia's essay.

REVISING WITH PEERS

Revising an essay is both a solitary and a social activity. Although you'll revise on your own, you also need feedback from other people. Peer revision is a group process in which your "peers"—students like yourself—help you evaluate and improve your work.

Peer revision helps you assess whether your writing is appropriate for your audience and purpose. Because your subject is so familiar to you, it can be difficult to anticipate how readers will react to what you've written. Ideas that seem clear to you may mystify your audience; misunderstandings and mistakes can creep in where you least expect them—like the computer "bugs" mentioned earlier. Peer editing helps you spot such problems, and group members may also have useful suggestions for correcting them.

Experienced writers recommend revising an essay at least twice—first on your own, and then with a group. The strategies below will help you get the maximum benefit from this process.

HOW PEER REVISING WORKS

At the beginning of the group revising process, a member reads his or her essay aloud. Others in the group discuss the essay's content and organization, offering suggestions for improvement where needed. Coaching, appreciation, and specific feedback are encouraged. The essay's author is free to accept or reject the group's suggestions; most of the time, however, these comments are useful and welcome. Finally, if time allows, the group also proofreads the paper. Then the process begins again with another student's essay.

Like most students, you'll probably find peer revision enormously beneficial to your growth as a writer. Be patient with the process, even if it seems unfamiliar at first. Resist the temptation to argue when a group member suggests a change in something you've written. Your group can tell you which elements in your essay are successful and which need improvement. Trust yourself, too: Don't be afraid to show appreciation and make suggestions to other group members.

Besides enhancing your writing skills, peer revision develops your ability to talk about writing—what works, what doesn't, and what strategies are needed for improvement. These skills are valuable both in college and the working world. Because many careers require committee reports, team writing is an important part of many responsible jobs. You can earn respect and appreciation by knowing how to write well both as an individual and a group member. Because peer revision in college is such an important learning opportunity, resolve to get as much benefit from the process as you can.

STRATEGIES FOR PEER REVISING

Work on one paper at a time. Have the author read the paper aloud to the group without stopping. Listeners may take notes about points they'd like to discuss. When the author is finished reading, group members can discuss the following points:

1. What was your overall reaction to the paper? This question is a useful starting point because it encourages the group to react to the writer's ideas and experiences, rather than usage and organizational details. How did you feel as you listened? Did any

points particularly interest you? What did you like best about the paper? Were any points confusing? Do you feel you understood the writer's main point?

2. Is the thesis effective? If it is unclear or omitted, the paper may need major changes.

3. Is the essay coherent? Evaluate the supporting ideas, which should be logical and consistent. If necessary, the group can offer suggestions for revising the outline.

4. Did the writer fulfill his or her purpose? If the essay is descriptive, did the author successfully communicate his or her feelings and the meaning of the experience described in the essay? If the writer's purpose is informative, what did readers learn? If the purpose is persuasive, how convincing were the ideas and examples in the essay?

5. Is the introduction effective? It should clarify the subject and the writer's point of view, provide sufficient background, stimulate the audience's interest, and state the essay's thesis.

6. Is each paragraph complete and consistent? Are there enough examples and transition words? Does each paragraph come to a satisfying close?

7. Is the conclusion effective? Does it match the rest of the essay? Does it leave a strong final impression on the audience?

Collaborative Activity: Peer Revising

Instructions: As you read the following essays on your own, evaluate the writer's organization and development. Check the outline for unity and coherence; look for transition words and well-developed supporting ideas. Then meet with a small group of other students to discuss how these essays could be improved. Follow the "Strategies for Peer Revising" described above. Have one student in the group read each essay aloud; then continue with the rest of the revision process. When you're finished, evaluate the group experience. Did the group process enhance your ability to react to and revise these essays? Why or why not? What changes could your group make next time to improve the process?

Good-bye, Liza

When I broke up with Liza last summer, I learned some important lessons about life and love. In the past I made fun of friends who felt bad after breaking up. I wasn't very helpful when they faced other problems either. For example, I didn't even call Joe when he was fired from the sporting-goods store. Now I know how it feels to be hurt.

I learned that emotional pain comes in unexpected ways. In the beginning I thought I'd be glad to be done with Liza because she'd been so difficult to get along with. But for months everything reminded me of the good times we'd had together. Sometimes I think about trying to get her back again, but I know it's hopeless. I'm glad I met another woman, Ginny, I really like.

In addition, I learned a lot. I used to act superior when one of my friends was having love problems. Now I know how they felt, and I'm grateful for the friends who understand what I was going through. My mother said some wise things too. I'm also glad I had some distractions to get me through the worst times. The football season helped a lot, and so did my job at the mall.

I found out it's hard to trust again. When I finally started dating again, I was sometimes very suspicious and distant with her. Finally my new girlfriend, Ginny, taught me a few things. She said she'd been hurt the same way more than once, and she knew it was hard to trust again. But it's like plunging into the cold water at the beach. You don't want to do it, but the results are worth it. My mother told me the same thing, but it wasn't as convincing because it happened to her before she married my dad.

The lessons I learned have helped me build a wonderful relationship with Ginny. I guess it's all part of life. Although the experience with Liza was so painful, it helped me mature into a better person. There are times when I find myself thinking that the pain was worth it after all. I also have more respect for my mother because I can see how much she knows about life and love.

Too Much TV?

Watching television is a popular American pastime. TV provides entertainment, information and cultural experiences to millions of people. Last month some family friends proudly announced that they'd sold both their TV sets. Now that they're not watching TV anymore, they say that life is much better. The children are doing better in school, and they're all having more family fun. I disagree. TV watching can enhance family life.

First, TV can help families communicate. Parents can ask children questions about what they're watching. Then they can exchange views and learn about one other's values and points of view. Sometimes my dad watches "The Simpsons" on TV with my eight-year-old brother, and they talk about good manners and family problems. My parents think I watch too many sports programs, but I learn a lot from them, too. I'm inspired by my sports heroes, and the programs give me something to talk about when I see my friends.

Watching TV also helps families relax together. When I'm home for the evening, we vote on one show to watch as a family. But I don't participate if I'm studying or have plans with my friends. My family and I like to watch quiz shows, national news, and some of the specials that are on. We really enjoy competing against each other when we watch "Jeopardy" and "The Price is Right."

Watching TV doesn't have to be a waste of time or a bore. My parents have always emphasized self-discipline, and their wisdom has helped all of us schedule our TV time wisely. Rather than banishing TV altogether, parents should teach their children how to make the best use of this wonderful resource. They should also encourage their children to develop other interests and hobbies. TV is here to stay. It's an important part of American family life, and that's unlikely to change.

SUMMARY

1. Most writing contains "bugs"—awkward sentences, misplaced ideas, organization mistakes—that can be fixed by careful revision.
2. Because feedback from others is so helpful, it's wise to practice peer revision whenever possible.
3. The Revision Checklist on page 138 can help you systematically and thoroughly revise your work.

LOOKING AHEAD

Computers are important writing tools. In Chapter Nine, "Writing with Computers," you'll learn how computers can help you develop your writing skills, broaden your writing audience, and discover new ideas.

CHAPTER NINE

Writing with Computers

Preview

Computers assist writers in three important ways. First, word-processing software facilitates the writing process. Because changes are so easy, many writers use a computer to explore, organize, and revise ideas. Second, the Internet provides a diverse real-world audience for your writing. Most important, the Internet is a vast source of ideas, information, and other resources for writing.

WHY WRITE WITH COMPUTERS?

Whether you're an experienced user or a novice, this chapter can help you use computer technology to improve your writing. If you're a newcomer, the first step is to learn some basic terms; others will be introduced later.

- *Software* means specialized computer programs that help you perform specific tasks.
- *Word processing* refers to software that transforms an old-fashioned typewriter keyboard into a powerful writing tool.
- The *Internet* is a worldwide network of electronic information tools.
- The *World Wide Web* (also called WWW and "the Web") is the part of the Internet familiar to most computer users. It consists of linked documents that use a special format called HTTP. (Many people use the terms *Internet* and *World Wide Web* interchangeably.) Computer users can view these documents (called "websites" and "web pages") on their computer screens; video and sound are available as well.
- A *search engine* is an online device that can help you find websites that interest you. *Yahoo.com* and *Altavista.com* are popular search engines.

Both word processing and the World Wide Web are so important to writers that skill with both is essential to many careers. Word processing simplifies typing: It's easier to make corrections and revisions on a computer than when you're using an old-fashioned typewriter. You can move text, fix errors, and insert new material rapidly, often with just a few keystrokes. Essays, letters, and reports produced with word-processing software have an attractive, professional look that's important in modern workplaces. In this chapter, you'll learn some tips for mastering word processing.

The World Wide Web puts you in touch with information sources from all over the world. Anyone (including you!) who has access to some basic computer equipment and software can put documents onto the Web. Specialized tools called "search engines" help computer users find the documents they want—a process called "surfing." "Surfers" use the Web for entertainment and a wide range of other activities—making travel reservations, shopping for bargains, communicating directly with experts, expanding knowledge about a vast array of topics, and finding answers to questions and problems. Professional people in many fields rely on the Web for information about developments in their fields. For writers, the Web is an amazing source of ideas and information.

If you haven't tried word processing before, or been introduced to the World Wide Web, magical experiences are in store for you. It's natural to be uneasy about computers if you're a novice. Remember, though, that huge numbers of people—including many children—quickly learn how to have great fun with computers. Many people report that it's a thrill to produce a professional-looking letter or essay on a computer the first time—and a great surprise to discover that basic word processing is easy. And the almost inconceivable possibilities of the World Wide Web are even more exciting.

If you're finding it difficult to imagine all these possibilities, you're not alone. The extraordinary powers of today's computers took almost everyone by surprise. (The 1993 edition of the *American Heritage Dictionary* doesn't even mention many computer terms that are widely used today—"Internet," "surfing," and "netiquette.") Even technology experts have had trouble imagining the possibilities. In 1943, the chairman of IBM predicted that there would someday be a world market for as many as *five* computers. In 1949, *Popular Mechanics* magazine thought technology would eventually shrink the size of computers to only one and a half tons! In 1977, the founder of Digital Equipment Corporation declared that there was no reason for anyone to have a computer at home.

Because this book is not a computer manual—and because technology changes so rapidly—the following pages focus primarily on computers as writing tools, not computer instruction. For up-to-date computer assistance, consult an experienced computer user, or read an instructional manual that teaches the computer skills you want to learn.

ADVANTAGES OF USING A WORD PROCESSOR

Whether you're a skilled keyboard user or a novice, a computer can help you improve the look, style, and content of your writing. Because mistakes are easy to correct, a computer can help you produce error-free writing. Spellcheckers automatically highlight misspelled words and help you choose the correct spelling of the word you're trying to write. When you're having trouble thinking of the exact word you want to use, a thesaurus in the software can guide you to the choice you want. It's easy to make changes and corrections, and you can rapidly move pieces of your writing to see where they fit best. And word processing allows you to experiment with type faces and other formatting features to give your writing eye appeal. Word processing manuals are sold in most bookstores, and colleges offer computer classes and computer labs staffed by experts who can help you improve your skills.

The time you spend developing computer expertise and keyboarding skill will pay off handsomely both in college and the workplace. Because writing is an important part of most professional careers, you'll have a big advantage if you can use word processing efficiently instead of having to wait for a typist to get your writing into shape. Furthermore, you'll have final control over the quality of the finished product: Errors can creep in when someone else has to redo all your paperwork.

TEN TIPS FOR EFFECTIVE WORD PROCESSING

1. Take a keyboarding course. Once you've learned the keyboard and begun performing writing tasks at the computer, your speed and accuracy will automatically improve. You can sign up for a class on campus or learn from a computer or video program.

2. To avoid losing your work and having to start over during a computer failure, save early and often. ("Saving" means making a permanent copy that you can retrieve if there's a computer failure.) Computers aren't perfect: Sometimes they shut down abruptly, erasing whatever you've been working on. Don't wait until a document is perfect to save it. Most experienced users save their work every five minutes or so. Many students learn about saving the hard way when a sudden computer shutdown destroys two hours of work and an almost-perfect writing assignment.

3. Make at least one backup of important documents—and remember that in college, almost anything you're writing qualifies as "important." Hard drives can "crash" (malfunction) without warning, erasing all your documents; a diskette you've been using for months may suddenly go bad and have to be thrown away. Many students and professionals always make a "hard copy" (printed copy) of ongoing writing projects, as well as putting a copy onto a diskette. (While writing this book, I kept backup diskettes both at home and at work as extra insurance.)

4. Have plenty of labeled diskettes handy. It's disastrous to lose a diskette containing an assignment you've worked on for weeks. If you've put your name, address, and phone number on the label, there's a chance your diskette will be returned.

5. Cultivate friendships with computer-savvy friends and staff members. Express sincere thanks to anyone who helps you solve computer problems and sharpen your skills. (When someone has given you extraordinary help, consider extending a lunch invitation, sending a thank-you card, or writing a letter to your helper's supervisor.) And remember that others around you may be having the same questions and problems: Be willing to share what you're learning.

6. Prepare for change. A diskette you're using today may not be compatible with technology a few years from now. Discuss long-term writing projects with computer experts to find ways to ensure that your electronic files will continue to be usable.

7. Be wary of grammar checkers. Remember that a computer is a machine, not a human brain: It can only guess at English grammar, based on a complex system of statistics and rules. When in doubt, consult an expert about the computer's grammar suggestions.

8. Learn the basics first. Word-processing teachers say that most novices can start producing professional-looking work after only an hour or two of instruction. Make sure you know how to do the following tasks: open a new document, indent paragraphs, double space, save and print your work, and operate the "undo" key (a marvelous aid that allows you to fix a document after you've accidentally messed it up). Be sure you also know how to start up and shut down the computer properly.

9. Plan a systematic program for upgrading your skills. If you have your own computer, you can easily set it to show you a new tip every time you turn it on. Borrow a computer manual from the library or—better yet—purchase one and read a page or two every day. Spend a few minutes every day experimenting with the menus and commands displayed on the screen.

10. Have fun. Deadlines and perfectionism spoil the excitement of the new discoveries you'll be making as you develop your computer skills. Most expert users report that they learned a great deal by playing and experimenting with various applications. Expect both highs and lows: Computers can be enormously frustrating, exhilarating, and surprising. Don't think you have to learn it all at once, or that there's something wrong with you (or your computer) when a command doesn't work the way you expected. A playful, relaxed attitude is your greatest asset while you're learning.

Collaborative Activity: Share What You Know

Instructions: Meet with a small group of other students to discuss word processing. If possible, your group should include both novices and experienced users. Choose one person to serve as recorder. Taking turns, have each person share experiences and impressions about word processing. The following questions may be helpful:

- Are you a computer user—or are you close to anyone who uses word processing regularly? What kinds of experiences have you had—or heard about from others?

- What kinds of apprehensions did you have (or do you have now) about starting to use word processing?

- If you've used a computer for business, personal, or academic writing, what are the two best pieces of advice you can give a new user?

- If you're a novice, what is the first writing task you'd like to learn to perform on a word processor?

- If you're an advanced user, what are two useful skills you'd be willing to teach to others in the group?

Working through the Writing Process on a Computer

Because typing is required for most academic and professional writing tasks, word processing skills are a great aid as you work through the writing process. How and when you work at a computer is an individual decision. If your typing skills are good, you may want to use the computer as a tool for discovering ideas—especially if you favor Discovery Activities that generate many words, such as brainstorming, freewriting, the journalist's questions, and the Thinking Tools. If you prefer drawing or clustering, or you feel more comfortable writing by hand, you may want to do most of your planning with a pen or pencil. In the planning stage, some writers switch back and forth between writing by hand and typing on the computer. Note there is one big advantage to doing your freewriting on the screen: You can save it onto a diskette and use it as the raw material for your essay. Word processing makes it easy to modify, move, delete and add to what you've already written.

Even if you don't use the computer for planning activities, it's a good idea to type your thesis statement and supporting ideas onto a computer diskette. The word processor makes it easy to develop your ideas, and you don't have to worry about forgetting anything important. (Be sure to print and save a hard copy as a backup.)

Some people handwrite their first drafts, which they then transcribe onto a computer diskette for revising. But most people find it more efficient to use the computer keyboard to draft their work. During the drafting stage, work quickly and ignore errors. Remember that your goal is to produce a complete draft that you can fix later. If the spellchecker and grammar checker distract you, turn them off until you're ready for editing. Save often during the drafting step, and when your draft is finished, be sure to print a hard copy as insurance against a computer failure.

The benefits of word processing software can best be appreciated during revising and editing. The computer makes it easy to delete ideas that don't work and substitute something better. Experimentation is easy and fun. For example, you can write two opening paragraphs, print both, and decide which you prefer. If you feel that a paragraph lacks a climax, you can move your examples around until you find an arrangement that works. When new ideas occur to you—or existing ideas seem dull—you can change them in an instant.

Editing is easy too because changes are so easy on a computer—and word processing software has a spellchecker and grammar checker to help you. When you're ready to edit, make sure the spellchecker is turned on, but keep a dictionary handy too. Some words may not have been programmed into the spellchecker, and it won't always recognize proper nouns—names of people, places, institutions, and businesses. Another limitation is that the spellchecker can't tell that a word has been used in the wrong place. If you substitute *since* for *sense*, the spellchecker won't notice the error. And, as noted before, be cautious about the grammar checker's suggestions. Remember that they are the product of a machine, not an educated human brain. Most important, don't be fooled by the professional look that word processing brings to your writing. It's always a good idea to put aside something you've written for at least a few hours, and then read it again. Proofreading a hard copy is always a good idea: Many people find that errors are easier to spot on paper than a computer screen. These two tips will help you find and correct weak spots that may have escaped your eye at first.

Word processing software won't magically transform weak writing into powerful prose. You—not the computer—are in charge of the writing process. Always think about content, organization, and interest before you turn to editing issues. If you're dissatisfied with the ideas, examples, or development of an assignment you're working on, seek help from someone who's knowledgeable about writing.

Too many students use the computer for tinkering rather than expert revision. Changing a word or punctuation mark here and there won't turn a dull essay into a fascinating one. Always revise before you edit: Write about the best ideas you can think of, organize them effectively, and consider how your work will be received by your readers. When you're satisfied that you have something worthwhile and interesting for your audience to read, you can use the spellchecker, grammar checker, and thesaurus for minor corrections.

Writing Assignment: Write on a Computer

Instructions: If you haven't used word processing before, schedule an hour or two for a basic orientation. (The computer lab on campus will be able to help you.) Then sit at the computer and write a paragraph about your learning. Include such details as how you acquired your basic skills, how the writing experience feels now, and the next step you plan to take as you learn about electronic technology.

THE WORLD WIDE WEB

Imagine an electronic device you can install in your home to access entertainment, information and news coverage from all over the world—a device that offers updates from experts and leaders in countless fields, as well unparalleled coverage of events in sports, music, and the arts. Services are available from a wide variety of providers, depending on the financial investment you want to make, and an astounding range of equipment is on the market. To get maximum benefit, you must learn to interpret an elaborate printout of offerings that is updated daily. Experienced users say that critical thinking is required to find your away among the possibilities and make worthwhile choices—but the potential benefits are astounding.

If all this seems overwhelming to you, think again: I've just the described the current state of the television industry. The analogy is important because the World Wide Web can be vast and intimidating to a person who has never used it—and an endless source of wonder and delight to those who take some time to discover its possibilities. If you are willing to invest some time learning about the World Wide Web, you'll soon feel as comfortable with your computer as you do with your television set.

READING TO WRITE: INTERNET DEBATE

Ann Landers is a newspaper advice columnist who answers readers' questions about a wide variety of problems and issues. In one column, Senator Patrick Leahy wrote to warn Landers's readers about the dangers of the Internet. A few days later, thousands of letters poured in to Landers's office as readers debated the benefits and risks associated with the World Wide Web. A selection from those letters appears below.

Before you begin reading, brainstorm your own list about the advantages and disadvantages of the Internet. If you are not yet a Web user, write what you have learned from conversations with friends, reading, television, and other sources.

Your list:

Vocabulary:

Web crawlers	(noun) World Wide Web users
condescending	(adjective) smug
netspeak	(noun) Internet jargon
cybersex	(noun) any sexual relationship that begins on the Internet
chat room	(noun) a Website that allows people to write informal messages to one another
pedophile	(noun) criminal who seeks sex with children
onliner	(adjective) person who uses the World Wide Web
deviants	(noun) people whose behavior doesn't meet current moral standards

Is the Internet Dangerous?
from the syndicated Ann Landers column

Dear Ann Landers: I recently read your response to Sen. Patrick Leahy. You said most Web crawlers are "fairly decent people." I object to that condescending classification. I am a well-spoken, well-mannered, married woman, neither lonely nor bored, and I consider myself thoroughly decent. IMHO (that's netspeak for "In My Humble Opinion"), you're off base, Ann.—Karen in Bryan, Texas

Dear Karen: You and thousands of others. The mail has been staggering, and most of the readers agree with you. Here's more:

From Eureka, Calif.: The Internet is feared because it is an equalizer, one of the few forums in which people can be judged solely by their words instead of their looks, dress or accent. Saying the Net is destructive because it can be used incorrectly is like saying humankind would be better off without fire because it can be dangerous.

Florida: I'm an Internet nut. People can and do make wholesome, healthy friendships on the Net. Same as in the workplace. It is no different from everyday life, made up of the good and the bad. Contrary to popular belief, the vast majority of surfers are not into cybersex. Whenever there is an open forum, you are bound to get a sampling of everything.

Detroit: My 20-year marriage is in ruins. My wife is convinced she has found her soul mate on the Internet. She is 42. We have two teenage daughters. Her "dream man" is an Air Force specialist from New Jersey. Please let your readers know there is danger lurking in those chat rooms.

Madison, Wis.: Get a clue, Ann. Condemning the Internet because some people meet scoundrels online is like condemning parks because some pedophile exposed himself to children in a park. You have to go looking for temptation on the Internet. It doesn't come find you. In a free society, people should be left alone to choose the path they want to take.

New York: After 19 years of marriage, my wife wants a divorce. She says the computer has opened her eyes to a whole new world. The woman has spent an average of five hours a day glued to that gadget, exchanging e-mail with pilots, business executives and poets. She also has been getting letters from prison inmates. If this is progress, I'll take vanilla.

El Dorado, Ark.: I have just taken a delightful "trip" on the Internet. It embraced art, anthropology, genealogy, music and literature. On other occasions, I have chatted with many interesting onliners but never felt inclined to form a close relationship with any of them. The problem with people and the Internet is not the Internet but what people do with it. The same is true of a knife. I was under the knife having lifesaving surgery the same day someone across town was murdered by one.

Reno, Nev.: People tend to focus on the small percentage of deviants in our society. For the most part, the people on the Internet are very bright and wonderful and do not prey on the weak. Imagine a world where there are no lines of distinction between color or class and where communication is as free and desirable as across the fence to your next-door neighbor. That's where the Internet is today. The people on it are creating a new and exciting method of communication for the next generation. Let us not fear it. Let's welcome it.

Responding to What You Have Read

1. Based on Ann Landers's column, list both the dangers and benefits of the World Wide Web.

2. Can you think of any dangers not mentioned in Landers's column? Of any benefits? List as many of each as you can.

3. Based on Landers's column and any Internet experiences you have had or heard about, list the kinds of writing a World Wide Web user might do.

4. Write a list of rules that might help a computer user avoid problems while on the World Wide Web.

5. Which do you think are more significant—the risks or rewards of surfing the Web? Explain your answer.

Collaborative Activity: Risks and Rewards

Instructions: Meet with a small group of other students to compare and discuss your answers to "Responding to What You Have Read." Then compile three group lists: the risks of Web surfing, the rewards, and a set of guidelines to help users avoid some of the problems associated with the World Wide Web. When you have finished, share your lists with other student groups in your class.

Online Correspondence

One of the marvels of the World Wide Web is its ability to put you in touch with people all over the world. Through search engines you can find websites and chat rooms that will link you to correspondents whose interests match yours. Some Internet services will even pair you up with a pen pal. Web correspondence is an excellent tool for broadening your knowledge and improving your ability to write about serious topics for a real-world, diverse audience.

Before you begin, you should be aware that online writing is different in two significant ways from traditional U.S. mail correspondence (often called "snail mail").

1. Security is a bigger issue. Often you'll be writing to someone completely unknown to you, especially in the "chat rooms" described below. And you can never know who is watching your online activities. Many people—some of them criminal types—secretly read online messages. Always assume that your messages are being read by a large group of people unknown to you. Be cautious with personal information such as your address, account numbers, and so on.

    If you're online at work or school, always assume that your email might go astray. Never use email to send information that might be damaging to yourself or others. Don't use email to discuss your intimate problems or to transmit gossip, unflattering opinions, profanity, or threats. Be especially careful with humor: Email that's read by the wrong person can be misunderstood and create serious problems for you and others.

2. Online correspondence is less formal than most academic and professional writing. Abbreviations are common—for example, in the Ann Landers column you saw that "IMHO" means "in my humble opinion." Typing and grammar mistakes are common, for several reasons. People online may get a great deal of email, so they tend to answer it quickly. And there's usually no printed copy to proofread, so many mistakes are never caught.

Here are some suggestions for finding correspondents online:

Websites

Many agencies, businesses, nonprofit organizations, newspapers, magazines, clubs, and other groups include lists of email addresses on their websites. If you're online, you can correspond with government officials, authors, celebrities, and experts in a vast number of fields. For example, you can write a congratulatory letter to a person you admire, request that a government agency investigate a problem, seek an expert answer to a question in a field that interests you, or ask a journalist how a particular article was written or researched.

A few basic rules—called "netiquette"—apply to this type of writing. Respect your correspondent's time: Keep your message short, and avoid long attachments that can tie up computer equipment. Proofread carefully. Above all, be courteous. If you disagree with a correspondent, state your position respectfully. Avoid rude, accusatory language, and don't use the CAPS LOCK key: Writing in capital letters is called "shouting."

When a correspondent responds with information you had requested, write a short thank-you note. Avoid pointing out mistakes that you spot when you read your email. And be especially careful with humor, which readers may misunderstand because they can't see your smile or the twinkle in your eyes.

Chat Rooms

A *chat room* is a website where people can post and read one another's messages. If you stay online while others are reading and replying to your message, you can respond instantly to what they have written. Many chat rooms are dedicated to a particular topic—anything from ballroom dancing to gourmet cooking to raising twins—and participants may meet online at a regular time.

Chat rooms are popular with computer users for a number of reasons. People with a particular concern or challenge—such as a health issue, a personal goal, or a family problem—can share information and offer support to one another. People who are passionately devoted to a hobby or special interest can exchange ideas and share experiences. Chat rooms are a great boon to anyone who has limited opportunities to meet others with similar problems or interests. Computer users who are shy or unable to travel can suddenly begin enjoying a wealth of new friendships.

But chat rooms have risks as well as benefits. Because live, face-to-face contact is missing, you can never be sure your new friends are representing themselves honestly. People with criminal tendencies sometimes monitor chat lines in hopes of finding victims. Even normal, healthy online friendships can get out of hand. Chat rooms offer an easy antidote to the loneliness many people feel today—too easy, according to some authorities. It's possible to become so involved in online chat that relationships with family members and old friends begin to wither and die.

You can minimize the risks by following a few simple rules. Monitor a chat room for a while before you begin sending messages. If the tone or subject matter in a chat room seems disturbing or suspicious, exit immediately and don't go back. Never give out information that others can use to find you—your location, telephone number, place of work. It's a good idea to use a nickname rather than your real name.

Don't throw yourself wholeheartedly into an intense relationship with an online acquaintance. Bring a combination of warmth and suspicion to online relationships. Don't believe everything you're told, and don't use the chat room as a substitute for friendships in your college, extended family, and community. If something happens that alarms you, notify your service provider, campus security, or the local police. These commonsense tips can help you enjoy rich and rewarding friendships online—and improve your writing skills at the same time.

Collaborative Activity: Send an Email message

Instructions: Begin by meeting with a small group of other students to discuss email possibilities, which might include:

- asking a professional writer about his or her working process
- sharing your opinion about a current issue with a government official
- asking a specific, thoughtful question of a famous person
- seeking specific information from a nonprofit organization devoted to a cause that interests you

Use a search engine to find a site sponsored by a legitimate business or nonprofit organization. Compose your email message, making sure it is brief, courteous, and purposeful. Ask your group and your instructor to review your message before you go online.

After you receive a response to your email, share it with your instructor and other class members. Write a thank-you message, if appropriate. Finally, meet with other group members to discuss what you learned from this activity.

Evaluating Online Information

The World Wide Web offers rapid access to an incredible array of information. Web addresses (called URLs—Uniform Resource Locators) are published in magazines and newspapers and advertised on television. You can browse the Web for information by typing keywords and questions into search engines.

This wealth of information has both advantages and disadvantages. A Web search can deluge you with so much information that you have difficulty sorting and evaluating it. The Web offers instant access to breaking news and cutting-edge developments, but some of it may be discredited as time passes. And while the Net allows you the convenience of independent research at any time of the day or night, you may sometimes need a professional's help to understand, and assess Website information. You can make many judgments on your own, however, if you understand some basic research principles and understand the nature of the World Wide Web.

Evaluating Websites

Anyone can publish a Website. The World Wide Web is very different from public and academic libraries, which must follow strict guidelines about adding material to their collections. Librarians carefully assess the quality of books, magazines, newspapers, videos, recordings, and other items before purchasing them. In general, you can expect a professional library to reject publications that are racist, pornographic, inaccurate, or suspect for other reasons. But the Web has no quality control whatsoever: You must make your own judgments about the quality of posted information.

Fortunately it's easy to make some basic judgments about a Website. Look for clues about the person or group that posted the information. First, look for well-known, reputable sources. You can trust the professionalism of site associated with a famous name—the *New York Times,* the Mayo Clinic, Stanford University, National Public Radio, the *Encyclopedia Britannica.*

The abbreviations at the end of Web addresses (called "domains") can be helpful:

- .org = nonprofit organization
- .com = commercial (profit-making) business
- .edu = nonprofit educational institution, such as a college or university
- .gov = government agency

It can make a great deal of difference whether a Website is designed to sell a product for profit (.com) or disseminate information for the public good (.org, .gov, .edu) . Still, some businesses are dedicated to high-quality, objective information (the *New York Times*), and nonprofit organizations often advocate a particular point of view on such issues as abortion, capital punishment, and animal rights.

Be cautious when experts speak on subjects outside their own specialties. Linus Pauling, who won a Nobel Prize for chemistry, is a famous spokesman for the benefits of Vitamin C—a subject outside his academic specialty; scientist Albert Einstein wrote political treatises about nuclear disarmament—as did religious leader Billy Graham. Skill and experience are necessary when you're assessing the writings of a person who's gone outside his or her field. You can't assume that a person with an outstanding reputation in one area is equally expert in another. In 1997, a famous political writer made news around the world when he declared that a U.S. Navy missile was responsible for the crash of TWA Flight 800 in New York. Pierre Salinger, former press chief for President John F. Kennedy, had a fine reputation for political knowledge, but he was not qualified to analyze the complex data associated with a plane crash. His erroneous statements (based on an amateurish explanation published on the Web) created great embarrassment for him.

The World Wide Web uses a special symbol—the tilde (~)—to show that an individual associated with an organization is presenting his or her own viewpoint. For example, college professors sometimes attach personal Web pages to a university Website. The tilde reminds you that these pages are not endorsed by the university; the expert is speaking on his or her own behalf, and you need to do your own evaluation of both the expert's qualifications and conclusions.

Other clues can tip you off to the overall quality of a Website. Look at the quality of the writing: Punctuation and spelling errors hint that the site isn't a professional one. Check the date of the most recent revision; reputable organizations keep their sites up to date. Beware of a site that does not acknowledge recent developments in a field. For years, scientists debated whether the earth's temperature was actually rising. In January 2000, the National Academy of Sciences finally settled the question by verifying that ground monitors have shown a sharp increase in the earth's temperature over the last twenty years. Any reputable Website about global warming will acknowledge the National Academy of Sciences report.

It's vital to educate yourself about resources that can help you evaluate Websites. Librarians, professors, and other experts can help you interpret and assess information. The *Encyclopedia Britannica* has a Website at www.Britannica.com that will direct you to reliable Web pages in countless fields. If your college is a subscriber, you can use the Britannica site free of charge: Ask a librarian how to access it on your own computer. Remember too that you can often email Web authors to ask them about their sources and conclusions. Most important, apply your own thinking skills, experience, and knowledge to Web information. As you increase your familiarity with a subject, it becomes easier to spot errors and muddy thinking.

Collaborative Activity: Experience the Web

Instructions: Meet with a group of other students to list topics to explore on the World Wide Web. Possibilities include:

- places you'd like to visit
- historical events

- current issues
- people who interest you

Have each group member choose two topics to explore. Using a search engine, Britannica.com, or other resources, explore the topics you've chosen. Look for clues about the reliability of the sites you visit. Take notes on your experience, and meet with your group to discuss what you have learned about the Web and the topics you slected.

World Wide Web Activity: Visit Your College

Instructions: Explore your college or university Website. (You can find the URL in the college or university catalog.) Click on the links that seem interesting or useful to you, and take notes on the information you find. When you're finished, meet with a group of other students to discuss your experience. List the ways the Website can be helpful to you during your college years. The following questions can help you discover the possibilities offered by your college Website:

- Is emergency information posted?
- Do professors post course-related material?
- What library services can you use online?
- How can you use email to ask questions and seek solutions to problems?
- Are there links to information and services outside your college?
- Is there a schedule of events and important dates?
- How much of the catalog is posted online?
- Can you perform college-related tasks online, such as submitting papers, registering for courses, and paying fees?

Writing Assignment: Use the Web as a Writing Resource

Instructions: Write an account of your experience reading about a topic on the World Wide Web. Begin by selecting a topic that interests you. Before you go online, freewrite about your topic and the additional information you'd like to have. Then use a search engine, Britannica.com, or other resources to find Websites about your topic. Take notes on what you're learning; print pages that have information you'd like to keep.

When you're finished with your online reading, write an essay about your experience. Begin by describing the information you wanted. Your thesis should state whether or not you were successful (or what degree of success you had). Develop your essay by describing the steps you took in your search, the knowledge and skills you gained, and any difficulties you encountered. Be sure to mention anyone who helped you find or evaluate information. Before submitting your essay to your instructor, submit it to a peer group for suggestions about revisions.

SUMMARY

1. Word-processing software can help you in every stage of the writing process.
2. Sending email can increase your knowledge and help you experience the challenges of real-world writing.
3. The World Wide Web offers many resources for writers.
4. It's important to develop skill in interpreting and evaluating information on the World Wide Web.

LOOKING AHEAD

In Part Two, you'll learn additional ways to develop your ideas. You'll gain more experience with descriptive, informative, and persuasive writing, and you'll practice using *process, classification, comparison/contrast, cause/effect, narration,* and *definition* to develop and write your essays.

PART TWO

DEVELOPING YOUR IDEAS

CHAPTER TEN

Using Processes In Writing

Preview

When you write about a process, you explain the steps in a task or procedure. The reading selections and writing activities in this chapter use processes for a variety of purposes. In this chapter you will write about processes in paragraphs, a personal essay, and an academic essay; you will also write a set of instructions.

INTRODUCING PROCESSES

When you write about a process, you outline the steps in a task or procedure, or you explain how something works. The ability to write about processes is vital in our rapidly changing world, which constantly challenges us to learn new tasks and perform old ones in new or better ways. "How-to" books are always in demand, and many jobs require the ability to write clear and accurate instructions. Your college catalog explains many processes that are important to campus life: applying for admission, registering for classes, getting a parking permit. If you've held a job or done volunteer work, you may have been asked to share your knowledge by writing instructions or explanations for others to read. In this chapter you will use process writing to describe, inform, and persuade; you'll also practice writing instructions.

Collaborative Activity: Talk about Processes

Instructions: Meet with a small group of other students to list the most useful processes you've learned since you started college. Consider college procedures (such as registering for classes) and instructions (such as the commands for the laser printer in the computer lab). Then brainstorm a list of the steps required to perform a process you've chosen.

USING PROCESS TO DESCRIBE AND INFORM

By writing in detail about every step in a process, a writer can help readers learn about an unfamiliar experience. In his book *Living in Space,* writer Peter Smolders shows that many simple actions—sleeping, eating, washing—are vastly different in outer space because there's no gravity and no twenty-four-hour rhythm of daylight and darkness. Readers can imagine how these activities feel because Smolders "makes meaning" (Chapter 2) of them with his vivid description of each step.

Sleeping in Space
adapted from Living in Space *by Peter Smolders*

Sleeping in space is a little different from on Earth, due to your being weightless. To an outsider it may appear that you are standing rather than sleeping, but in space the position is completely immaterial. On Earth, where your weight is normal, your body sinks into the mattress. In the Space Station, you'll hardly feel the hard board beneath you.

If you feel sleepy (every day you'll witness sixteen sunsets, so you can't depend on those!), you take off your clothes and carefully store them, so that you'll not be rudely awakened by a shoe hitting your nose. Tighten the two belts across your chest so that you are held firmly in your sleeping bag. In each bedroom a mask and ear-muffs are available in case you wish to sleep undisturbed. Before going to sleep adjust the ventilation and switch off the light (the switches are close to your head), after which you slide your arms under one of the belts to stop them from floating in front of your face. Good night!

Responding to What You Have Read

1. Effective process writing requires more than making just a list of steps. What information does Smolders include *besides* the actual steps you would take to get ready for bed in a space module? Why does he share this information?
2. What kind of readers do you think Smolders had in mind as he was writing—experts in space travel or the general public? Explain your answer.
3. Write a short (three or four sentences) summary of this reading selection.

Collaborative Activity: A Fresh Look at a Familiar Process

As new technology develops, we become accustomed to activities that might have amazed people from the past, such as talking on a telephone, reading e-mail on a computer, preparing a meal in a microwave oven, and taping a conversation.

Instructions: Meet with a small group of other students to choose a process you know well that might surprise a "time traveler"—a person from long ago who has magically entered today's world. Working with your group, choose a time from the past when your "time traveler" would have lived. Then compose a letter telling the "time traveler" the purpose of the activity you've chosen, the steps involved, and any other information he or she might find interesting.

USING PROCESS TO INFORM

Process writing often has an informative purpose. Readers can gain valuable information by learning how to do a task or procedure of benefit to them.

The following paragraph, written by a first-year college student named Daniel, has an informative purpose—teaching readers how to set up a study schedule:

Hitting the Books

When my college classes started in September, I couldn't keep up with my homework. Although I had graduated from high school with honors, I had been out of school so long that I'd forgotten how to study. My two-year-old son, Gary, created difficulties too. I wanted to spend plenty of time with him, but I wasn't getting my assignments done on time. I was starting to feel that maybe I didn't belong in college at all. Finally Angela, my wife, showed me how to make a study plan. She graduated from a community college as an R.N. several years ago and is an expert student. Angela showed me that breaking my study time into half-hour blocks can keep me from getting bored and help me learn more material. I study several subjects every evening, and I can concentrate much better. After only a month, I'm making a B in both math and chemistry. She also encouraged me to plan blocks of time for playing with Gary, watching TV with him, and taking him on outings. He's too little to be on a schedule all the time, but there are much fewer interruptions from him now. I'm using my time better, and I feel more confident about college. I've stopped believing that only students with superior brains can be successful in college.

Exercise 1: Analyze Daniel's Paragraph

1. Who is Daniel's audience likely to be?
2. What was his purpose when he wrote this paragraph?
3. Underline and label Daniel's topic sentence and conclusion.
4. List the steps Daniel used to make his study plan.

Writing Activity: How Do You Study?

Instructions: Write a paragraph describing the steps in your study process.

READING TO WRITE: TEACHING TOLERANCE

In this selection you'll learn how a fifth-grade teacher uses an art project to teach her students about tolerance.

A Rainbow of Colors
from the *Los Angeles Times* by Jane Gross

Randy Haege spreads a fan of construction paper before a roomful of eager fifth-graders whose faces are a living color wheel of black, brown, yellow, white and every shade in between.

There is paper of burnt umber and bronze, gold ocher and taupe, coffee and portrait pink; paper of raw sienna and sandalwood, terra-cotta and copper, almond and peach.

There are colors enough for all 26 children in Haege's class at the Anatola Avenue Elementary School in Van Nuys, who are making masks of their faces. There is a mirror on the wall to help them choose the colors. All this because Haege wants the skin color just right.

"Take a moment to think about it," the teacher tells them. "Look in the mirror. Hold your hands in a circle and compare. Now, I don't want any put-downs. But I do want us to try and get as close as we can to who we really are."

Once upon a time, no one bothered to produce a rainbow of colored paper for children's self-portraits. Once upon a time, adults corrected the manners of a youngster who dared mention race. But those days are long gone in Los Angeles, where nearly nine out of 10 schoolchildren are nonwhite and teaching tolerance is a desperate preoccupation.

Responding to What You Have Read

1. List the steps Randy Haege follows to teach her class about tolerance.
2. What is the purpose of the process she is teaching?
3. Do you think her teaching method is effective?
4. Do you think children should be encouraged to talk about race? Why or why not?
5. Write a short (three or four sentences) summary of this reading selection.

Writing Activity: Lessons about Life

Instructions: Write a paragraph about one of the following topics.

1. Describe the process someone in your own life used to teach you a value that you still hold today.
2. Describe how you might teach another person a value important to you.

READING TO WRITE: BREAKING STARCH

My American Journey is the autobiography of Colin L. Powell, a four-star general and former Chairman of the Joint Chiefs of Staff. Reminiscing about his Army career, Powell explained that the term STRAC (a shortened form of "Strategic Army Corps") meant "a state of being, a sharpness, a readiness, an esprit de corps." Soldiers tried to show that they were "STRAC" by arriving for work in heavily starched and pressed "fatigues" (work uniforms). Here Powell describes the process of putting on these stiff pants for work. More important, he "makes meaning" by explaining that his attitude towards "breaking starch" has changed since the early years of his military career.

Breaking Starch
Adapted from My American Journey *(1995) by Colin L. Powell*

Being STRAC came to mean looking sharp more than being combat ready. We had our field uniforms starched stiff as boards to achieve knife-edge creases. "Breaking starch" meant using a broom handle to open up the pants so that we could get into our fatigues without ripping off our skin. We dressed for inspection at the last possible minute; we left the pants unbuttoned and the fly unzippered; we put on our boots last—all in the interest of dressing without wrinkling the uniform. The effort was pointless, since within an hour everybody's uniform was a mass of wrinkles. But being STRAC meant breaking starch, and I broke starch with the best of them. It was tradition. And, as often happens in the Army, we overdid it. Style overran substance.

Responding to What You Have Read

1. List the steps in "breaking starch."
2. What was the original purpose of "breaking starch?"
3. What does Powell think of "breaking starch" now that he is looking back and retired from military service?
4. What do you think Powell meant when he wrote, "Style overran substance"?
5. What did you learn about Powell himself from this selection? How did his thinking change during his Army career?
6. What "meaning" was Powell communicating in his comments about "breaking starch"?
7. Do you think Powell was writing for a military audience, or for the general public? Explain.
8. Write a short (three or four sentences) summary of this reading selection.

Writing Activity: Style Versus Substance

Instructions: Think about a process (such as a task or a social custom) that you consider pointless. Write a paragraph describing the process and explaining why you consider it unnecessary.

WRITING AN ESSAY ABOUT A PROCESS

You've learned that writers can "make meaning" by explaining why a process is important, interesting, useful, enjoyable, unpleasant, or harmful. You can communicate your ideas about any process: frying hamburgers, taking inventory in your store, cleaning your basement, arranging flowers, teaching your teen-aged daughter how to drive. One student wrote about her struggle to assemble a lawn mower; another described the fun he and his wife had bathing their infant son every evening.

You're about to see how a first-year college student named Jamie wrote a personal essay to "make meaning" about a process she disliked—cleaning hotel rooms to earn money for college. Later you will write an essay of your own about a process you know well that has "meaning" for you.

Here is Jamie's essay:

Cleaning Hotel Rooms

Last summer I cleaned hotel rooms to earn money for college. I expected the work to be easy. After all, my family often stays in hotels, and we never leave a big mess behind us. My father always tips the cleaning staff generously, so I expected to make a lot of money. But it turned out to be the worst job I ever had.

The first step was pushing a heavy supply cart and a vacuum cleaner to each room I was cleaning. Then I opened the curtains, stripped the beds, emptied wastebaskets and ashtrays, and sprayed cleaning solution around the bathroom. Walking back and forth, bending, and straightening up over and over became tiring very quickly.

After I stuffed the used linen into the laundry bag, I pulled out fresh linen and made the beds. Then I had to stretch a large, heavy bedspread across the whole bed. Because the beds were king size, I usually had to walk around them several times, pulling on the linens and spread, until the bed looked neat.

The next task was tidying the room. I wiped spills, threw away leftover food, and straightened furniture. If guests had been partying in their room, it could take an extra fifteen minutes to wipe ketchup out of the wastebaskets, remove empty bottles, and pick up all the broken pretzels and potato chips.

I still wasn't finished. It was time for the bathroom and more bending and stretching. Often there was a mess in the sink for me to clean up—dried shaving cream, whiskers, and smeared toothpaste. Next was mopping the floor, followed by taking used towels to the laundry bag, and bringing in a pile of fresh ones.

The part I hated most came last—dragging the huge vacuum cleaner around the room. At first I thought that would be easy because the rooms were small. But I quickly discovered that there was little space to move the vacuum around the furniture. Often I banged my knees and shins on the dresser and chairs. The loud noise from the big motor made the job even more annoying.

When I was finally finished, it was time to move the supply cart and vacuum to another room and start over. My boss thought I should be able to clean a room thoroughly in only twenty minutes. Because he'd never done it himself, he had no idea why it sometimes took half an hour or even longer. Often I skipped breaks and shortened my lunch hour to get done on time.

I was glad when the summer ended. It was hard work, and the only thing I learned was that most people aren't as tidy as my family is—and they don't tip the way my father does either. I've signed up for a lifeguard class, and I'm going to spend next summer at the hotel pool.

Exercise 2: Analyze Jamie's Essay

Instructions: Answer the questions below.

1. How did Jamie "make meaning" about her job?
2. Jamie used many details to make her job sound difficult. Circle three details you found most convincing.

3. Few jobs are totally bad—or good. What positive features of the job do you think Jamie may have omitted so that her essay would have unity?

4. Suppose Jamie wanted to rewrite this essay with a different purpose—persuading her boss to allow more time for cleaning each room. What changes would you suggest to her?

Jamie's Planning Process

Before she drafted her essay, Jamie used the "plus, minus, interesting" activity you met in Chapter Two to discover ideas. Here is her planning sheet:

Jamie's "Plus, Minus, Interesting" Lists

+	—	Interesting
tips	heavy equipment	hotel chain employs
use of pool	stretching	traveling inspectors
air conditioned	bending	some guests are
nice guests	back and forth	careless about
	disgusting spills	valuables
played radio, TV		
while working	time pressure	retired people are
		good tippers
short drive from	uncaring boss	
home		guests often leave
	banging into	items behind after
not watched	furniture	checkout, usually
closely		clothes and jewelry
	cranky guests	
fun to see what		
goes on in	guest complaints	
people's rooms	low pay	

Jamie wanted to emphasize only the unpleasant parts of her job, so she worked primarily with her "minus" list. She also decided to include some items listed under "interesting" to make her essay more lively.

PLANNING WITH A FLOWCHART

Jamie also used a *flowchart*—a series of boxes and arrows showing steps in a process—to plan her essay. First, she drew a box for each step she followed in cleaning a hotel room; then she connected the boxes with arrows:

Jamie Cleans a Hotel Room

The following information and activities will help you plan and write an essay about a process you know well.

Using Thinking Tools: Discover Ideas for a Process Essay

Instructions: Complete the following activities.

1. Use the "plus, minus, interesting" thinking tool (page 42) to discover ideas for an essay about a job or task. Here are suggested topics:
   - A task you'll never do again or hope to do again
   - A business process

- A process your family uses to celebrate holidays
- A process that improves or damages health
- A natural process that is beneficial or harmful
- A process college students should learn
- A process all adults should learn

    When you've finished making your "plus, minus, interesting" sheet, circle the information you will probably use in an essay about the task; cross out anything you will probably omit from the essay. (Your essay assignment appears on page 170).

2. Make a flowchart (p. 168) representing the steps in the process you have chosen.

Save your "plus, minus, interesting" sheet and flowchart to use later, when you draft your essay.

DRAFTING THE ESSAY

Remember that the process you're describing must "make meaning" for your readers. Be sure your essay has a point: Avoid simply listing the steps in the process. During the drafting step, consider the purpose of each part of your essay: introduction, body, and conclusion. Use transition words to help readers move smoothly from one idea to the next.

Here is Jamie's essay once again, with the parts labeled: introduction, thesis statement (underlined), important transition words (**bold type**), conclusion, and other features.

Cleaning Hotel Rooms

[Introduction] Last summer I cleaned hotel rooms to earn money for college. I expected the work to be easy. **After all**, my family often stays in hotels, and we never leave a big mess behind us. My father always tips the cleaning staff generously, so I expected to make a lot of money. **But** it turned out to be the worst job I ever had.

The first step was pushing a heavy supply cart and a vacuum cleaner to each room I was cleaning. **Then** I opened the curtains, stripped the beds, emptied wastebaskets and ashtrays, and sprayed cleaning solution around the bathroom. Walking back and forth, bending, and straightening up over and over became tiring very quickly.

After I stuffed the used linen into the laundry bag, I pulled out fresh linen and made the beds. **Then** I had to make the bed. **Because** the beds were king size, I usually had to walk around them several times, pulling on the linens and spread, until the bed looked neat.

The next task was tidying the room. I wiped spills, threw away leftover food, and straightened furniture. If guests had been partying in their room, it could take an extra fifteen minutes to wipe ketchup out of the wastebaskets, remove empty bottles, and pick up all the broken pretzels and potato chips.

I **still** wasn't finished. **It was time** for the bathroom and more bending and stretching. Often there was a mess in the sink for me to clean up—dried shaving cream, whiskers, and smeared toothpaste. **Next** was mopping the floor, followed by taking used towels to the laundry bag, and bringing in a pile of fresh ones.

The part I hated most came **last**—dragging the huge vacuum cleaner around the room. **At first** I thought that would be easy because the rooms were small. **But** I quickly discovered that there was little space to move the vacuum around the furniture. Often I banged my knees and shins on the dresser and chairs. The loud noise from the big motor made the job even more annoying.

When I was finally finished, it was time to move the supply cart and vacuum to another room and start over. My boss thought I should be able to clean a room thoroughly in only twenty minutes. **Because** he'd never done it himself, he had no idea why it sometimes took half an hour or even longer. Often I skipped breaks and shortened my lunch hour to get done on time.

[Conclusion] I was glad when the summer ended. It was hard work, and the only thing I learned was that most people aren't as tidy as my family is—and they don't tip the way my father does either. I've signed up for a lifeguard class, and I'm going to spend **next summer** at the hotel pool.

Writing Assignment: "Make Meaning" about a Process

Instructions: Develop your "plus, minus, interesting" sheet (page 168) and flowchart (page 169) into a college essay. Be sure to decide what "meaning" your process will have for your readers. The guidelines that follow will help you write an effective essay.

GUIDELINES FOR WRITING A PROCESS ESSAY

1. Choose a process you know well. To refresh your memory, work through the process, if possible, taking notes to use in your essay.

2. Use critical thinking to clarify your purpose. Does the process have a special meaning for you? If you want to communicate an attitude, atmosphere, or feeling, your purpose will be descriptive. If your primary goal is to share information, consider what facts and ideas you want to emphasize.

3. Think about your audience. What do they know about the process already? How will you "make meaning" for them? Will you have to provide background information? Should you explain terminology, equipment, or procedures for them?

4. Use one or more Discovery Activities (Chapter Two) to generate ideas for your essay. Brainstorming the steps in the process works well for many students, since it helps organize your ideas. Other Discovery Activities may also help you get in touch with memories and feelings. Even if you are writing primarily to inform, lively descriptions and vivid details will add interest to your essay. Freewriting may also help you get in touch with memories and feelings about a process. Other possibilities include drawing a simple picture of a place you associate with the process, or talking about it with a friend.

5. Use your "writer's eyes" (Chapter Four) to discover details and information that "make meaning." Peter Smolders uses a sleeping bag, mask, and set of earmuffs to make sleeping in a space station vivid and real.

6. Review Chapter Six for tips about organizing your essay. These suggestions may also prove helpful:

   ■ First paragraph: Aim to stimulate interest in your subject. Write a thesis statement that identifies your process and explains its "meaning" for your readers.

   ■ Body paragraphs: Describe the steps in the process in order. Use transition words to help readers understand the process: first, second, third, next, after, then, later, following, last, finally.

   ■ Conclusion: Restate the point your essay is making about the process you've chosen. Use a conclusion strategy (page 126 in Chapter Seven) that emphasizes the meaning you're communicating to your readers.

USING PROCESS TO WRITE INSTRUCTIONS

Throughout your life you will learn new skills and share what you know with other people. If you've ever struggled to assemble a toy or learn a new computer program, you understand the importance of precise, easy-to-follow directions. Keep the following points in mind when you're writing instructions:

1. *Consider your audience.* If your readers are familiar with the kind of process you're teaching, you can assume they already know some of the vocabulary you'll be using. Less experienced readers need more explanation. For example, you don't have to tell a professional cook how to "clarify" butter or "separate" eggs. But readers accustomed to microwave meals and fast food may not have learned these skills. In that case, you'll need to write step-by-step explanations (and perhaps provide drawings or photographs) in your directions. If you're writing computer instructions, remember that experienced computer users understand such terms as "log on," "format," and "directory," but novices may not. When in doubt, explain.

2. *Consider your purpose.* If you're writing numbered steps (like the instructions you're reading now), strive for clarity and simplicity. Don't clutter the steps with details and descriptions that aren't needed. Do give readers enough help to guide them through the process successfully.

3. *State your purpose clearly.* Explain why the process is useful or important. For example, before you tell readers how to clean the battery terminals in an automobile engine, tell readers that corroded, dirty terminals cause battery failures.

4. *Before you begin writing, try one or more Discovery Activities.* The flowchart that Jamie used (p. 168) often works well. Freewriting about the task can also be helpful.

5. *Write an effective introduction.* Introduce the process, explain its purpose, and clarify your reason for writing. Are you teaching readers to perform a task that's new to them,

or are you offering an improvement of something they already know? List any materials needed and include any advice that may be helpful. Some kinds of baking can't be done in humid weather; gardeners need advice about climatic and seasonal conditions; students should be advised to begin working on a research paper early in the semester.

Offer helpful information about social concerns, health, finances, or similar issues. If you're teaching basic automobile maintenance, urge readers to recycle their used oil. Toy-assembly directions should include safety tips for playing with the toy. If you're teaching students how to do their own laundry, mention that they can save money by using a store-brand bleach rather than an expensive name brand.

6. *Organize the steps logically.* A Chevrolet owner's manual offered directions for finding and removing the jack stored in the trunk. But those instructions appeared *after* the directions for changing the tire—even though that's when the jack would be needed. Avoid that mistake by arranging your instructions logically. If your recipe for macaroni and cheese calls for a pound of cooked macaroni and a quarter-cup of melted butter, instruct readers to prepare those ingredients first. Consider numbering the steps.

7. *Provide "checkpoints" for your readers.* Help readers assess their success in following your directions, like this: "If you've performed these steps correctly so far, the sauce will be brown and thick." "If you've pruned your shrub correctly, it will have a much more attractive shape than when you started."

8. *Ensure that your instructions are complete.* A frustrated amateur photographer returned his new camera to the manufacturer because it didn't seem to have a rewind button. They mailed him a letter explaining that the button was on the bottom of the camera—a detail omitted from the illustration in the instruction manual. Authors of cookbooks sometimes forget to mention whether a casserole dish should be covered or uncovered. You can avoid such mistakes by going through the process yourself, taking notes about each step.

9. *At the end of your instructions, restate the purpose of the task.* Predictions work particularly well as conclusions for directions: Tell readers again how much they'll benefit by following the instructions you've given them.

10. *Double-check your instructions when you're finished.* Because you're familiar with the process you're describing, it's easy to omit important information. Ask a friend to read your instructions and offer feedback about them. If possible, have your friend actually use your instructions to perform the task.

READING TO WRITE: QUITTING SMOKING

The next selection is from a self-help book about becoming a happier person. Here psychiatrist David D. Burns offers instructions for a difficult task—breaking the smoking habit.

As you read the selection by Dr. Burns, notice how he motivates readers and guides them through each step of the process. Notice too how the instructions are organized, using the transition words *first, second,* and *third.* Before you begin, you will try a "prereading" activity designed to help you gain more benefit from reading.

INTRODUCING PREREADING ACTIVITIES

"Prereading"—activities that prepare you for reading—can help you improve your reading, thinking, and writing skills. They may also stimulate ideas that you can write about later on. Most of the reading selections in this book begin with a prereading activity—answering questions or freewriting. Notice how the following activity prepares you to read Dr. Burns's advice about quitting smoking.

Prereading Activity: Breaking a Habit

Instructions: Before you start reading, write a response to one or more of these questions:

1. Have you ever tried to break a habit? What happened?
2. Have you ever tried to quit smoking—or have you watched another person go through the process? What happened?
3. What strategies do you think would be helpful to a person who's trying to quit smoking?

How to Quit Smoking
from Feeling Good *by David D. Burns, M.D.*

Suppose you want to quit smoking. You may be reminding yourself about cancer and all the other dangers of smoking. These fear tactics make you so nervous that you immediately reach for another cigarette; they don't work. Here's a three-step method that does work.

The first step is to make a list of all the positive consequences that will result when you become a nonsmoker.

Once you have prepared the list, you're ready for the second step. Every night before you go to sleep, fantasize you are in your favorite spot—walking through the woods in the mountains, on a crisp autumn day, or maybe lying on a quiet beach near a crystal-blue ocean. Whatever fantasy you choose, visualize every enjoyable detail as vividly as possible, and let your body relax and let go. Allow every muscle to unwind. Notice how peaceful you feel.

Now you are ready for the third step. Fantasize that you are still in that scene, and you have become a nonsmoker. Go through your list of benefits and repeat each one to yourself in the following way: "Now I have improved health and I like it. I can run along the beach, and I want this. The air around me is clean and fresh, and I feel good about myself. I respect myself."

This method of habit management through the power of positive suggestion works amazingly well. You can do it easily, and you'll find it's well worth your efforts. It can be used for self-improvement in losing weight, getting up on time in the morning, sticking to a jogging routine, or any other habit you'd like to modify.

Responding to What You Have Read

1. Reread the suggestions for writing instructions. How effectively did Dr. Burns follow each suggestion? Give reasons for your answer.

2. Reread your responses to the Prereading Activity on page 173. Were your ideas similar to Dr. Burns's suggestions? Did you or he omit any advice that might have been helpful to a person trying to break a habit?

3. Most instructions don't include long descriptions. Why did Dr. Burns include descriptions of scenery?

4. Make a flowchart to represent the steps in breaking another bad habit, such as procrastination or overeating.

5. Write a short (three or four sentences) summary of this reading selection.

Writing Activity: Breaking a Habit

Instructions: Write a paragraph describing how you succeeding in breaking a habit. When you have finished, share your final draft with a group of students, and consider incorporating their suggestions into a revision.

READING TO WRITE: HANDY AT HOME?

In this selection, essayist Robert Fulghum takes a light-hearted look at a familiar task—making repairs around the house.

Advice from Mr. Fixit
from Maybe (Maybe Not) *by Robert Fulghum*

At least half your basic home fixit jobs call for a screwdriver. You don't really need to go out in the garage and spend ten minutes looking for that sixty-dollar twenty-piece matching set of screwdrivers with three styles of magnetic tips. Many screwdrivers are nearby. Fingernails. A dime, nickel, or quarter. But you really can't beat the all-purpose combination of a butter knife and a nail file. In fact, the kitchen is full of knives that make great screwdrivers. So what if you snap the tip off one? No problem—you've got yourself an improved screwdriver.

Spoons also work quite nicely when the knives don't. Even forks will pry the lids off cans, though forks should be reserved for mixing paint. The point is, you have at hand all the screwdrivers you'll ever need. Right there in the kitchen.

Need a lightweight saw? That's what serrated bread knives are for.

As to pliers: fingers. Or fingers with a dishtowel wrapped around the top of something that won't come off after you've pounded the edge of it with the handle end of a butcher knife. Tweezers and clothespins work as pliers for small jobs. But the best pliers are in your own mouth—teeth, of course, teeth. Just don't let your kids catch you.

And while I'm mentioning body parts, let's talk about *power* tools—knees, elbows, fists, and feet. A great many things can be fixed by kicking, pounding, shaking, and throwing.

To cut and open things, there are, of course, all those knives in the kitchen, and the razor blades and manicure sets in the bathroom, which is a good place to use them because you are closer to the Band-Aids, which you will need sooner or later when you use sharp tools. . . .

See, the truth is, at home, in private and in secret, we mostly make do. That's how we run our lives most of the time. We might as well accept that. And feel good about it. And get good at it.

Responding to What You Have Read

1. Did Fulghum intend to write a set of instructions about home repairs—or do you think he might have had another purpose?
2. Fulghum writes, "at home, in private and in secret, we mostly make do." Do you agree or disagree? Why?
3. Do you think "making do" is ever appropriate in other areas of life? Why or why not?
4. Write a short (three or four sentences) summary of this reading selection.

Writing Assignment: Writing Directions

Instructions: Write a set of directions—either serious or humorous—for a process you know well. Choose a process you learned at school, at work, at home or from friends. A number of topics appear below, but feel free to choose a different task if you wish.

personalizing a dorm room	finding a book in the college library
putting a child to bed	adjusting a microscope to view a slide
doing a push-up	converting a fraction to a decimal
operating a cash register	waiting on a customer
making a credit-card phone call	cooking a favorite dish
using a self-service gasoline pump	asking for a date
using a stick shift to put a car into reverse	bathing a dog

Collaborative Activity: Share Your Directions

Instructions: Meet with a small group of other students to exchange and discuss the instructions you've written. If possible, carry out the actual instructions; if not, read them carefully and give feedback to the writer. Finally, return the instructions to the author, along with your suggestions, for revising and editing.

USING PROCESS TO PERSUADE

In addition to the purposes you've already explored, process writing can be persuasive. If you explain how sluggishly the circulatory system operates when it's blocked by cholesterol, readers may decide to exercise more and improve their eating habits. An account of how jurors reach a verdict may convince citizens that serving on a jury is a privilege as well as a duty.

Sometimes persuasion is linked to another purpose. In a previous "Reading to Write" selection, Dr. Burns offered instructions about quitting smoking. But he also had a persuasive purpose—convincing them that giving up cigarettes was important to their well-being. Persuasive writing often includes descriptions and information that clarify and strengthen the author's viewpoint.

The following excerpt is from a book with a persuasive purpose—asking readers to stop eating beef.

Prereading Activity: Writing to Persuade

Instructions: Write your answers to these questions before you read the selection from *Beyond Beef.*

1. Persuasive writing often includes vivid descriptions that stimulate readers' feelings. What descriptions do you think an author might use to convince readers not to eat beef?
2. Persuasive writing also relies on information. What facts might convince readers not to eat beef?

READING TO WRITE: THE MEAT INDUSTRY

Beyond Beef: The Rise and Fall of the Cattle Culture was written by animal-rights advocate Jeremy Rifkin. To make his point, Rifkin describes processes he considers cruel to cattle. In this excerpt, he describes how cattle are transported to slaughterhouses:

Cattle to the Slaughter
from Beyond Beef *by Jeremy Rifkin*

Cattle are often transported for hours or days along interstate highways without rest or nourishment and frequently without water. At the end of their journey, those animals still standing are deposited in a holding pen at the slaughterhouse. "Downers," however, often must wait hours in great pain to be unloaded. These are the animals that suffered broken legs, necks, backs or pelvises during the journey. Often spread-eagled on the floor of the trailers, unable to stand or walk, these hapless animals are chained by their necks or broken legs and dragged from the truck onto the loading ramp to await their turn for slaughter.

Responding to What You Have Read

1. List the descriptive details that Rifkin uses to persuade readers that the cows are cruelly treated. Are they similar to the details you listed in the Prereading Activity?
2. Do you think Rifkin's descriptions might persuade readers to stop eating beef? Why or why not?

3. What information did Rifkin include in this excerpt? Is it effective? Why or why not?

4. How do you think a writer hired by the beef industry would describe this process?

5. What "meaning" do you think Rifkin was trying to communicate to his readers?

6. Write a short (three or four sentences) summary of this reading selection.

A STUDENT WRITES A PERSUASIVE ESSAY

You're about to read a persuasive essay written by a first-year college student named Kevin. As you read, notice how many processes Kevin included in his essay about depression—and how they help him make his point about getting help for depression.

Advances against Depression

Depression is a serious illness. According to the National Institute of Mental Health, more than seventeen million Americans suffer from depression every year. Severe depression causes thirty-five thousand suicides annually. Unfortunately, many depressed people refuse to get help. Some are ashamed of their condition, and others are afraid of becoming addicted to antidepressants. Life could improve for many of these people if they learned about treatment options.

Since the 1950s, researchers have developed medications that often help depressed people. Although some medications artificially alter people's moods, others work naturally. For example, the human brain naturally produces a chemical called "serotonin" that makes people feel content and happy. But serotonin quickly breaks down in the brains of depressed people. A class of medications called "Selective Substance Reuptake Inhibitors," or SSRIs, helps serotonin last longer before it begins to break down. Patients who take this medication do not get "high," so there is no risk of addiction. Prozac is the most famous of these "inhibitors," but there are many other medications as well.

Professional counseling can help depressed people by teaching them new skills and encouraging them to make choices that improve their lives. Often counseling causes depressed people to feel better without medication.

For some people, both medication and counseling are necessary. Because every person is different, treatment must be supervised by a professional. Within a month of treatment, many people start to improve.

People who are seriously depressed should seek professional help without embarrassment. Many successful and famous people have experienced depression, including Abraham Lincoln, Beethoven, Mary Tyler Moore, and Ernest Hemingway.

A life is a terrible thing to waste. Because depression is so common, everyone should know that help is available. There's nothing to be ashamed of and much to be gained by seeking help.

Exercise 3: Analyze Kevin's Essay

Instructions: Answer the questions below.

1. What processes did Kevin include in his essay?
2. What was his purpose in writing the essay?
3. Label the parts of Kevin's essay: introduction, thesis statement, transition words, conclusions.
4. What readers did Kevin have in mind when he wrote his essay?
5. How would Kevin's essay been different if his purpose had been strictly informative?
6. Write a short (three or four sentences) summary of this reading selection.

WRITING A PERSUASIVE ESSAY ABOUT A PROCESS

1. List as many viewpoints as you can think of about the issue you've chosen. Write an introductory paragraph that stimulates readers' interest in your subject. A vivid description, startling fact, dramatic story, or stimulating idea may catch readers' attention right away.
2. State your position early—usually in the first or second paragraph.
3. Choose convincing examples to make your point. Use your "writer's eyes" to stimulate readers' thoughts and feelings.
4. Avoid offending readers who disagree with you. Don't use offensive labels; treat all viewpoints with respect.
5. Restate your viewpoint in your concluding paragraph, and reinforce it with a vivid fact, idea, or story.
6. Use transition words to help readers understand your reasoning. The words suggested earlier for process writing (page 171) will probably be useful: first, second, third, next, after, then, later, following, last, finally. (Suggested transition words for persuasive writing appear on page 107 in Chapter Six.)

Writing Assignment Write a Persuasive Essay

Instructions: Plan, draft, and revise a process essay with a persuasive purpose. Because you are trying to change people's thinking, choose a process that affects many people. Here are three ways to start thinking about your topic:

1. Choose a process that people need to understand better. (This was Kevin's approach.)
2. Choose a process that should be encouraged. (One student wrote about a reservation that started a program to help Native Americans open their own successful small businesses.)
3. Choose a process that should be discouraged. (This was Jeremy Rifkin's approach when he wrote about transporting cattle to the slaughterhouse.)

LEARNING MORE ABOUT PROCESS WRITING

This chapter ends with two more "Reading to Write" activities. Seeing how others have used processes in their writing can help you develop your own skills. The next reading selection is a true story about a college student who produced an unusual process essay.

READING TO WRITE: A STUDENT AT WORK

Prereading Activity: Students at Work

1. Who usually reads the papers written in a college writing course?
2. Imagine that you worked with incapacitated patients in a nursing home. What behaviors, sights, sounds, and smells might you experience on the job?
3. Think of a job you've had or a task you've done (not necessarily for money). What kinds of processes did you perform? What was your attitude towards the job?

Vocabulary:

laconic	(adjective) using few words, concise
searing	(adjective) scorching
agitated	(adjective) shaken, upset
libel	(noun) crime of publicly damaging someone's name or reputation
publicized	(verb) printed for the public to read
potent	(adjective) powerful

Millie
from Uptaught *by Ken Macrorie*

When time came to hand in a case-history of some process the student knew well, she presented me with a story of her working day at a nearby hospital and care home. It was laconic and powerful.

The students looked at Millie wondering where she had been all that time. She let a few facts open up that world of loneliness and slidings in and out of reality, and ended the account like this: "The hall was dark. As I walked toward the time clock, I heard a few moans. Someone called out, 'I want to go home.' I punched the time clock, walked out the door."

Millie could walk out; they couldn't. That was the story—told in such exquisitely painful particulars that three hours after it was printed in a campus publication with an 11,000 copy press run, I received a phone call from the president of the university. "That story in *The Review* this morning about the patients in the home. Was that written by one of your students?"

"Yes."

"Well, it's a good story, full of feeling, but there's one trouble. All the names in it are real."

Millie was so deeply embarrassed that I didn't think I'd be able to pull her out. The editors and she and I drove to the home and talked to the director. She was agitated, fearing her patients' personal lives would be spread around the county. But she felt comforted to know we admitted wrong. She said she would take all precautions possible to keep copies of *The Review* from reaching the patients. Neither she nor any of them pressed charges against the university. Millie said she could not return to our university next fall, but I insisted she had written a compassionate if searing report on the human condition and we needed students like her. I showed her a letter in which the president said we must not let her turn away from our university for what was only a human mistake.

She came back in the fall, joined the staff of *The Review,* and contributed good writing to it.

Never before had my students written anything alive and honest enough to be dangerous. I was going to have to treat them as potent.

Responding to What You Have Read

1. In a few sentences, summarize this story about Millie and her essay. Reread your pre-reading activity. Did the questions help you understand this reading selection?

2. Did Millie effectively consider her audience and purpose when she wrote her essay? Give reasons for your answer.

3. Although the author doesn't identify the nursing-home process Millie described in her essay, he offers some hints. What are they? What was Millie's purpose in writing the essay? Use your imagination to think of a process she might have used.

4. Evaluate the professor's effectiveness as a teacher. (Making a "plus, minus, interesting" sheet may be helpful.)

5. What "meaning" do you think the professor was trying to communicate when he wrote about Millie's experience?

Writing Assignment: People and Processes

Millie wrote a moving essay about a process she saw every evening in the nursing home. She "made meaning" from the process by showing how trapped the residents felt.

Instructions: Write an essay about a process you're familiar with that might cause a person to feel happy, sad, valued, or hurt.

READING TO WRITE: RAY KROC SOLVES A PROBLEM

Although this reading selection is primarily about cooking french fries, it also reveals a great deal about Ray Kroc and McDonald's, the fast-food chain he founded. Kroc's remarkable career began when he was a sales representative for a company that sold milkshake machines. Curious about a small restaurant called "McDonald's" that kept ordering more milkshake machines, he dropped in to see why their business was doing so well. There Kroc met the McDonald brothers, who owned the business, and Kroc tasted the foods on their menu. Impressed, he bought their business and gradually opened new McDonald's restaurants all over the country. In this excerpt from Kroc's autobiography, he explains how he solved a perplexing problem in 1955, when he was opening the first store in the McDonald's chain.

Prereading Activity: Think about French Fries

1. Have you heard of Ray Kroc? If so, what do you know about him?
2. What do you know about McDonald's and its french fries?
3. What do you think the "french-fry flop" might have been?

Vocabulary:

aghast   (adjective) horrified

baffled   (adjective) hopelessly confused

curing   (adjective) ripening

spud   (noun) potato

The Great French-Fry Flop
adapted from Grinding it Out *by Ray Kroc*

A subject of great concern to me was the great french-fry flop. I had explained to my associate Ed MacLuckie with great pride the McDonald's secret for making french fries. I showed him how to peel the potatoes, leaving just a bit of the skin to add flavor. Then I cut them into shoestring strips and dumped them into a sink of cold water. I rolled my sleeves to the elbows and, after scrubbing down in proper hospital fashion, I immersed my arms and gently stirred the potatoes until the water went white with starch. Then I rinsed them thoroughly and put them into a basket for deep frying in fresh oil.

The result was a perfectly fine looking, golden brown potato that snuggled up against the palate with a taste like . . . well, like mush. I was aghast. What could I have done wrong? I went back over the whole thing once more. The result was the same—bland, mushy french fries. They were as good, actually, as the french fries you could buy at other places. But that was not what I wanted. They were not the wonderful french fries I had discovered in California. I got on the telephone and talked it over with the McDonald brothers. They couldn't figure it out either.

This was a tremendously frustrating situation. My whole idea depended on carrying out the McDonald's standard of taste and quality in hundreds of stores, and here I couldn't even do it in the first one!

I contacted the experts at the Potato & Onion Association and explained my problem to them. They were baffled too, at first, but then one of their laboratory men asked me to describe the McDonald's San Bernardino procedure step-by-step from the time they bought the potatoes from the grower up in Idaho. I detailed it all, and when I got to the point where they stored them in the shaded chicken-wire bins, he said, "That's it!" He went on to explain that when potatoes are dug, they are mostly water. The taste improves as they dry out and the sugars change to starch. The McDonald brothers had, without knowing it, a natural curing process in their open bins, which allowed the desert breeze to blow over the potatoes.

With the help of the potato people, I devised a curing system of my own. I had the potatoes stored in the basement so the older ones would always be next in line for the kitchen. I also put a big electric fan down there and gave the spuds a continuous blast of air, which greatly amused Ed MacLuckie.

"We have the world's most pampered potatoes," he said. "I almost feel guilty about cooking them."

One of my suppliers told me, "Ray, you know you aren't in the hamburger business at all. You're in the french-fry business. You've got the best french fries in town, and that's what's selling folks on your place."

Responding to What You Have Read

1. Reread your answers to the Prereading Activity on page 181. Did the questions help you read more attentively? Would you answer the questions differently now that you've read this selection about Ray Kroc?
2. List the steps in the french-fry making process described by Ray Kroc.
3. List the steps Kroc used to solve the french-fry problem.
4. What does this selection teach you about potatoes? French fries? Success in business? Ray Kroc's personality?
5. Underline the descriptive words and phrases in this selection, and label them D. Then underline the informative sentences in this selection, and label them I.
6. Write a short (three or four sentences) summary of this reading selection.

Writing Assignment: Solve a Problem

Instructions: Write an essay about a process you have used to solve a problem of your own. Consider the purpose of your essay—descriptive, informative, or persuasive. Include both the steps you followed and any feelings you experienced: confusion, frustration, embarrassment, excitement, triumph.

SUMMARY

1. Process writing can have a descriptive, informative, or persuasive purpose.
2. Besides outlining steps and procedures, an essay about a process should "make meaning" for your readers by showing the benefits of learning about the process you've chosen.

LOOKING AHEAD

In Chapter Eleven, you'll practice writing about classifications—ways of grouping similar things together, or dividing a category into several parts. You can use classifications for descriptive and informative writing—to increase readers' knowledge and understanding. A classification essay can also have a persuasive purpose.

Using Classifications in Writing

Preview

A *classification* essay sorts related items into three or more groups or divides a concept or thing into three or more categories. A classification essay can be informative or persuasive.

INTRODUCING CLASSIFICATION

If you're a bargain shopper, you're probably familiar with the classified advertisements in newspapers. The groupings you find there—Help Wanted, Apartments for Rent, Musical Instruments, Pets, and Supplies—help organize a wide assortment of information.

Writers frequently use *classifications* (categories) to "make meaning" by grouping and organizing information for their readers. The term "classification" covers two ways of organizing information. One involves placing items into groups: students, professors, transportation, foods, governments. The second strategy involves dividing a concept or thing into variations, levels, degrees, or types: first-degree, second-degree, and third-degree burns; gold, silver, and bronze Olympic medals. At the end of this chapter John Holt uses this strategy to persuade readers that discipline is more complex than they might expect.

Here is a descriptive paragraph by a first-year college student named Kiri. When Kiri enrolled in college, she needed someone to look after her two young daughters. The search for a suitable person took almost two weeks, involving many telephone calls and visits. Kiri realized that listing each place she had considered would make her essay too long and repetitious. Instead she grouped the places into three *classifications*—family members, babysitters, and preschools. The result is an effective essay that describes how she made her final choice.

A Place for My Children

When I enrolled in college last year, I began looking for a place to leave my two daughters when I was in class. Doris is four, and Belle is two. At first I thought about asking family members to help out because Belle and Doris really like their grandmother and Aunt Betty. But neither relative has the energy or desire to play with two lively little girls. Also my mother and sister don't like following my instructions about snacks and naptimes. They want to do things their way. Next I considered hiring a babysitter. But the ones near my home don't have insurance, licenses, or training. When I visited their homes, I saw only a few toys, and there weren't any other children there. Finally I visited a few preschools in town. I quickly found a place with young, caring teachers. The toys and playground equipment impress me, and the director is very professional. Now I can concentrate on my classes instead of worrying about Doris and Belle while I'm on campus. Best of all, my daughters look forward to seeing their friends at the preschool.

SELECTING CLASSIFICATIONS THAT "MAKE MEANING"

Writers use classifications to sort information in ways that "make meaning" for their readers. Think about baseball: To a person who doesn't know much about the game, all the pitches may look the same. But an avid fan can easily distinguish between curve balls, fast balls, knuckleballs, and sliders. Familiarity with this information opens up a whole new dimension in baseball, making every game more interesting to watch. If you're knowledgeable about the sport, you might write a classification essay that begins like this:

> You'll enjoy your next baseball game more if you can recognize these four pitches.
>   EFFECTIVE THESIS

Besides introducing the subject of the essay, this thesis statement "makes meaning" by explaining why baseball fans should know about these four pitches.

When you plan an essay about classifications, set up your categories carefully. Avoid categories that are too obvious, such as the differences between houses, apartments, and mobile homes. Anyone planning to rent or purchase a residence is probably familiar with these categories already: Your essay won't add much information. But you might write an effective essay about types of leases, mortgages, or realtors.

Similarly an essay comparing sports cars, subcompacts, and minivans won't be helpful to someone buying a new car: Most people already know the type of vehicle they want to buy before they even walk into a dealership. A family with a limited budget and four children won't even consider buying a sports car; a single person who spends many weekends at the beach probably won't be interested in a minivan. But you can write about vehicles if you choose a topic that readers will find useful. For example, a person buying a light truck might want to know about types of transmissions, engines, and cabs.

Make sure your classifications are realistic. An essay about acting careers might mention high school and college drama departments, dinner theaters, community theaters, film companies, and television studios. But starring in a major motion picture is not a practical option for most actors, and therefore it should not be included as a classification.

Finally, make sure the classifications in your essay are clear and distinct. If you're writing about nursing careers, "private agencies" and "hospitals" are workable classifications. But "operating rooms" can't serve as the third type because it overlaps with your second category, hospitals. The following exercise will give you practice in evaluating classifications.

Exercise 1: Evaluate Classifications

Instructions: Put a check in front of each statement that contains effective classifications. Put an X in front of any statement with ineffective classifications.

_____   1. A job seeker can look for work as a volunteer, a part-time employee, or a full-time employee.

_____   2. If you're low in cash, you can furnish an apartment by asking friends and family for their unwanted furniture, shopping at thrift stores, and investigating classified ads.

_____   3. Popular eating places include fast-food establishments, cafeterias, diners, and fine restaurants.

_____   4. The financial aid office has information about three kinds of tuition assistance.

_____   5. Before you buy a nonprescription pain reliever, you should know about the types available and their potential side effects.

_____   6. Student travelers can see Europe on a budget by staying in bed-and-breakfast homes, youth hostels, and out-of-the-way hotels.

_____   7. After college graduation, an athlete can play as an amateur, join a professional team, or obtain a coaching position.

_____   8. If you're trying to get back into shape, consider working out on your own, forming a fitness partnership with a friend, or joining a health club.

_____   9. Towing companies report three major reasons why cars break down on the road.

_____ 10. Students interested in a military career should consider these four options.

Collaborative Activity: List Your Choices

Instructions: Meet with a small group of other students to list occasions when you had to choose from three (or more) classifications. Be sure to consider *types* rather than particular choices. Pizza Hut, Red Lobster, and Denny's are too specific to be considered classifications. But you could write about types of cuisine, such as Italian, Chinese, and Mexican. The list below may help you choose a subject, but feel free to use other classifications if you wish.

- Education: community college, public or private four-year college, public or private university, vocational or business school
- Living arrangements: home, dormitory, shared apartment off campus, living alone off campus
- Weddings: elopement, home ceremony, church ceremony, another setting
- Trips: car, airplane, ship; resort, hotel, motel, relative's home; travel alone, travel with a friend, guided tour

USING CLASSIFICATIONS IN AN ESSAY

The following suggestions will help you use classifications to write an effective essay:

1. Your introductory paragraph should catch readers' interest, provide background information, state your thesis, and explain the importance of usefulness of the subject you've chosen. Be sure to explain any terms that are unfamiliar.
2. In the body paragraphs, name and describe the classifications you've selected. Include enough examples and details to "make meaning" for your readers. Consider introducing each classification with a transition word, such as "first," "second," "third," "next," "last," "final," "worst," and "best."
3. Your conclusion should restate your purpose in writing the essay. Use a fact, story, or similar strategy to emphasize your main point once again.

A STUDENT WRITES A CLASSIFICATION ESSAY

The essay below, written by a student named Larry, uses classifications for an informative purpose: Teaching restaurant servers how to do their jobs effectively. Larry used three consistent categories—food, money, and customers—and included many examples in his essay. He planned the essay carefully to make sure his classifications were useful. When Larry showed this essay to his supervisor, she asked to use it as a training aid for new employees.

Working as a Restaurant Server

I've been working part-time as a server at McKay's Inn on Ninth Street for three years. I was nervous when I started because there's so much to remember. The pace is so hectic that it's easy to forget about coffee refills, credit-card validations, and special orders. In the beginning I made many mistakes, and my supervisor had to spend extra time straightening them out. The job became simpler when I started sorting it into three kinds of tasks: food, money, and customers. Repeating those three words to myself helps me stay on top of the job.

The word "food" reminds me to make sure the entrees are hot and attractively garnished. It also helps me think about special orders and condiments such as horseradish sauce and Parmesan cheese. A little extra concentration as I pick up the plates from the kitchen can prevent many difficulties later. Sometimes I can solve a problem before the customer even finds out about it. If someone orders french fries, I make sure he doesn't get mashed potatoes by mistake.

The word "money" helps me keep track of customers' bills. When the restaurant is busy, it's easy to forget write down some of the items, especially if customers order desserts and extra drinks. I also have to remember the steps to follow when a customer uses a credit card. If I omit a step, the transaction will be canceled later, causing problems with my supervisor. During busy times it's easy even to forget to return a customer's change or credit card. Thinking about the word "money" as I approach a table helps me handle all these matters correctly.

Most important of all are the customers themselves. Even when the pace is hectic and the kitchen is making mistakes, the word "customer" reminds me to smile and act helpful. A little extra effort, like bringing prompt coffee refills or an extra basket of hot rolls, can pay off in large tips. Now that I've been at McKay's for three years, many customers ask for me by name. My commitment to good service has paid off.

Working at McKay's has taught me how to concentrate, get along with people, and pace myself during long hours of carrying heavy trays back and forth. My three-word system simplifies my job and helps me satisfy my customers. Whether you're working as a server or performing a different kind of job, I encourage you to adopt a similar system. The small extra effort is well worth it.

Collaborative Activity: Evaluate Larry's Essay

Instructions: A Checklist for Writing about Classifications appears below. Working with a small group of students, use the Checklist to evaluate Larry's essay. (You may also want to look again at the suggestions on page 186.) If you could talk to Larry, what feedback would you give him?

■ ■ ■ Checklist for Writing about Classifications

_____ 1. Are your classifications useful and interesting to readers?

_____ 2. Have you avoided classifications that are too obvious to be interesting?

_____ 3. Have you checked your categories to ensure that they don't overlap?

_____ 4. Have you explained the categories clearly?

_____ 5. Does your introductory paragraph catch readers' interest?

_____ 6. Have you provided sufficient background information?

_____ 7. Is your purpose clearly stated?

_____ 8. In your body paragraphs, did you provide enough explanations and examples?

_____ 9. Did you use transition words such as "first," "second," "third," "next," "last," "final," "worst," and "best"?

_____10. Does your conclusion restate your purpose?

Writing Assignment: Inform or Describe

Instructions: Write a classification essay with an informative or descriptive purpose. The following list may be helpful in choosing your subject; you may also write about a subject you've chosen yourself. When you have finished your essay, use the checklist above to evaluate what you have written.

college courses	computer programs
homes	cars
families	professors
part-time jobs	parties
dates	co-workers

types of people you don't want as friends
types of students who shouldn't work while they're in college

USING CLASSIFICATIONS TO PERSUADE

In addition to informing and describing, classifications can persuade readers to change their thinking about an issue. One strategy is to set up classifications to demonstrate that an issue is more complex than readers might have thought. This is the strategy John Holt used in his essay about discipline at the end of this chapter. Readers who think "discipline" has only one meaning—spanking—are likely to be surprised when they read Holt's three classifications.

A second strategy is to sort items into those you disagree and agree with. Consider putting the item (or items) you agree with at the end of your essay for greater emphasis. A student named Joni used this strategy to organize an essay about problem-solving techniques. Her first two categories—aggression and submission—describe methods she dislikes. She saved her favorite method—negotiation—for last so that readers would continue to think about it after they finished her essay.

Here is Joni's essay:

Resolving Conflicts

Conflicts are a fact of life. For most of us, hardly a day or two goes by without a disagreement with a friend, family member, neighbor, or co-worker. Most of us learn how to solve problems at home or from friends. Typical methods include threats, shouting, crying, pouting, scolding, arguing, or negotiating. These techniques can be grouped into three approaches to problem-solving.

The first approach is called "aggression," and it includes threats, shouting, scolding and arguing. Aggressive problem-solvers use force or a superior position to get what they want. These techniques are especially popular with people in positions of authority. For example, some supervisors humiliate their employees to get work done, and some parents use threats to frighten disobedient children.

Crying and pouting are typical behaviors of the second approach, which is called "submission." Most submissive problem-solvers lack a position of authority. Because they can't win a power contest, they win through manipulation. Unhappy employees may act depressed or helpless to get what they want. Children sometimes cry or pout to make their parents feel guilty.

A repeated cycle of aggression and submission may last for years without solving anything. An angry husband raises his voice and shakes his fists to get what he wants. His wife agrees because she is afraid to show her anger. But her pitiful crying makes him feel guilty, and he later gives in to her. Soon the cycle begins again. At times the partners may switch roles, so that the woman is aggressive, and the man is submissive.

The best approach to problem solving is called negotiation. It includes listening, bargaining and creative thinking. The emphasis is on understanding and fulfilling both persons' needs.

I know a couple who argued constantly about how to spend their free time. She enjoyed fishing and wanted to enjoy nature with her husband, but he found it boring.

After many arguments, the wife reminded her husband that he'd once been interested in nature photography. He liked the idea of trying it again, so they purchased a 35-millimeter camera and a zoom lens. From then on their nature trips included both good fishing and opportunities for photographs—and their marriage improved.

Since we will always have conflicts, it makes sense to develop problem-solving techniques that preserve relationships. Anyone can benefit by working on negotiation and thinking skills. With patience and practice, arguing friends, family members, neighbors, and co-workers can enjoy new levels of harmony and mutual respect.

Writing Assignment: Be Persuasive

Instructions: Write a classification essay with a persuasive purpose. Begin by choosing a subject and selecting one of these two strategies:

Strategy One: Use classifications to convince readers that a concept or thing is more complex than they expected. For example, you could argue against teenage curfews by showing that teenagers are so varied that it's not fair to subject all of them to a single rule. Or you could argue against racial prejudice by showing that it takes many forms that few people ever think about.

Strategy Two: Sort items into those you disagree with (placed early in your paper) and those you agree with (placed near the end of your paper). For example, you could describe three or four ways to invest money, and convince readers that one is safest and most productive. Possible topics include study methods, fitness programs, eating habits, and behavior at the mall, in a movie theater, or on the freeway.

READING TO WRITE: DISCIPLINING CHILDREN

The next selection is from the book *Freedom and Beyond* by educator John Holt (1923–1985). Holt uses three classifications to persuade readers that there's more to discipline than the traditional methods used by most parents.

Prereading Activity: Think about Discipline

Instructions: In the space below, brainstorm a list of methods that parents and teachers might use to discipline children. Put a + in front of the methods you consider appropriate for children, and a – in front of the methods you consider inappropriate.

Three Kinds of Discipline
From Freedom and Beyond *by John Holt*

A child, in growing up, may meet and learn from three different kinds of disciplines. The first and most important is what we might call the Discipline of Nature or of Reality. When he is trying to do something real, if he does the wrong thing or doesn't do the right one, he doesn't get the result he wants. If he doesn't pile one block right on top of another, or tries to build on a slanting surface, his tower falls down. If he hits the wrong key, he hears the wrong note. If he doesn't hit the nail squarely on the head, it bends, and he has to pull it out and start with another. If he doesn't measure properly what he is trying to build, it won't open, close, fit, stand up, fly, float, whistle, or do whatever he wants it to do. If he closes his eyes when he swings, he doesn't hit the ball. A child meets this kind of discipline every time he tries to *do* something, which is why it is so important in school to give children more chances to do things, instead of just reading or listening to someone talk (or pretending to). This discipline is a good teacher. The learner never has to wait long for his answer, it usually comes quickly, often instantly. Also it is clear, and very often points toward the needed correction; from what happened he can not only see what he did was wrong, but also why, and what he needs to do instead. Finally, and most important, the giver of the answer, call it Nature, is impersonal, impartial, and indifferent. She does not give opinions, or make judgments; she cannot be wheedled, bullied, or fooled; she does not get angry or disappointed; she does not praise or blame; she does not remember past failures or hold grudges; with her one always gets a fresh start; this time is the one that counts.

The next discipline we might call the Discipline of Culture, of Society, of What People Really Do. Man is a social, a cultural animal. Children sense around them this culture, this network of agreements, customs, habits and rules binding the adults together. They want to understand it and be a part of it. They watch very carefully what people around them are doing and want to do the same. They want to do right, unless they become convinced they can't do right. Thus children rarely misbehave seriously in church, but sit as quietly as they can. Some mysterious ritual is going on, and children, who like rituals, want to be part of it. In the same way, the little children that I see at concerts or operas, though they may fidget a little, or perhaps take a nap now and then, rarely make any disturbance. With all those grownups sitting there, neither moving nor talking, it is the most natural thing in the world to imitate them. Children who live among adults who are habitually courteous to each other, and to them, will soon learn to be courteous. Children who live surrounded by people who speak a certain way will speak that way, however much we may try to tell them that speaking that way is bad or wrong.

The third discipline is the one most people mean when they speak of discipline—the Discipline of Superior Force, of sergeant to private, of "You do what I tell you or I'll make you wish you had." There is bound to be some of this in a child's life. Living as we do surrounded by things that can hurt children, or that children can hurt, we cannot avoid it. We can't afford to let a small child find out from experience the danger of playing in a busy street, or of fooling with the pots on the top of a stove, or of eating up the pills in the medicine cabinet. So, along with other precautions, we say to him, "Don't play in the street, or touch things on the stove, or go into the medicine cabinet, or I'll punish you." Between him and the danger too great for him to imagine we put a lesser danger, but one he can imagine and maybe therefore wants to avoid. He can have no idea of what it would be like to be hit by a car, but he can imagine being shouted out, or spanked, or sent to his room. He avoids these substitutes for the greater danger until he can understand it and avoid it for its own sake. But we ought to use this discipline only when it is necessary to protect the life, health, safety, or well-being of people or other living creatures, or to prevent destruction of things that people care about. We ought not to assume too long, as we usually do, that a child cannot understand the real nature of the danger from which we want to protect him. The sooner he avoids the danger, not to escape our punishment, but as a matter of good sense, the better.

Collaborative Activity: Talk about Discipline

Instructions: Meet with a small group of students to compare your brainstorming lists (page 189). Then discuss John Holt's essay. Did reading it stimulate any new ideas about discipline?

Responding to What You Have Read

1. List Holt's three types of discipline.
2. What is Holt's attitude towards each of these types?
3. What kinds of readers do you think Holt had in mind when he wrote this selection?
4. List three examples from the essay. What is the purpose of each?
5. Write a response to Holt's ideas about discipline. Do you agree or disagree with him? Why?
6. Write a brief (five to ten sentences) summary of this essay.

Writing Assignment: Freedom and Beyond

Instructions: Write an essay about one of the following topics:

- discipline methods in your family (past or present)
- types of self-discipline
- an experience of your own that fits one of Holt's categories
- three kinds of discipline you've experienced or observed
- three kinds of freedom you've experienced—or would like to experience

SUMMARY

1. An essay about classifications should employ categories that readers will find useful and interesting.
2. In a persuasive essay, you can show that an issue is more complex than readers might have expected.
3. Another persuasive strategy is to write about three or more categories and place the category you favor first or last.

LOOKING AHEAD

Both comparisons and contrasts can help you develop the main point of an essay. In Chapter Twelve you will learn two ways to organize a comparison or contrast essay: the block method and the point-by-point method.

Using Comparison and Contrast in Writing

Preview

Comparison essays make a point by emphasizing similarities; contrast essays make a point by emphasizing differences. Comparison and contrast essays can be developed using either block or point-by-point organization. Comparisons and contrasts can be used for a variety of writing purposes.

INTRODUCING COMPARISONS AND CONTRASTS

When you use comparisons or contrasts in an essay, you make a point by bringing two related things together. Comparisons emphasize similarities; contrasts emphasize differences.

To be effective, your comparisons and contrasts must "make meaning." It's not enough to list the differences between planning a vacation yourself and using a travel agent, or to describe the similarities between major-league and minor-league baseball. Your writing must make a point worth reading. For example, you could show readers that they'll save time and money by using a travel agent instead of making their own reservations. Or you could convince readers to support a local baseball team by showing that minor league and major league games are very similar.

This descriptive paragraph, written by a student named Peggy, uses *contrasts* to explain the benefits of living at home:

Missing Home

Now that I've grown up and I have my own apartment, I realize that living at home had its advantages. Cleaning house and taking care of the yard were a group effort when I was at home; my brother and sisters and I had our own assigned chores. My parents split up the shopping and cooking until we children were old enough to help. Now I am on my own doing all the housework, including the heavy work that my brother Charles used to do. Another advantage I didn't appreciate then was my required eleven o'clock bedtime. Now that I can stay up as late as I want, I'm too tired to enjoy it. When eleven o'clock arrives, I'm still doing homework and chores around the apartment. Many other benefits of living alone have turned out to be mixed blessings. I don't have to wait in line for the bathroom any more, but I have to clean up the mess I make there. I can eat when I want to, but Mom's not there to cook. Living by myself has advantages, but sometimes I miss the good times I had at home.

The comparison paragraph below has an informative purpose—explaining how children benefit from playing baseball. To emphasize his point, psychologist Paul M. Lerner uses similarities to *compare* baseball to life:

Baseball Lessons
From "Learning from the Game" by Paul M. Lerner

In teaching baseball to a child, the parent also conveys a set of attitudes toward life. Ballplayers give the best of themselves to the game. They are prompted by a sense of responsibility to live up to their special talents. A growing boy, though realizing one day that he may not make it to the major leagues, learns through the sport the importance of making full use of his unique abilities and inner resources. He begins to sense the responsibility to do his best. A youngster also learns that a baseball attitude towards life places a high premium on consistency and patience. In baseball, the necessity for consistency outweighs the need for inspiration.

Collaborative Activity: Explore Comparisons and Contrasts

Instructions: Meet with a small group of students to compare and contrast high school and college. Begin by comparing the two, listing as many similarities as you can. Then contrast the two, listing as many differences as you can.

A Closer Look at Comparisons

Comparisons are useful when you want readers to see that two things have much in common, as in the following situations:

1. You can show readers how to save time or money.
   - A store brand of a product is identical to the name brand.
   - A low-cost item performs as well as a more expensive one.
   - Nurse practitioners perform some medical procedures as effectively as physicians do; the cost is lower, and waiting time is shorter.
   - Catalog customers have the same choices as customers who drive to a downtown store.
2. You can ease readers' fears about something unfamiliar.
   - Electronic word processing is easy for people who already know how to type.
   - A first-time political candidate is much like a famous relative who held political office in the past.
   - Reading skills required for college assignments are similar to the skills taught in high school.

The following essay fulfills Purpose 1. The author, a student named Mitchell, explains why public schools are as good as private ones that charge expensive tuition fees.

Just as Good

My parents made sacrifices to send me to private schools from first to third grade. I received a fine education, and I'll always be grateful to them. But if I have children myself someday, I'm going to send them to public schools.

Students and staff are much the same in both private and public schools. People are people, after all. Most teachers graduate from the same kinds of colleges. Most students come from similar families. My private-school friends weren't much different from the children I played with in my neighborhood.

The lessons taught in both types of schools are very similar, too. After school and on weekends I used to talk about school with my friends from public school. Our books and homework were much the same. We all studied long division, the table of elements, and the Civil War at the same time.

I've seen my neighborhood friends do just as well in college as my classmates from private school. Students who are lucky enough to have parents who encourage them, as mine did, can be very successful without a private education. The money saved on tuition can be used for educational trips, a computer, books, and college expenses. There isn't any good reason to pay high tuition fees when public schools do a fine job free of charge.

Collaborative Activity: Think about Comparisons

Instructions: Meet with a small group of students to list two comparisons that might help readers do each of the following:

a) save money
b) save time
c) overcome their fear of something unfamiliar

A Closer Look at Contrasts

Contrasts are useful to show that two things are different. Often you will use contrasts to emphasize that one thing is better or worse than another.

1. You can encourage readers to make a change in their behavior.
   - Computer research is easier than research with print databases.
   - Watching a Shakespeare play is more enjoyable than reading it.
   - Driving in a winter storm requires more skill than driving in clear weather.
2. You can encourage readers to change an opinion.
   - Mail-in ballots cost less and encourage more citizen participation than balloting booths.

- Because assault weapons are more destructive than hand weapons, they should have stricter regulations.
- Community-based programs for youthful offenders cut crime more effectively than traditional prison sentences.

3. You can analyze changes in legislation, institutions, and people's behavior.
   - American corporations are less tolerant of sexual harassment and racial prejudice than they used to be.
   - Fewer designers and clothing manufacturers are featuring garments made with fur.
   - The rules of amateur figure skating now emphasize showmanship more than they used to.

The following essay fulfills Purpose 2. A first-year student named Angie used contrasts to encourage readers to change their thinking about coed and single-sex softball. Many softball fans assume that coed games are more exciting because men are powerful hitters and fielders. But Angie thinks women's softball is more fun for both players and fans.

Play Ball!

Four years ago, I started playing softball with two local teams—a women's team, and a coed one. Although coed softball is a lot of fun, I enjoy playing in the Women's League much more.

To begin, competition is more equal when only women play. I'm a right fielder, and the men's strength makes balls harder to catch. In a coed game, the team with more men is likely to win because male players overpower the women. When only women are playing, skill counts more than strength. Games are more fun to watch because talent really stands out in the Women's League. When men are playing, an accomplished woman player may be overshadowed by a man who looks more impressive because of his size.

Furthermore, playing with all women is safer. Because most men hit and throw the ball harder than women, I worry about injuries in coed games. As a result, I don't play as well. Once I saw a woman player hit on the back of the head by a ball during a double play. She was in the hospital for two days. A week later I was hit by a ball during the same kind of play, but I wasn't hurt because a woman had thrown it.

I have good friends in both the women's and the coed teams, and I look forward to every game. But it's always more exciting and more fun to play in the Women's League.

Collaborative Activity: Think about Contrasts

Instructions: Meet with a small group of students to list contrasts that might encourage readers to a) change their thinking or b) change their behavior.

Using Comparisons and Contrasts to "Make Meaning"

Whether you're writing about comparisons or contrasts, ensure that your essay "makes meaning" by planning your thesis statement carefully. Avoid empty words like "different," "change," and "alike" that don't express a definite viewpoint. Make sure your essay makes a point rather than merely listing similarities and differences. Compare these thesis statements:

> Living at home is different from life in a college dorm. WEAK
>
> I'm enjoying college more now that I'm living in a dorm instead of at home. BETTER
>
> The members of a church are much like a family. WEAK
>
> People who feel lonely and isolated can feel they are part of a family by joining a church. BETTER
>
> Today's public schools are different from public schools thirty years ago. WEAK
>
> Teachers in today's public schools face greater challenges than teachers from thirty years ago. BETTER

Exercise 1: Evaluate Thesis Statements

Instructions: Put a check before each effective thesis statement. Remember that essays about comparisons and contrasts should "make meaning" rather than simply list similarities and differences.

_____ 1. Laptop and desktop computers are different in many ways.

_____ 2. Etiquette rules have changed in the last fifty years.

_____ 3. Yoga offers more health benefits than traditional calisthenics.

_____ 4. Joan and Jean are twins, but they're not at all alike.

_____ 5. News reporting on public radio is better than the reporting on commercial radio stations.

_____ 6. The Spanish and Portuguese languages are similar.

_____ 7. Most college courses are taught at twice the pace of high-school courses.

_____ 8. College demands more intense study skills than high school.

_____ 9. The alcohol in beer and wine coolers is as intoxicating as the alcohol in hard liquor.

_____ 10. Ice hockey and field hockey are very different games.

Exercise 2: Write Thesis Statements Using Comparisons

Instructions: Choose five of the topics below. For each choice, name two items that could be compared. Then write a thesis statement that makes a point about your topic. For example, "something that has not changed much over the years" could prompt this thesis statement: The quality of most television entertainment has not improved since I was a child.

    a) something that has not changed much over the years: an institution, organization, company, profession, place, or product

b) groups: couples, families, clubs, teams, performers

c) government: policies, officials or candidates

d) customs: traditions, holidays, observances, rituals

e) products: manufactured items or foods

f) locations: two places where you've lived, worked, or attended school

Exercise 3: Write Thesis Statements Using Contrasts

Instructions: Choose five of the categories below. For each choice, name two items that could be contrasted. Then state a *point* your contrast could make. For example, shopping malls fit the first category: "something that has changed over the years." You could show that malls have changed to fit the needs of today's lifestyles: Senior citizens, community leaders, business owners, and young people use malls to meet a variety of needs.

a) something that has not changed much over the years: an institution, organization, company, profession, place, or product

b) groups: couples, families, clubs, teams, performers

c) government: policies, officials, or candidates

d) customs: traditions, holidays, observances, rituals

e) products: manufactured items or foods

f) locations: two places where you've lived, worked, or attended school

Useful Transitions for Comparison and Contrast

For similarities: also, like, both, similarly, same, in common, too, likewise, in the same way

For contrasts: however, nevertheless, on the contrary, on the other hand, instead, unlike, in contrast, although, but, even though, yet

USING COMPARISONS AND CONTRASTS IN ESSAYS

The following suggestions will help you write an effective comparison or contrast essay.

1. Choose a topic you know well, or do enough research to increase your knowledge. Make sure there are enough similarities to justify writing your essay: Don't compare a wood-burning stove to a microwave oven. And make sure you can make a strong point about your subject. Avoid planning an essay that will simply list similarities or differences.

2. Decide whether your purpose is primarily descriptive or informative. Will you be emphasizing knowledge (for an informative essay) or experience and impressions (for a descriptive essay)?

3. Use the discovery strategies you've already learned—freewriting, brainstorming, clustering—to explore your subject. Your "writer's eyes" and personal experiences will be

helpful in choosing a point worth making. Every student essay in this chapter begins with personal experience—attending school, baking a pie, hunting, working with a computer.

4. When you know what point you wish to make, decide whether you will emphasize similarities (in a comparison essay) or differences (in a contrast essay). Rereading the preceding pages may help you decide how you can make your point most effectively.

5. Use critical thinking to determine whether comparison or contrast will work better for your purpose. Rereading pages 194–196 may be helpful.

6. Plan your essay thoughtfully. Your first paragraph will introduce both of the items you're comparing and contrasting; it will also state your purpose. In the body of your essay, you can choose between block and point-by-point organization (below). The choice is usually yours. But if your essay will be more than a few pages long, point-by-point organization will probably be easier for your readers to follow, since you'll constantly be going back and forth between the two items you're describing.

7. Make sure your conclusion restates and reinforces your purpose. Use one of the concluding strategies in Chapter Seven to leave a powerful impression on readers.

ORGANIZING A COMPARISON/CONTRAST ESSAY

When you organize an essay around comparisons or contrasts, you can use either block or point-by-point organization to develop your thesis statement.

Block Organization

In *block organization,* you present information about one item in the first part of your essay. Then you switch to the other item in the rest of your essay. If you were contrasting high school and college clubs, you would discuss high school clubs in the first part of your essay. The second part would explain how college clubs are different.

A student named Benjamin used block organization to contrast the baking methods he and his grandmother use. Benjamin's first paragraph explains how he bakes an apple pie. Then he uses the rest of the essay to show that his grandmother's baking methods are better.

A Better Pie

Until I watched Grandma make an apple pie, I thought I was a terrific baker. I always choose fresh, red apples, and I use a name-brand mix for the crust. The whole process—slicing the apples, mixing the ingredients, preparing the crust, and baking it—takes almost three hours. I add cinnamon for extra flavor, and I time the baking process carefully. After all that effort, my pies are better than the heat-and-serve ones sold in supermarkets. But they're never as good as Grandma's, and I've always wondered why.

After I spent a weekend visiting Grandma and watching her in the kitchen, I began to understand why her pies are special. Her first bag of apples went back to the store because they weren't tasty enough. The next apples were better, but

Grandma didn't put them right into the piecrust. First she tasted them; then she added small amounts of lemon juice, cinnamon, nutmeg, cornstarch, vanilla, and sugar until she was satisfied with the texture and flavor.

As I watched Grandma preheat the oven, she told me that the crust won't bake properly if it's started in a cold oven. A technician adjusts her oven every year so that there are no cold or hot spots to spoil her pies.

Her crust was homemade, not from a box, and she used lard rather than shortening to make it tender. She sprinkled it with sugar and cinnamon and refrigerated it overnight before it went into the oven. Even her spices were fresh. She threw away a tin of cinnamon because it was three months old.

After watching Grandma put all that time and effort into her pie, I'm not sure I want to be an expert baker. But I do know better than to brag about my "homemade" baking next time. And I'll never say "easy as pie" again.

Many readers like block organization because it organizes ideas into two easy-to-read sections: There's no jumping back and forth from one item to another. Block organization works best in paragraphs and short essays because readers can easily remember the points that were made about both items. But in a longer essay—one several pages long—block organization may be confusing. By the time readers finish the second half of the essay, they may have forgotten about the item that was discussed at the beginning of the essay.

Writing Assignment: Use Block Organization

Instructions: Using block organization, as Benjamin did, write an essay comparing or contrasting two ways of performing a task. "Make meaning" by showing that the two ways are equally good (comparison) or that one is better than the other (contrast).

Point-by-Point Organization

Point-by-point organization is another way to develop your thesis statement. Here you go back and forth from one item to the other throughout the body of your essay. Every time you make a point about one item, you immediately compare or contrast it to the other item. Point-by-point organization is especially good for long essays because both items are mentioned in every body paragraph: Readers are unlikely to lose track of what you're writing about.

On page 195, Mitchell used point-by-point development to compare private and public schooling in her essay "Just as Good." This outline shows that Mitchell made an important point about both private and public schools in each paragraph of the body of her essay.

Mitchell's Outline

Thesis: If I have children myself someday, I'm going to send them to public schools.

First topic sentence: Students and staff are much the same in both private and public schools.

Second topic sentence: The lessons taught in both types of schools are very similar too.

Third topic sentence: I've seen my neighborhood friends do just as well in college as my classmates from private school.

Conclusion: I'll be enrolling my children in public school as soon as they're old enough for kindergarten.

The next student essay uses point-by-point organization. Notice that the author makes a point both about typewriters and computers in each paragraph.

Word Processing

Although I was nervous about using a computer at first, I've discovered that a computer is much easier to use for college papers than a typewriter. I took a one-credit course in word processing one weekend, and I started saving time on writing assignments almost immediately.

I discovered that corrections are much easier on a computer. Instead of using an eraser or correction tape, I just tap a few keys to make the changes I want. The time saved helps me complete homework much faster than I used to. My instructors appreciate neat written work, so my grades are better too. Next, the computer helps me with spelling. Correcting spelling errors with a big dictionary takes a long time, and I can't always find the words I want. But the computer's spellchecker quickly fixes most of my spelling errors.

Best of all, revisions are easy. Because I store all my college papers on a disk, I can quickly make any changes a professor wants. I don't have to spend an hour or two retyping the whole paper from the beginning. Changes are so simple that I'm doing more revising than ever before. After making B's and C's in English all my life, I'm expecting an A this semester.

I wish I'd had a computer instead of a typewriter when I was in high school. My grades would probably have been higher, and I would have been better prepared for college. Now that I've discovered that word processing is easy and fun, I'm encouraging all my friends to try it too.

Writing Assignment: Use Point-by-Point Development in an Essay

Instructions: Use point-by-point development to write an essay about something new you've experienced recently. You may write a comparison essay, emphasizing that the experience was comfortable for you because it seemed familiar; or you can write a contrast essay, emphasizing features that made this experience different from anything that had already happened to you.

USING COMPARISON AND CONTRAST TO PERSUADE

Comparisons and contrasts are often useful when you're writing with a persuasive purpose. Comparisons—showing that one thing is as good as another—can convince readers to change their minds about a product, a place, or an institution; so can contrasts, which often show that one thing is better or worse than another.

A Student Writes a Persuasive Essay

The following student essay uses contrasts for a persuasive purpose: Jon is trying to convince readers that hunting is not really a sport. Although this essay has descriptive and informative qualities, Jon's primary purpose is to challenge readers' thinking.

Is Hunting a Sport?

When my brother and I were small, our father taught us how to hunt, just as his father had done for him. I grew up proud of my ability to bag a deer and bring down a duck flying high above me. I used to boast that hunting requires fitness, skill, and courage, just as other sports do. Lately I've changed my thinking. Hunting is not a sport, and Americans should stop taking pride in this cruel pastime.

Hunting does not require fitness, as real sports do. Football, basketball, track, and boxing make severe physical demands on athletes. Endurance, strength, and flexibility are a must. But hunters aren't athletes. Often they're overweight and out of shape. The running, chasing, and cornering are often done by dogs. Many hunters sit in a duck blind or a deer stand all day, and others ride in an open truck looking for deer or wild hogs. Pulling the trigger—the climax of this activity—requires little strength.

Hunting is an unequal contest between a human and an animal. True sports match opponents at the same level of experience, size, and skill. Heavyweight boxers don't take on featherweights; amateur soccer players don't compete with professionals. But a hunter's quarry rarely meets its opponent in an equal contest. Birds, rabbits, and other small animals are defenseless against humans. Larger animals rarely confront the humans who stalk them. The sophisticated paraphernalia carried by hunters eliminates any chance of an equal encounter.

Most important, hunting doesn't requires much skill. Unlike real sports, hunters don't need strength, agility, speed, or strategy. Hunters rely heavily on chance, equipment, and manipulation. Duck calls, shotguns, decoys, rifle scopes, and other equipment do most of the work. Many hunting preserves are deliberately overpopulated with animals so that even small children can hunt successfully, as my brother and I did. Often the owners feed the deer in designated spots, giving hunters an even greater advantage.

I gave up hunting a year ago, after going directly from an all-day track meet to a weekend of hunting with my father and uncle. Fresh from the exciting challenges of track, I realized for the first time that hunting has little in common with true sports. You'll still find me in the woods, but I'll be jogging down a picturesque trail instead of shooting. My hunting days are over.

Exercise 4: Analyze Jon's Essay

Instructions: Reread Jon's essay and answer the following questions.

1. Underline Jon's thesis statement and topic sentences.

2. Although "Is Hunting a Sport?" is persuasive, it also contains some information about hunting. List the facts you learn about hunting from Jon's essay.

3. Did Jon use block or point-by-point organization in his essay? Explain your answer.

4. What transitions did Jon use? How effective are they?

5. Evaluate Jon's essay. If you were a member of his editing group, would you recommend any changes? Explain your answer.

USING COMPARISONS AND CONTRASTS IN A PERSUASIVE ESSAY

In addition to the ideas on page 106, these suggestions may be helpful if you're writing a persuasive essay.

1. Persuasive essays usually focus on contrasts, showing that one thing is better than another. But you can also use similarities as your focus, showing that one thing is as good (or as bad) as another. For example, experts say that ordinary unleaded gasoline is just as good as premium for most cars.

2. Avoid similarities that may offend readers. Don't make comparisons to Nazis, the Ku Klux Klan, or other disagreeable groups.

3. Choose a main point that is interesting and worth reading. Don't tell readers that an automobile is more practical for city transportation than a horse-drawn buggy—that's too obvious. But you could describe the advantages of horses or bicycles over automobiles for police work in metropolitan areas.

Writing Assignment: Be Persuasive!

Instructions: Write a comparison or contrast essay with a persuasive purpose. Rereading "A Closer Look at Comparisons" and "A Closer Look at Contrasts" earlier in this chapter will help you write an effective essay. Be prepared to share an advanced draft with a group of students, and consider incorporating their suggestions into a revision.

READING TO WRITE: INSURANCE INVESTMENTS

Morton Shulman is the author of two books that teach ordinary people the basics of money management. In this reading selection, he tries to persuade readers to purchase term rather than whole-life insurance. As you read, notice how Shulman uses contrasts to emphasize the point he's making.

Prereading Activity: Is Life Insurance Important to You?

1. What do you already know about life insurance?
2. Do you have a life insurance policy? Why or why not?

Life Insurance
from Anyone Can Be A Milliionaire *by Morton Shulman*

The single most common individual investment in North America today is life insurance. It is also the least productive; in fact, insurance should not be considered an investment at all.

Life insurance is bought for two reasons—protection and savings. As pure survivor protection, there can be no quarrel with insurance. By paying small premiums, each individual helps alleviate the risk of untimely death of many others. This is term insurance; its cost is very low, and it allows the breadwinner to be sure that the family will have an adequate income in case of an unexpected death. The person who buys term insurance is showing love for the family.

Unfortunately most insurance that is sold is not term insurance. All other insurance plans contain a combination of protection and savings, and they cost much more than term insurance. The names may be ordinary life, 20-year-pay or endowment, or whole life; these terms refer only to the varying percentages of protection and savings in each policy. When we consider the three basics of any investment—yield, safety, and possible capital appreciation, it soon becomes clear that insurance is probably the worst investment described in this book.

Responding to What You Have Read

1. How do you know that this reading selection is primarily persuasive? List the words that provide clues to Shulman's purpose.

2. Does Shulman use block or point-by-point development in this selection? Explain your answer.

3. Besides contrasting whole-life and term insurance, this selection also contrasts insurance and investments. Explain the difference. (Refer to the dictionary if necessary.)

4. Do you agree with Shulman's conclusions about term and whole-life insurance? If you need more information about insurance before making your decision, what strategies might you use to find answers to your questions?

5. Look again at your answers to the Prereading Activity on page 203. What did you learn from this reading selection?

6. Do you agree with Shulman's preference for term insurance over whole-life insurance? Why or why not?

7. Write a short (five to ten sentences) summary of this selection.

READING TO WRITE: AN ENGLISH-SPEAKING CHILD IN CALCUTTA

You're about to read a reminiscence of a man who spent part of his boyhood with relatives in Calcutta, a large city in India. Before you begin reading, complete the activities below.

Prereading Activities: Growing up in Another Culture

1. Recall your first experiences with people different from your family—anyone whose nationality, religion, or lifestyle was different from the one familiar to you. What can you remember about the thoughts and feelings you had then?

2. Recall the stories you most enjoyed reading and hearing as a child. Where were you when you encountered these stories? What attracted you about them then?

Vocabulary:

puja   (noun) a Hindu prayer ritual

Bengali   (noun) the language of western Bengal (a region in India) and Bangladesh (a country in Southeast Asia)

Their Books and Mine
Adapted from Beyond Translation *by Amit Chaudhuri*

The Dakkhinee Bookshop, at the turning of Lansdowne Road and Rash Behari Avenue, was really no more than a pavement bookstall. It stands there even now, still doing business—though, with more than half its books gone, it is a shadow of its former self.

When I was a boy, visiting my cousins' house in Calcutta, this was the main bookshop in the area. Although it was a good half hour away from where my cousins lived, we would trek to it on foot. Any car passing the bookshop at that time would have seen three boys, their backs to the road, their heads bent. Then we would return home with books in our hands: adventure annuals and mystery stories—my book in English and my cousins' books in Bengali. Childhood was a time when I read nothing in Bengali and my cousins read nothing in English. Sitting side by side, we would begin to read almost immediately, enveloped in the same contentment, as we read our books in different languages and inhabited different imaginary worlds.

While we were reading, the routines of the house continued around us. The maid might be swabbing the floor, leaving dark, moist arcs on the red stone, which dried and disappeared soon after. Downstairs, my aunt might be overseeing something in the kitchen while my uncle prepared to eat an early lunch before going out to work at his small business.

We sat just anywhere while we read—on the stairs, on the floor, against the side of a bed—suspending activity, waiting for a story or a book to be finished. The years passed. And we still sat reading side by side, of worlds that could not be translated into each other; changes came to us as sounds in the street, adornments to our consciousness.

But did the future matter then? While we read, my aunt would come upstairs, perhaps to rearrange something—a pillow on the bed—or to have her bath and do her *puja,* or to call us downstairs for food. I would be reading about lighthouses, boating adventures, or mountain expeditions, while my cousins read about mad scientists and mysteries, about holy men and the seven seas and bloodthirsty kings. While we sat with our books in our hands, our minds racing with demons, usurped kingdoms, seashores, and collapsing houses, my aunt hovered around us. She had a gift with children, drawing an enchantment around them without any apparent effort, and the spell lasted all of my childhood.

Not having grown up in Bengal, I never learned to read or write Bengali in school. I lived, an only child, in Bombay with my parents. My father worked in the corporate world of tall buildings and offices, the Marine Drive and the Arabian Sea. My sojourns in Calcutta, during the summer holidays, and sometimes in the winter, lasted no more than two months. But once there I was plunged into the lives of my cousins and never thought of going back until I had to. I never thought of myself as a visitor.

What were my cousins' thoughts? I never entirely knew. When we finished reading our stories in our different languages, we looked up and became conscious once more of the house, with secret flashlight signals and demons who could grow eight times their size still in our heads.

Once finished, our books lost their interest, but they remained precious as material objects, and we would pretend to sell them to each other as make-believe hawkers. But, essentially, our worlds remained locked from each other; we never read one another's stories, though I admired the covers of their books, with severed heads dripping blood, and princesses as frail as dragonfly wings. They would never know what it meant, as I did, to live outside this world of magic and small means; and I would never know what it meant to grow up reading their stories—by Saradindu and Sukumar Ray and Hemendra Kumar Ray—and be transported, as I believed they were for those half hours, more completely into another world than I was.

Responding to What You Have Read

1. Write any questions that came to mind as you read this essay. What strategies can you use to find the answers?
2. In a few sentences, summarize the experiences Chaudhuri described in this essay.
3. Reread what you wrote during the Prereading Activities. How are your memories similar to Chaudhuri's? How are they different?
4. Is this essay primarily about comparisons, contrasts, or both? Explain your answer.
5. What do you think was Chaudhuri's purpose in writing this essay?
6. Write a short (five to eight sentences) summary of this selection.

Writing Assignment: Write about a Memory

Instructions: Write a comparison or contrast essay about either of the topics below. While you are planning your essay, ensure that it will "make meaning" with a strong thesis statement.

1. Write an essay comparing or contrasting your family with another family, real or imaginary—a family you know, or one from a book, television show, play, or movie.

2. Write an essay about an experience you've had at home, on vacation, at school, or at work. Compare or contrast your experience with a similar one you're familiar with from a friend, book, television show, or movie.

SUMMARY

1. Comparisons emphasize similarities; contrasts emphasize differences.
2. Comparisons and contrasts can be used to describe, inform, and persuade.
3. Comparison-contrast essays can be developed using block or point-by-point organization.

LOOKING AHEAD

In Chapter Thirteen you'll learn about using causes and effects in writing. Causes explain *why* something happens; effects show the *results* of an event or process. You can use causes and effects to write essays that describe, inform, and persuade.

CHAPTER THIRTEEN

Using Causes and Effects in Writing

Preview

Preview

Writing about causes and effects helps readers understand *why* something happens. Causes and effects have a time relationship: Causes come first, and effects happen later. Causes are the factors that make events happen; effects are short-term and long-term results. You can use causes and effects in descriptive, informative, and persuasive essays.

INTRODUCING CAUSES AND EFFECTS

When you write about causes and effects, you help readers understand *why* something happens. Usually causes and effects have a time relationship. *Causes*, the factors that make something happen, come first; *effects* are results, or outcomes, that happen later. By exploring causes, effects, or both in an essay, you can broaden your readers' understanding of your subject.

In her book *Alcohol and You,* author Jane Claypool uses both causes and effects to explain *fetal alcohol syndrome*—the damage done to an unborn baby when its mother drinks alcoholic beverages. The following paragraph focuses on *causes:*

Fetal Alcohol Syndrome
from Alcohol and You *by Jane Claypool*

It is easy to see why alcohol can have such serious effects on the developing fetus, for when a pregnant woman has a drink, the alcohol crosses through the placenta to the fetus. The alcohol travels through the baby's bloodstream in the same concentration as through the mother's. If the pregnant mother becomes drunk, so does the unborn baby. However, the unborn child does not have the ability to handle alcohol as well as the mother does. An unborn baby's liver burns up alcohol at a much slower rate; thus the alcohol stays in the system longer. Unborn babies can't say no to that last drink. Nor can newborns say no when more alcohol is transmitted through the breast milk of the nursing mother.

In the next paragraph, Claypool focuses on the *effects* of alcohol during pregnancy—what happens after the baby is born:

> Children with the fetal alcohol syndrome do not "catch up" even when special care is provided after birth. Some of these babies have abnormally small heads, severe facial irregularities, joint and limb abnormalities, heart defects, and poor coordination. Many are mentally retarded and experience behavioral problems, including hyperactivity, extreme nervousness, and poor attention spans.

Exercise 1: Analyze Causes and Effects

1. What purpose do you think Claypool had in mind when she wrote these two paragraphs? Was her purpose primarily informative or persuasive?
2. Think of a social problem that concerns you. List as many causes and effects as you can think of. If you were trying to persuade others to solve the problem, which list would you show them?
3. Think of a choice you've made recently. Write down as many causes and effects as you can think of. Decide which list is more interesting, and write a paragraph about it.

Collaborative Activity: Identify Causes and Effects

Instructions: Label each selection below either "cause" or "effect." Next, write a sentence explaining your answer. Finally, meet with a small group of students to discuss your answers.

_____ a) From the article "A Boy and His Gun" in *Time* magazine:

> Steve, 14, stopped walking home alone from school last year when many of his fellow seventh-graders at Hale Junior High started taking up guns. "Some guys just started to change. It became cool to say you could get a gun," he says. "Nobody messes with you if they even think you may have a gun."

_____ b) From a speech by psychologist Ken Magid:

> If you have a half-million American teenagers having babies, and those teens are having to go through their own identity crisis at the same time, they aren't able to give a value structure to their own infants.

_____ c) From the article "The Nose-Job Generation" by David Sharp:

> But over summer vacation last year, Ashley went to a plastic surgeon and had the hump removed. The bridge of her nose is now about a 16th of an inch lower, and her confidence is about a mile higher. She no longer hides her profile.

_____ e) From the newspaper article "Cooking the Books" by Sean Loughlin:

> Each year a larger percentage of the country's total economic output is consumed by interest payments on the national debt. That means there's less

money available for new projects or programs, such as worker retraining, education, road and bridge repair, or even defense.

READING TO WRITE: A HERO FOR TODAY

In the following selection, a journalist explains why youthful golf champion Tiger Woods is so widely admired.

Prereading Activity: What's a Hero?

In the space below, make a list of the athletes you admire and your reasons for admiring them. (If you're not a sports fan, make a list of admirable people in other fields.)

Vocabulary:

adulation	(noun) strong admiration
hyped	(adjective) receiving exaggerated publicity
braggart	(noun) person who shows off
denigration	(noun) negative criticism
lucrative	(adjective) financially rewarding
anarchism	(noun) lack of rules
schtick	(noun) gimmick
mensch	(Yiddish noun) admirable person
lout	(noun) rude, coarse person
freebooter	(noun) person who steals
mesmerized	(verb) hypnotized
paragon	(noun) fine example

Why We Admire Tiger Woods
from the Los Angeles Times *by Charles Krauthammer*

Yes, he's good, very good. Record-breakingly good. But there are dozens of other great athletes in the country, and golf is generally not a sport that quickens America's pulse.

Yes, he's young. But we've had 7-year-old tennis champions. We've had gymnastics champions barely out of infancy.

Of course, there is race. An African- and Asian-American Masters champion is as rare as April snow in Augusta. But almost as rare is a black hockey player, and nothing remotely like the Woods phenomenon greeted Grant Fuhr, an extremely talented black goalie who in the '80s won five Stanley Cups with the Edmonton Oilers. And Hideo Nomo—splendid pitcher, rookie of the year, Dodger and Japanese—became a local hero but hardly a national obsession.

Yes, excellence, youth and ethnicity account for much of the Woods mania. But they are not quite enough to explain the wave of adulation.

Woods is more than just good, young, black and Asian. He is gracious. In an age of the commercially hyped, trash-talking, in-your-face sports star, here is someone who combines great athleticism with decency, politeness and respectfulness.

And not just respect for his parents, his elders, his competitors. He has a deep respect for the difficulty of his craft. For all of his greatness and his awareness of it, he is anchored in the history and mystery of his game.

This is not exactly humility. One does not expect humility from someone who drives a ball 350 yards with accuracy and wins six of his first 19 pro tournaments, including the Masters, with an all-time record score. But Woods's pride in his game does not extend to the braggart denigration of the competition and the naked promotion of self over sport that you find in so many young stars today.

This, after all, is the age of the athlete with attitude. Andre Agassi and Deion Sanders have mastered this very lucrative chest-beating individualism. Dennis Rodman has taken it to its conclusion with his groin-kicking, body-piercing anarchism.

The bad boys, by the way, did not start with young black basketballers. It began with young white tennis players like Jimmy Connors and John McEnroe who turned bad manners and quick tempers into a schtick and a ticket to celebrity that took them beyond tennis.

Americans are overcome with relief to find, rising out of this swamp of rotten behavior, a *mensch* like Woods.

A paragon in sports is easy to define: someone whom you would be pleased to have your child emulate. One of the main reasons baseball is dying is that, with the exception of Cal Ripken and a handful of others, the best players are louts. Who cares about the fortunes of a sport populated by growling freebooters with contempt for their followers and their game?

Enter Tiger. Woods's final-round Masters performance earned the highest television ratings in recent golf history. It is not that we tuned in to see possibly the best golfer ever. We tuned in to see a good man excel. America is mesmerized not just because he is a great athlete. Not just because he is a gifted young African- and Asian-American athlete. But because he is a paragon and a rarity: a gentleman athlete.

Responding to What You Have Read

1. List the causes of Tiger Woods's popularity cited by Charles Krauthammer.
2. Do you agree or disagree with Krauthammer's statement that baseball is "dying out" because most players are "louts"? Why?
3. Look again at the list of admirable people you made on page 210. Did any of Tiger Woods's special qualities appear on your list?
4. Think of an athlete or other public figure you disapprove of. List as many reasons as you can for your disapproval.
5. What are the *effects* of Tiger Woods's good manners and sportsmanship? List as many as you can.
6. Write a brief (three or four sentences) summary of this selection.

Collaborative Activity: Talk about Heroes

Meet with a small group of other students to discuss the reasons you admire certain public figures. Begin by listing people the group considers admirable; then list the causes for your approval. Next, make a list of the effects these people have had on their admirers.

Writing Assignment: Someone to Admire

Write a paragraph about a person you admire. You are free to write about anyone you choose, living or dead: a relative, friend, public figure, or literary character. Focus your paragraph on either causes—the reasons for your admiration—or effects—the person's positive influence on your life.

STUDENTS WRITE ABOUT CAUSES AND EFFECTS

The two student paragraphs that follow are good illustrations of descriptive writing about causes and effects. The first, written by a student named Dinh, is about *causes*—the reasons she enjoys working at an Oriental music store:

Music to My Ears

I enjoy working as a cashier at a small store that sells recordings of Oriental music. I've been there for a year and a half, and it's a perfect job for me. The boss treats me like her best friend. May, my boss, is six years older than I am, but we're very close. We can talk about almost anything, and she's very understanding. Most of the time I'm able to do my homework there during slow periods. Other bosses would get angry about that, but May encourages me to do well in college. Furthermore, my salary is good. I started at seven dollars an hour, even though it was only my first job. I've had two raises in only eighteen months. Best of all, I get a chance to work on my Mandarin. My native language is Cantonese, and I used to speak only a little

Mandarin. But about half our customers speak Mandarin, so I've learned a lot from them. This job has been a great experience for me.

In the next paragraph, a student named Rolf describes the *effects,* or results, of enrolling in a college-success seminar.

A Semester of Success

I was puzzled when my college counselor encouraged me to enroll in a college success seminar. I was a good student in high school and won several academic awards. I expected to do even better in college because I thought my courses would be more interesting. It took some convincing for Mr. Paul to persuade me to enroll in the course. Now I think it was a good decision because I learned two valuable kinds of information. One was better study skills. College turned out to be harder than I thought because the pace is so fast. The seminar covered memory techniques, testing skills, notetaking, and other strategies. The other benefit was useful information about college life. Guest speakers shared many tips about college policies, financial aid, and services for students. Thanks to the seminar, I really am doing better in college than in high school, and I feel more confident and more at home on campus.

Exercise 2: Analyze Causes and Effects

Reread Dinh's and Rolf's passages. Did Dinh include any effects in her paragraph about her reasons for liking her job? Did Rolf include any causes in his paragraph about the effects of his college-success seminar? Explain your answer.

A CLOSER LOOK AT CAUSES AND EFFECTS

Like Dinh's and Rolf's paragraphs, essays often focus primarily on causes or effects, rather than both. Your instructor may give you an assignment asking for either causes or effects, or the choice between the two may be yours to make.

Your critical thinking skills can help you decide which to emphasize. After you've decided on a subject, make two lists on a sheet of paper: Causes and Effects. Include as many items as you can think of—you can always make deletions later. When your lists are complete, evaluate what you have written: Is one list longer or more vivid than the other? Will readers find the items in one list more interesting than the other? These questions can help you decide whether to emphasize causes or effects in your essay.

Two students named Paul and Fatima used this listing method to discover and evaluate ideas for a cause/effect writing assignment. Although both wrote about the same idea—a satisfactory purchase of a used car—they organized their essays differently. As you read Paul's planning sheet, you can see that his "causes" list is more interesting:

Buying a Good Used Car

Causes

—listened to Grandpa
—read classifieds
—visited dealers
—took my time

—checked friends'
experiences and suggestions
—had engine checked
by Gramp's mechanic

Effects
—happy with car!
—saved $$$—couldn't afford new car
—proud of car
—independent—no more bumming rides

Since his "causes" list had several interesting item, Paul decided to use it as the basis for his essay:

A Million More Miles

My grandfather jokes that a car isn't broken in until it's gone a million miles. He always buys secondhand cars and has been happy with them. The lessons I've learned from him helped me buy a good used car two years ago.

He began by telling me to take plenty of time to look at classified ads and visit dealers. For two weeks I made phone calls and drove around to look at used cars. I soon learned which cars were bargains and which ones weren't. It was hard to pass up a few nice cars that might have been good buys. But Grandpa assured me that other good deals would come along if I studied the market first.

Talking to friends about their experiences with car ownership, as Grandpa suggested, was also helpful. I found out about laws in our state that protect people who buy cars. For example, car buyers have the right to call the previous owner to find out if anything major is wrong with the car. I also learned which cars my friends found most reliable, and which ones seemed prone to problems. And I picked up many other useful tips, like how to tell if the odometer was moved back or the car had been in an accident.

Grandpa told me the most important step is having the car checked for engine problems before I buy it. A friend gave me the name of a good mechanic who agreed to look at the Honda Civic I wanted to buy. Everything checked out, and the mechanic assured me I was getting a good deal on it.

Thanks to Grandpa, I now have a car I'm happy with. He says that I should keep learning about cars so I can make a good decision when it's time to buy another one. But he says that won't happen for a while because I'll be driving my Civic for a million more miles.

Exercise 3: Analyze Paul's Essay

Instructions: Reread Paul's essay, and answer these questions.

1. Is Paul's essay informative, persuasive, or both? Give reasons for your answer.
2. Label the thesis statement, topic sentences, and transitions in Paul's essay.
3. Paul's essay is primarily about causes—the reasons his purchase worked well for him. But he also mentions some of the *effects* of his purchase. List as many as you can find.

Unlike Paul, Fatima wrote about the *effects* of her purchase of a used car. Here is her planning sheet:

Buying Michael's Car

Causes
–I trust him
–nice car
–couldn't afford new one
–nervous about negotiating at a used car lot
–simplest option for me

Effects
–nicer car than I could buy new
–extras: tinted windows, thick carpet,
  terrific stereo, plays compact disks!
–low monthly payments
–low insurance
–even with a few repairs, I'm saving money

Here is Fatima's essay:

Better than New

Last year when I was thinking about buying a new car, my brother-in-law Michael offered to sell me his Cavalier. I hesitated because I really wanted a new car, and I was nervous about doing business with a relative. After I bought the Cavalier, though, I was glad I did. I love the car, and the savings are a big help in paying for college.

Michael told me I'd save money on insurance, and he was right. Because the Cavalier has lower book value than a new car, my premiums are smaller. I've already saved almost a hundred dollars.

I was worried about repair costs, but so far the Cavalier has had only minor problems. The water pump had to be replaced, and I bought a new battery last November when I was worried about starting the car on cold mornings. My low car payments more than make up for those expenses.

Now I own a car that's nicer than any new one I could have afforded to buy. I love its tinted windows and luxurious carpeting. Because music is important to Michael, the Cavalier has a better sound system than I would have bought for myself. I can play both compact disks and tapes in my car, and they make driving to work and classes much more enjoyable.

I expected to have some regrets at first because I had looked forward to driving a sharp-looking new car. But the extra money in my checking account every month quickly eased my disappointment. Right now Michael is driving a red Caprice, and I hope to buy it from him in a few years when he's ready for a new car.

Exercise 4: Analyze Fatima's Essay

Instructions: Reread Fatima's essay, and answer these questions.

1. Is Fatima's essay informative, persuasive, or both? Give reasons for your answer.
2. Label the thesis statement, topic sentences, and transitions in Fatima's essay.
4. Fatima's essay is primarily about effects—the results of her car purchase. What were the *causes* of her purchase? List as many as you can.

Collaborative Activity: Discuss Causes

Instructions: Read the next essay, written by a first-year college student named Lisa. She recently ended a relationship with Thad, whom she had dated throughout high school. In this essay she is emphasizing the *effects* of the breakup. After you've read the essay, meet with a small group of students to list possible *causes* for Lisa's breakup with Thad. Be as creative as you wish.

Time to Say Goodbye

It wasn't easy for me to break up with Thad last summer. We'd been together for two years and were thinking about getting married after college. We knew each other well, and I depended on him a lot. I was afraid to start all over looking for a new relationship. After being with Thad for so long, I thought I'd never find someone else to love. I cried for days, but now that I've gotten over the pain, I'm glad I had the courage to say goodbye to Thad. Since the breakup I've seen some positive changes in myself.

My attitude is much better. Everybody tells me that. Because Thad and I took each other for granted, I had allowed my appearance and my personality to deteriorate. I realize now that I was often short-tempered and abrupt with Thad, and I had stopped caring about how I looked. Since we broke up in July, I've lost five pounds, changed my hairstyle, and signed up for an aerobics class.

I also manage my time better now. At the end of our relationship Thad and I weren't enjoying each other very much, but I spent almost every evening with him because I couldn't think of anything better to do. Now I've renewed some old friendships and have started to participate in campus activities. Last week I had a fantastic time at a dance, even though I didn't have a date.

The biggest improvement has been in my family. My parents and I used to argue about Thad constantly. They disliked his casual manners, which I found refreshing, and they blamed him for my impatience with their curfews and other rules. Now that Thad is out of the picture, my parents have relaxed, and they're giving me more freedom. Carl and Jerry, the men I'm dating right now, are more polite and polished than Thad was. I'm beginning to agree with Mom and Dad: Why did I put up with Thad's lax manners for so long?

The whole experience, despite the pain, has taught me a lot. I've learned that life really can be better when I trust my instincts and have the courage to change. I only wish I'd broken up with Thad before I invested so much in a relationship that was doomed to failure.

Collaborative Activity: Discuss Effects

Instructions: The following essay was written by a first-year student named Dennis. In this essay he is exploring *causes*—his reasons for becoming involved in student government at his community college. Meet with a small group of students to discuss the possible *effects* of his decision.

Taking the Lead

In high school I was so busy with football that I never paid attention to student government. In fact I thought our student representatives led very dull lives compared to mine. Because I was a good defensive player, I was mentioned in the newspaper pretty often. Everybody in high school knew who I was. I thought the student representatives just sat around in meetings all the time.

But student government started to look interesting when I enrolled in community college. I decided not to continue with football after high school, so I needed another way to make friends. The student representatives seemed like interesting people, and I thought I would enjoy their company.

A talk with my older sister also influenced my decision. She is an administrator in a big hospital and spends a lot of time in committees working with government officials at the local and state level. She told me she wished she had done more to develop leadership skills at college. Since I'm aiming for a leadership position in the insurance field, I need that kind of experience.

I was very nervous about running for election, but I decided the lessons I learned would be worth it, whether I won or lost. I was a good student in my high school speech class but hadn't made a speech since eleventh grade. I looked forward to sharpening my speaking skills, and I also knew I'd enjoy the election process because I thrive on challenges.

I think my biggest motivation was the desire to learn more about how decisions are made at my college, and finally become one of the decision-makers myself. In the short time since I enrolled, I thought of a few changes I'd like to see on campus.

For example, I think entering freshmen should be able to sign up for a weekend re-treat to get to know each other and learn what to expect their first year.

I'm happy to report that I was elected to the student government. I've learned that student government needs volunteers for many interesting tasks that don't re-quire an election. I encourage any student who wants to get maximum benefit from college to become involved in student government.

Writing Assignment: A Good Decision

Write a paragraph about the causes or effects of a wise decision you've made since high school graduation. When you are finished, read your final draft to a group of other students; consider incorporating their suggestions into your paragraph, and revise it if necessary.

Exercise 5: Explore Causes and Effects

Choose five items from this list; then list at least three causes and three effects of each. Be as creative as you wish. Save your lists to use in a writing assignment on page 219.

- a) A student makes a perfect score on a biology test
- b) Students litter on campus
- c) A student moves from the dorm to her own apartment
- d) An evening student changes to a full-time day program
- e) A student isn't selected for the swimming team
- f) The college library shortens its hours
- g) College tuition goes up
- h) A downtown public health center is closed
- i) The age for legal drinking is raised by two years
- j) A college begins a major recycling program

USING CAUSES AND EFFECTS TO WRITE AN ESSAY

An essay assignment about causes and effects appears on page 219. The following sugges-tions will help you plan and write an effective essay.

1. Look for an interesting point to make about your subject: Don't write an essay that simply lists causes and effects. Clarify your purpose—descriptive or informative. (Re-member that the two often overlap.)
2. Decide whether to focus on causes or effects in your essay. Use critical thinking to de-cide which would help make your point more effectively. Asking yourself these ques-tions may help you: Are you more interested in the *whys* (causes) of your subject or the *results* (effects)? Which would be more interesting to your readers? Do you want them to gain a new, deeper understanding of why something happens? If so, your purpose

will primarily be informative. Or do you want them to share an experience? In that case, your primary purpose will be descriptive.

3. Use Discovery Activities to explore your subject thoroughly. Remember that vivid details and convincing examples are essential elements in an effective essay.

4. Try this plan for your first draft: Write an introductory paragraph that catches readers' interest, clarifies your subject, provides background, and explains why your subject is important to you. (See page 112 in Chapter Seven for more detailed suggestions.) Begin each body paragraph with a topic sentence about a cause or an effect (whichever you chose as your focus). Finally, write a conclusion according to the guidelines on pages 125–126 in Chapter Seven.

5. In the revision step, make sure your essay has unity (is consistent). Does your introductory paragraph clearly state the focus for the entire essay? Did you stick to that focus throughout the essay? Check for coherence as well: Do the causes or effects in your essay make sense? Are they arranged logically?

6. Read an advanced draft to a small group of students. After you've listened to their feedback, make any changes that you think will enhance your essay.

■ ■ ■ **Useful Transitions for Cause and Effect**

For causes: because, since, when, before, first, if
For effects: after, as a result, consequently, so, then, therefore, thus

---

Writing Assignment: Causes and Effects

Instructions: Choose a list you made for Exercise 4 on page 218. Write an informative paragraph about the list you've chosen. Read an advanced draft to a small group of students, and consider incorporating their suggestions into a revision of your paragraph.

A STUDENT WRITES AN ESSAY ABOUT CAUSES

The essay that follows explores the reasons, or causes, for a student's career choice. Jessica plans to become a counselor for juvenile offenders. During the planning step, she began listing her reasons for choosing this career. After she had made a partial list, another idea occurred to her: She remembered a troubled girl she had met and helped through basketball.

When Jessica began freewriting about this experience, memories came flooding back. She remembered that her interest in counseling began in her junior year of high school. She had persuaded several students to try high school basketball, and that experience inspired her to seek a career helping young people. Jessica decided to develop this freewriting into this essay.

Passing the Ball

I became interested in juvenile counseling during my junior year in high school. At that time I was excited about playing basketball, which had helped me make new friends and build up my self-confidence. I tried to persuade other girls in my high school to try basketball too. Through my influence, several of them joined the team. That experience changed their lives, and it made me see the importance of counseling troubled teenagers.

I started to get interested in troubled young people when I saw that many teens desperately need someone to care about them. I met one unhappy girl who was shooting baskets all alone at a playground. I found out that she hadn't made any friends in town, and her parents were getting a divorce. She was so lonely that she was considering suicide. I persuaded her to call the Crisis Line, and things got better. Later she joined the basketball team and made some good friends there. That experience convinced me that a caring person can make a big difference.

Another thing I learned is that teens need role models. One athletic girl had never joined a team because her grades were low. Her friends didn't care about school, so she didn't either. We started studying together, and her grades went up. Now she's on a college basketball team.

As a counselor, I hope I can persuade young people to avoid drugs. When I talked to teenagers in my high school, I saw that they didn't understand the dangers of drugs. On the team we try to keep ourselves in top physical condition. I persuaded one girl to try out for basketball, and she stopped spending her free time with friends who are users.

Now that I know I can influence teenagers in positive ways, I'm looking forward to a counseling career. I plan to major in criminal justice. Then I will spend my time helping teenagers make positive changes in their lives.

Exercise 6: Freewrite about Causes

1. Select a career that interests you. (You need not be seriously committed to this career.) Informally list experiences you've had and personal qualities that have caused you to become interested in this career.

2. Freewrite about the reasons for a decision you've made recently. Possibilities include deciding to come to college, choosing a job or a place to live, and entering or ending a relationship.

3. Freewrite about a behavior—either positive or negative—that you've observed in many other people. Explore its causes.

4. Choose a current issue that you've observed on your campus or in your community. List as many causes as you can think of.

Writing Assignment: Write about Causes

Instructions: Expand one freewriting activity from the previous exercise into a college essay. Note that an essay about item #1 or #2 will probably have a descriptive purpose. An essay about #3 or #4 may be descriptive or informative. Decide your purpose before you begin your first draft. Completing additional Discovery Activities may be helpful. When you've written an advanced draft, share it with a group of students, and consider making any changes they recommend.

A STUDENT WRITES ABOUT EFFECTS

Charles, a Spanish major, wrote the following paper about becoming a successful student. In the planning step, he intended to write about the study habits that had helped him win a college scholarship. But freewriting and other planning activities stimulated other ideas. He realized that his mature attitude towards school was the *effect* of a negative experience in the seventh grade. Notice that his paper emphasizes the kind of student he is now: Every paragraph begins with an *effect,* or result, of his seventh-grade struggle.

From Failure to Success

I've had many wonderful experiences in school. But the greatest benefits came from a bad experience in the seventh grade. I had a nervous and disorganized new math teacher who lasted only a year in our district. She and I didn't get along at all, and I wasn't sorry to see her go. I realize now, though, that I learned a great deal about success that year.

One change was that I started to take responsibility for my own learning. This teacher didn't follow any lesson plans, so the tests didn't cover the material she'd taught. Even worse, she got angry when we asked her too many questions. I failed my first three tests in her class. Several parents, including mine, called the principal about her, but the class didn't get much better. I finally realized that I couldn't depend on her to teach me math. Deciding to study harder on my own was an important step for me.

I also learned to look for help when I needed it. Before the seventh grade, I always had an easy time in school. It was embarrassing to have to ask for help. But I persisted, and a friend's older brother agreed to look over my homework several times a week. An eighth-grader in my study hall helped me too, and so did my parents. After a while I stopped being ashamed when I was having trouble with math.

The biggest change was learning how to organize my schoolwork. Most of my teachers back then reminded us about big assignments and tests. But my math teacher often forgot about them until they were due. Sometimes she also forgot to collect homework. If we didn't show it to her, she would just enter a zero into her record book. I began filling out a calendar each day, and I laid my homework on my desk at the beginning of each period so she would see that I had done it.

At the end of the year, I had a disappointing C in math instead of the A I wanted. For a long time I was unhappy with myself and angry at the teacher. But now I see that I learned many important lessons about academic success. That year was a hard one for me, but many benefits came from it.

Exercise 7: Explore Effects

Instructions: Complete the activities below.

1. Think about a decision you've made. Then list the short-term and long-term effects, or results, of your decision.
2. Think about a significant event from your past. Did it have a positive or negative long-term effect on you? Freewrite about it.
3. Reread your freewriting for Exercise 6, #3, on page 220. Then freewrite about the *effects* of the behavior you selected.
4. Freewrite about the *effects* of the current issue you chose for Exercise 6, #4, on page 220.

Writing Assignment: Write about Effects

Instructions: Expand one freewriting activity from Exercise 5 into a college essay. Before you begin writing, decide whether your purpose will be informative, descriptive, or persuasive. Complete additional Discovery Activities if necessary. Share an advanced draft of your essay with a group of students, and consider making any changes they recommend.

USING CAUSES AND EFFECTS TO WRITE PERSUASIVE ESSAYS

The student essays that follow demonstrate how causes and effects can be used for a persuasive purpose. Both students—Murray and Calvin—were concerned about young people who risk their lives and the lives of others by combining alcohol and driving. Although they chose the same topic, their essays are very different. After you have read each essay, ask yourself the following questions:

1. What audience did the student author have in mind?
2. What is the author's purpose?
3. Does the author focus more on causes or effects?

Two Students Write Persuasive Essays

The following essay was written by Murray.

The Sobering Truth

Every Monday morning I hear students in the Activities Center bragging about the drinking they did over the weekend. It's depressing to talk to so many students who think that excessive drinking is the only way to enjoy a weekend. What's even worse is that many of these students drive while under the influence of alcohol. They don't seem to care about the risks they're taking.

One possible consequence is a conviction for drunk driving. In our state, fines begin at one hundred dollars. Drunk drivers risk losing their driving privileges, and their cars may be impounded. Even worse, they may be sentenced to jail.

And drunk drivers may cause severe injuries to themselves and others. Not even air bags and seat belts can protect passengers from severe injuries caused by an intoxicated driver. Last year Marjorie, my best friend from high school, suffered a concussion when her Fiesta collided with a sport utility vehicle. Marjorie's boyfriend was worried because she had too much to drink at a party, so he made sure she was buckled up, and he followed her in his own car while she drove home. Even though his Honda was right behind her Fiesta, he couldn't prevent the accident. Marjorie missed six months of school and did not graduate with our class. She still has blackouts and headaches as a result of the accident.

Worst of all is the possibility of death. A fragile human being has little chance of surviving a high-speed automobile crash. And the danger is not limited to drunk drivers. Innocent passengers, even people in nearby cars, can lose their lives in an instant.

Drinking and driving should never be laughed off as youthful fun. Anyone who combines driving and alcohol, or tolerates such behavior in others, may be guilty of damaging or ending a life. It doesn't have to happen, and it shouldn't.

Here is Calvin's essay:

An Ounce of Prevention

Every time the newspaper prints an account of a drinking-and-driving accident, I see people shaking their heads in amazement. Why, they ask, would anyone be stupid enough to drink and drive? Of course these people have a point. But I wish that instead of wondering about it, they would get involved in preventing these accidents. If more people understood why young people drink and drive, we could work together to change this behavior.

One problem is boredom. When I was in high school, my town had very few activities for teenagers. Church and community leaders preached about the dangers of drinking, but they didn't plan alternatives for local teenagers. Some of my friends went to drinking parties even though they didn't like alcohol. Watching TV with their parents every weekend was just too dull, and there was little else to do.

Another problem is the lack of adult guidance. My mother and father avoid alcohol, but other parents drink and drive regularly. Many times I was offered beer and mixed drinks by my friends' parents, even though they knew I was underage. I heard adults bragging about the amount they drank and the fun they used to have drinking at college parties. Not surprisingly, their children behave the same way.

The teen years can be a lonely and confusing time. Young people are still learning about life, and they may not realize that alcohol can impair their driving. I've heard a number of college students brag that they drive better when they're drunk. Unfortunately one of them was in jail overnight because of his reckless driving.

Parents and community leaders should do more than complain about teenage drinking. By offering safe choices to teens, and serving as good models themselves, they can make the highways safer for everyone.

Collaborative Activity: Write Persuasively

Instructions: Write answers to the following questions about both student essays you just read. Then discuss your answers with a small group of students.

1. What audience did each student author have in mind?
2. What was each author's purpose?
3. Do the essays focus primarily on causes or effects?
4. How convincing is each essay?
5. If you could talk to the author of each essay, would you recommend any changes?

SUGGESTIONS FOR USING CAUSES AND EFFECTS IN A PERSUASIVE ESSAY

In addition to the ideas on page 222 earlier in this chapter, the following three suggestions may help you write an effective persuasive essay about causes or effects.

1. Use powerful examples to convince readers about the importance of the effects you're describing. Stories, statistics (available in libraries), and vivid details help reinforce your message. Whether you're writing about health, pollution, crime, personal relationships, or another subject, look for striking illustrations for your essay.
2. When you're writing about causes, relate them clearly and convincingly to the problem you're describing. For example, a pregnant woman may have difficulty connecting a glass of wine or beer to the unborn child she's carrying. But after reading Jane Claypool's explanation, she can vividly imagine the risks involved.
3. Be persistent. If you're having trouble connecting causes or effects to the point you're making, try additional Discovery Activities. Talking and reading can be especially helpful. If you're writing about a current issue, a librarian can direct you to a wealth of information.

Writing Assignment: Write Persuasively

Instructions: Write a persuasive essay about one of the following topics. Use either causes or effects to develop your thesis.

- risky behavior you've observed in others
- a college policy that should be changed
- a law that should be changed
- a change needed in your community
- a change needed on your campus
- a better way to do a familiar task

READING TO WRITE: YOUTHFUL VIOLENCE

In the article that follows, journalist Peter Applebome explores both the causes and effects of a serious problem in high schools.

Prereading Activities: Think about Violence

Instructions: As preparation for reading, write your answers to the questions below.

1. Why do some young people choose to commit violent acts? List as many causes as you can.
2. What are the short-term and long-term effects of these violent acts? List as many effects as you can.
3. Freewrite about ways society could prevent young people from committing violent acts.

Alma Maters: Two Words Behind the Massacre
from the New York Times *by Peter Applebome*

If much about the murderous assault by two students in Littleton, Colo., seemed so alien and bizarre as to be almost ungraspable, there was at least one part of the story that seemed as familiar as Big Macs and oldies radio.

It was the world of jocks and nerds, preps and geeks, winners and losers that defined life at Columbine High School before the killing of a teacher and 14 students, including the suicides of the two gunmen. It was something that is burned like a tattoo into the memory bank of most adults. It was high school.

The incident and other school shootings in places like Pearl, Miss.; West Paducah, Ky.; Jonesboro, Ark.; and Springfield, Ore. (Jonesboro was a middle school, the rest high schools) have been viewed through many prisms—guns and violence in the media, values and parenting. Clearly, no single factor will ever explain any of the incidents. But the fact that these horrors keep playing out in the nation's high schools tracks closely longstanding and growing concerns about the kind of educational and social environments they provide.

Many students, of course, have wonderful high school experiences. And any view of high school life would do well to remember the ways it mimics the world outside. But the most comprehensive recent report on American high schools, "Breaking Ranks," by the National Association of Secondary School Principals, concluded in 1996 that "high schools continue to go about their business in ways that sometimes bear startling resemblance to the flawed practices of the past."

And, like the high school bloodletting in films like "Carrie" or "Heathers" or the savage Darwinian hierarchy portrayed in films like "Jawbreaker," "Varsity Blues," or "Cruel Intentions," the images our culture presents of high school life are so routinely destructive as to prompt warning flags that go beyond spasms of horrific violence like Littleton.

Of course, strutting jocks and imperious prom queens lorded over high schools well before aggrieved teen-agers turned corridors into killing fields.

Writing last week in the Internet magazine *Salon,* social critic Camille Paglia described clique formation in high schools as "a pitiless process that has remained amazingly consistent for the past 60 years." She then lamented the way high schools have become anachronisms that warehouse students in the sterile regimentation of a world of cubical classrooms and cramped rows of seats.

And, though some elements of high school may seem eternal, increasingly questions are being asked about an educational model that has remained little changed since after World War I when high school—rather than work—became the norm for Americans in their mid-teens.

The most familiar professional critique is that despite some attempts at smaller, more experimental programs, high schools are too big, too impersonal and too out of touch with the youngsters in them. That perhaps was tolerable in days of two-parent families and close ties to churches and social organizations. It is not now.

Peter Scales, a psychologist and senior fellow with the research organization Search Institute, said the group's studies of 100,000 students from 6th grade through 12th found that only one in four said they went to a school where adults and other students cared about them.

The "Breaking Ranks" report, for example, called for smaller high schools or bigger ones broken down into "houses" or "teams" of no more than 600 students to create more intimate environments, and an adult advocate responsible for each student. Others call for team teaching arrangements that enable groups of teachers to monitor individual students and teaching plans that allow teachers to follow students from year to year.

Littleton was a 1,950-student school. Grades were not broken down into smaller groupings, and the school was organized along largely traditional lines.

The "Breaking Ranks" recommendations are more common in middle schools than high schools.

"You hear the principal and the others talking about what a wonderful school Columbine is," said Frank Smith, a professor of educational administration at Teachers College of Columbia University. "But what it means is a wonderful traditional model and a very expensive physical facility. In many ways, it's a wonderful version of an outdated school."

Jon Katz, a writer on new technologies, whose Web site has attracted 4,000 posts in recent days from self-styled outsiders terrified that the main effect of Littleton will be an effort to further marginalize the marginalized, said what has most changed the social dynamic of high school is technology.

Yesterday's high school outcasts, he said, were truly powerless. But youngsters drawn to the Internet and to the electronic culture of violent games like Tribe, Doom and Quake find a life outside high school that is exciting, engaging and intellectually stimulating, where they have friends, community and power. Only in school are they back at the mercy of the old kings and queens and a world of teachers talking at them while they sit in cramped desks just as students did when the radio was high-tech.

"Outside of school, these kids are empowered and stimulated," he said. "And school then becomes a nightmare, dull and claustrophobic and oppressive, where you have kids constantly dumping on them for being different. These are not violent kids. You look at the numbers, and it's absurd to say that. But what's happening is making them very alienated and very angry."

The solution, he says, is for schools to recognize and respect the world of the online subculture with, for example, a gaming club supported the way sports are, and more use of technology and less traditional and more interactive teaching styles.

Responding to What You Have Read

1. Look again at your responses to the prereading questions. In what ways were your ideas similar to the ones stated in the article? In what ways were your ideas different?

2. Review the questions you wrote as you read the selection. What strategies can you use to find the answers?

3. Prepare two lists—causes and effects—based on the ideas in "Alma Maters: Two Words Behind the Massacre."

4. What was the author's purpose in writing? Did this selection achieve his purpose?

5. Does this selection focus more on causes or effects? Explain your answer.

6. Is this selection primarily informative or persuasive? Explain your answer.

7. Freewrite about your own secondary education. What kinds of experiences did you have? What were the strengths of your educational experience? What problems did you encounter?

Writing Assignment: High School Life

Instructions: Plan, draft, and revise an essay about the reasons you liked or disliked your secondary education experience (causes) or the effects it had on you after graduation. Read an advanced draft to a small group of students, and consider using their suggestions.

SUMMARY

1. *Causes* are the factors that make things happen; *effects* are short-term and long-term results.

2. Causes and effects are useful in descriptive, informative, and persuasive writing.

LOOKING AHEAD

In Chapter Fourteen, "Using Narration in Writing," you'll practice using stories to develop your ideas.

CHAPTER FOURTEEN

Using Narration in Writing

Preview

A narrative is a story that can entertain, inform, or persuade. Well-told stories engage readers' emotions in powerful ways. The meaning of a story can change as time passes, different details are emphasized, or the storyteller decides to use a different viewpoint.

INTRODUCING NARRATION

Narratives—stories—are one of the most popular ways to teach a lesson or entertain an audience. Humans have always told stories for a variety of purposes. Historical stories educate their listeners and promote patriotism; religious tales and parables teach values and moral lessons; funny, sad, and touching stories entertain people and bring them together. Stories are told regularly in churches, classrooms, kitchens, and auditoriums. The ability to tell a story can help you make a point at a business meeting—or forge a new friendship at a picnic or party.

Notice how the following narrative paragraph, by a student named Ricky, makes a point about seat belts more effectively than a lecture about automobile safety:

The $7,500 Decision

A story saved my life. One of my friends is a car-racing fan, and he told me this story when we were both taking driver's ed. When he was in elementary school, he saw professional driver Chuck Brown briefly stop his car during a race he was winning. Brown lost the race and the $7,500 prize. Afterwards he told his amazed fans that his seat belt had come undone. Even though nobody else noticed, he didn't want to drive without his seat belt. Even though that stop cost Brown $7,500, he made the right decision. A week later he was involved in a racing wreck, and his seat belt saved his life. Last summer I had a collision with another car because of a driving mistake I made. The state trooper who came to the scene told me that my seat belt kept me from being thrown through the windshield. I might have died if I hadn't buckled my seat belt. Thanks, Chuck Brown, for teaching me a lifesaving lesson.

Author A. L. Williams used two true stories to emphasize the importance of perseverance in his motivational book, *All You Can Do Is All You Can Do*. Both the first narrative, about golfer Gary Player, and the second, about an unnamed violinist, make the same point:

> When Player was competing in a tournament, people constantly came up to him and made the same remark: "I'd give anything if I could hit a golf ball like you."
>
> On one particularly tough day, Player was tired and frustrated when, once again, he heard the comment; "I'd give anything if I could hit a golf ball like you."
>
> Player's usual politeness failed him as he replied to the spectator, "No, you wouldn't. You'd give anything to hit a golf ball like me if it was easy. Do you know what you've got to do to hit a golf ball like me? You've got to get up at five o'clock in the morning, go out on the course, and hit one thousand golf balls. Your hand starts bleeding, and you walk up to the clubhouse, wash the blood off your hand, slap a bandage on it, and go out and hit another one thousand golf balls. That's what it takes to hit a golf ball like me."
>
> I heard a similar story recently. A famous violinist was approached by a woman who gushed, "I'd give my life to play like you do." The violinist responded simply, "Madam, I did."

Collaborative Activity: Teach a Lesson

Instructions: Meet with a small group of other students to share stories. Choose either an entertaining or a teaching story to tell to the group. When everyone is finished, discuss the storytelling experience. Which features of the stories were particularly effective? What did you learn from this experience?

Writing Assignment: Write a Teaching Narrative

Instructions: Write down the story you told your group in the previous activity. Then read what you've written to group members and ask for feedback; consider incorporating their suggestions into a revised version of your story.

SUGGESTIONS FOR WRITING NARRATIVES

The following suggestions will help you write effective narrative paragraphs and essays:

1. Focus on your purpose. Remember that your narrative must "make meaning." If you're writing an informative or persuasive narrative, having a good story to tell is only the beginning. You must know what point you're making, and you have to select details that will reinforce that point.

2. Use your "writer's eyes" to help readers feel they are part of your story. Colors, sounds, and smells make a narrative come to life. Describe actions vividly so that readers can imagine themselves as participants. In a story that appears later in this chapter, Thelma Wells lists her actions to help readers "see" how angry she felt about her boss's behavior:

> I walked out of his office, covered my typewriter, and left the building.
> At home, I fumed and stomped.
> "How dare he?" I said, as I bundled Little George into the car.
> "How dare he?" I said, as I drove to the doctor's office.

3. Remember that it's up to you—the writer—to decide what point your story will make. The meaning of a story may change as time passes: You may have learned that a trusted friend was actually manipulating you, or that an adult you disliked actually had your best interests at heart. Family gatherings are prime examples: The same story might be told two or three different ways, according to the point of view of the storyteller.

4. Put the meaning first. If a narrative has a teaching purpose, begin by briefly stating the point you're making. When you state your purpose early, you are likely to have a stronger impact on your audience: Every detail in your narrative reinforces your purpose.

5. Use transitions to help readers follow the events in your narrative. The following words may be helpful: first, second, next, while, before, after, when, since, until, then, during, finally, last.

A STUDENT WRITES A NARRATIVE ESSAY

The following narrative, by a student named Deon, recounts a childhood experience that had an important effect on him. Notice that Deon "made meaning" before he told his story—and that his final paragraph reinforces that meaning.

When the Fun Stopped

The cold is gone, and it's time to go sign up for baseball. This was my routine for six years when I was growing up. I loved getting out on the field, throwing, running around and batting; baseball was my favorite sport. I use that in the past tense because it was ruined by overzealous adults who acted as if a baseball game was a matter of life and death.

Baseball was fun until I was twelve. I started playing when I was six. Although I was never a spectacular player, my skills improved every year. My favorite position was catcher, and I was lucky enough to be selected for a good team. My parents bought me my own gear, which made it even more fun.

But as I got older, it wasn't as much fun. I can clearly remember the first time a parent's behavior disturbed me. I was playing catcher, and a nervous young boy came to bat. His father was right behind me, shouting instructions to his son and belittling him when the boy made a mistake. I felt so bad for the batter that I couldn't concentrate on catching. The boy struck out, but for the first time I didn't feel happy for my team.

The following year I became the target of that kind of rudeness. My parents always relaxed and enjoyed coming to my games. But my coach was very serious about baseball, to the point that he spoiled it for all the kids on the team. He constantly yelled at us, drilled us to the point of exhaustion, and blew up over mistakes. After every game we had to sit in the dugout while he told us about all the things we did wrong. I began to dread the games. The new gear my parents bought me that year didn't cheer me up at all. I was falling out of love with baseball.

Maybe because I was older, I began to take more notice of the parents in the bleachers. They acted as if they were watching the World Series, not a bunch of boys having fun on a beautiful afternoon. I couldn't face the abuse I heard when I dropped a ball or struck out. Suddenly it seemed like I was letting everybody down if I did something wrong. I couldn't handle the pressure that the parents were putting on the team when all I wanted was to play the sport I loved with other kids who felt the same way I did. I finally refused to go to any more practices or games.

Since then, I always feel the same longing when signs of spring appear. I want to put on a uniform, grab my catcher's mitt, and head for the baseball diamond. But the wonderful feeling I used to have has been replaced by an icy pit deep in my stomach. No more baseball for me, please.

Exercise 1: Analyze Deon's Narrative

1. What is Deon's main point? How effectively do you think he made his point? Give reasons for your answer.
2. Deon put the beginning of his story into his second paragraph. What did he try to accomplish in his first paragraph? Was he successful?
3. List the "time" words (transitions like "after" and "when," for example).
4. Do you think Deon used his "writer's eyes" to write this essay? Why or why not? Give examples to back up your answer.

Writing Activity: Let There Be Fun

Instructions: Write an informal paragraph explaining how adults can help children have a good time at school, a community event, an organized sport, a family vacation or celebration, or some other activity. Tell at least one story to illustrate the point you're making.

READING TO WRITE: TWO STORIES THAT CHANGED AS TIME PASSED

You're about to read two stories that changed as time passed. The first, by an African-American business woman, is about an act of discrimination that began to look different as time passed. The second is a story about a high school student's decision that seemed like a good idea but later turned out to be a mistake.

Before you begin reading, freewrite about one of these two topics:

■ a story from your own life that you still think about years later
■ a decision you made that you wish you could change

Your freewriting:

Thelma Wells is an author and motivational speaker who founded her own company, Thelma Wells & Associates. This is a story about a problem she faced on her first job with her boss ("Mr. Harris" is not his real name), who is white.

Vocabulary:

| finesse | (noun) elegant skillfulness |
| prerequisites | (noun) requirements |

Fight, Flight, or Finesse
from Bumblebees Fly Anyway *by Thelma Wells*

Grannie called me at work one day, just before noon, telling me my son Little George was ill with a high fever. "The school nurse sent him home, Thelma, and said he ought to see a doctor today," she said. "He's a pretty sick little boy."

The common dilemma of the working mother, I thought, as I began trying to figure out how I could work until closing time, five o'clock, *and* get Little George to the doctor's office before it closed at five. I couldn't. I'd have to leave a little early. I knocked on Mr. Harris's door.

"Sir," I said, "My son is sick and I need to take him to the doctor."

Mr. Harris frowned.

"If I leave fifteen minutes early this afternoon I can get him in before the doctor closes for the day," I said. "Of course, I'll work through my afternoon break to make up for it."

Mr. Harris shook his head.

"No, Thelma."

No? Did he say no?

I couldn't believe what I'd heard.

"And I don't like you asking for favors," he added.

Favors? I thought, *what favors?* A bolt of hot anger surged through me. "I'm asking for what's mine," I said, holding my temper in a tight rein. "Those fifteen minutes are mine, and I need to use them to get my son to the doctor. And furthermore, I'm taking them, with or without your approval. In fact," I said, "I think I'll leave right now."

I walked out of his office, covered my typewriter, and left the building.

At home, I fumed and stomped.

"How dare he?" I said, as I bundled Little George into the car.

"How dare he?" I said, as I drove to the doctor's office.

That was on Wednesday. For the next three days I seethed with anger and refused to return to work. I called the plant manager—I thought I ought to explain my actions to someone—and when he heard what had happened, he apologized for Mr. Harris's behavior.

"That's not good enough," I said, still angry and reluctant to return to the office.

"I'm sure he's sorry, Thelma," the plant manager said, hoping to smooth things over. "Please come back."

The following Monday, I drove back to the plant. Mr. Harris was waiting for me with an apology, of sorts.

"I am truly sorry, Thelma," Mr. Harris said. "But you have to understand, I thought this was just the beginning—you know, you'd be asking for time off all the time. I know how you people are, always asking for favors and taking advantage . . . Well, I just didn't want to let that get started."

The anger that had burned down to hot coals over five days flared up again, hotter than before.

"You people?" I bellowed. "Did you say you people? I don't believe this . . ." I was nearly stuttering now with fury. "Do you think we're really all that different, you and me? Do you think we don't love our children as much as you love yours? Mr. Harris, I love my son just as much as you love yours, and when he needs me I'll be there, just like you'll be there when your son needs you. If that means leaving early to take him to the doctor, then that's what I'll do, just like you would. And it won't be taking advantage, or asking for favors. I'll pull my weight around here, just like I always have. So don't you ever worry about me expecting anything that isn't already mine!"

Panting, I left his office and sat down heavily at my desk. I seethed as I typed, pounding the keys and throwing the carriage ferociously.

The anger I felt toward Mr. Harris did not dissipate quickly. For days, maybe weeks, I felt myself grow hot every time I thought about that confrontation. And worse, I felt a huge amount of stress that I hadn't ever known before, and I knew that most of it stemmed from uncertainty. What would happen when I faced a similar situation in the future? And there would be similar situations—I was a mother with children, and I would, at times, be needed at home during office hours.

Would Mr. Harris be difficult every time I needed special consideration? Would I be forced to fight for any small adjustment that might be needed to accommodate my personal life? If I challenged him, would I be forced to quit? Would he fire me?

I worked for Mr. Harris for four more years after that first disagreement. We were wary of each other and careful to try to maintain an uneasy peace. In time, I began to realize that, while race was a factor with Mr. Harris, our personality differences were also something to be considered. We were destined to collide, regardless of our skin color.

Now, thirty years later, I'm a little smarter about how personalities interact in the workplace. I know a little more about collision prevention, and I know that my reaction to Mr. Harris was all wrong. My response was an instinctive one, not an educated one. Nor was it a constructive one. My animal instincts, which direct us to fight or take flight, took over, and I had flown out of the office in fury. When I returned a few days later, I had followed my instincts again, only this time, I had chosen to fight. Now I know that there are better, more constructive approaches to conflict with a manager or boss. Today, I know I'd do things differently. Much differently.

Today, I would be sure I was *prepared* before I approached my manager about a sudden, unexpected change in the work routine.

Preparation is essential if an employee is going to be able to deal successfully with a difficult situation involving the boss. And that preparation means the employee has worked hard to accomplish these three prerequisites:

- Know the boss's personality type
- Document your work record
- Communicate regularly and candidly with your boss

Responding to What You Have Read

1. In a few sentences, summarize Wells's story.
2. How did Wells interpret the conflict with her boss when it happened?
3. How did she interpret the story after time had passed?
4. Does Wells still think that racism was involved in the original incident? Do you agree with her?
5. At the end of the story, Wells lists three things she could have done to be better prepared before taking her request to her boss. Explain what you think she meant by each of the following:
    - Know the boss's personality type
    - Document your work record
    - Communicate regularly and candidly with your boss
6. Many working mothers have to deal with child-care emergencies like Thelma's. What workplace policies could have made the situation easier for both her and her boss?

Writing Assignment: A Job Conflict

Instructions: Write an essay about a job or task problem that you solved. Possibilities include a paying job, a task related to school, friendship or family life, or work you performed as a volunteer. Begin the writing process by freewriting (or look at your freewriting on page 231). Be sure your story "makes meaning." The next reading selection is a letter from a high school junior telling a story that looks different now that several years have passed.

Good Teachers Aren't Always Fun
from the Ann Landers syndicated column

DEAR ANN LANDERS: I am in my junior year of high school and not doing very well. When I was in the ninth grade, I had a very demanding history teacher whose reputation was well known. He assigned killer research papers, tough book reports and loads of outside library work. His tests were murder.

I complained to my parents because I didn't want to work that hard. Also, the chemistry between us wasn't the greatest. My parents came to school and had a meeting with the principal. I was taken out of that teacher's class and placed in another class where the kids had very little homework, watched films a lot and never flunked.

Now, when I look around, I see the students who sweated it out with that tough teacher, and they are doing a lot better than I am. They learned discipline and good study habits.

I wish my parents had insisted that I stay in that class and do the work. I still don't like the teacher, but I have to admit there was no horsing around in his classes. He did what a teacher was supposed to do. He taught.

Please tell kids not to take the easy way out. Tough teachers and hard courses may not be a barrel of fun, but they teach you something.

TOO LATE SMART, CASPER, WYOMING

Responding to What You Have Read

1. Briefly summarize the student's story as he would have told it when he was in the ninth grade. Then retell it as it looks to him now.
2. Do you agree with the student that he is "too late smart"? Why or why not?
3. Pretend you are Ann Landers and write a short response to the student.
4. Evaluate the student's letter. Do you think he told his story effectively? Why or why not?

Writing Assignment: A School Story

Instructions: Tell a story from the past that used to have one meaning for you but now has another. Include vivid details to make your story personal and interesting. When you have finished, meet with a small group of other students to share your stories. What insights do the stories give you about the people who wrote them?

SUMMARY

1. Narratives—stories—can entertain, inform, and persuade.
2. Since a story can be told in many ways, it's important to decide what point you want the story to make.

3. Vivid details can engage readers and increase the impact of your narrative.

4. Always state the point of a narrative at the beginning so that the story's details "make meaning" for your readers.

LOOKING AHEAD

In Chapter Fifteen, "Using Definitions in Writing," you'll practice defining a variety of terms in both informative and persuasive writing.

CHAPTER FIFTEEN

Using Definitions in Writing

Preview

A definition explains the meaning of a term and clarifies it with specific examples. Definitions are important because so many terms have different meanings for different people. Definitions are useful in both professional and college writing. Definitions can have descriptive, informative, or persuasive purposes.

INTRODUCING DEFINITIONS

Most people think of a dictionary when they hear the term "definition." But working out definitions is a task for everyone, not just the people who compile dictionaries. The complexities of modern life often require precise definitions of important terms.

Dr. Philip Maffetone, author of *Everyone Is an Athlete,* warns that athletes can suffer serious illness—even death—if they don't understand the definitions of *health* and *fitness.* Jim Fixx, a famous runner, died of a heart attack despite his devotion to fitness. Maffetone explains that fitness is "the physical ability to perform athletic activity," while health is "the state where all the systems of the body—nervous, muscular, skeletal, circulatory, digestive, lymphatic, hormonal, etc.—are working in an optimal way." Practice and training can help an athlete perform astounding feats, but health requires much more. For maximum health, athletes need to eat a balanced diet, see a physician regularly, get adequate sleep, and avoid harmful substances. Anyone who watches news programs regularly is aware that famous athletes can be spectacularly fit without achieving health. For an athlete, precise definitions of "fitness" and "health" can be lifesaving.

Clear definitions are just as important in the routines of everyday life: They facilitate communication and strengthen relationships by helping people understand and cooperate with one another. Family life is much easier when parents and children work out satisfactory definitions of *bedtime, curfew,* and *allowance;* couples need to agree about what constitutes a *wonderful vacation,* a *workable budget,* and a *fair division of labor.* Friends often need to work out definitions as well. In the following paragraph, a student named Betsy offered a definition of a term that was triggering arguments with her roommate: *neatness.*

A Place for Everything

Neatness is a wonderful quality that makes a room attractive and orderly without sacrificing comfort. It means that furniture is always ready for sitting, working, or sleeping. Beds, chairs, desks, and tables are cleared of clutter. Neatness welcomes visitors with fresh smells and shiny surfaces. People who stop by know they will not soil their clothes with dust, crumbs, or spilled liquids, and they will never see a dirty razor, a grimy sponge, or a plate of decaying food. Most important, neatness strengthens relationships. Papers, books, and personal items are easily located; breakage and accidents are rare. Neatness can be accomplished in a few minutes a day with a minimum of equipment and effort. It does not require scrubbing corners with a toothbrush, buffing floors with a waxing machine, or measuring the spaces between venetian blinds. All that is needed is a spirit of cooperation and a small investment in time and energy.

Collaborative Activity: Aim for Consensus

Instructions: Meet with a small group of other students to compile a list of ten or more everyday terms that might cause disagreements between family members, friends, roommates, or co-workers. Include ten or more terms in your list. When you have finished, evaluate the group process. What did you learn about the meanings of words? About communication? About group problem solving?

"MAKING MEANING" WITH DEFINITIONS

Definitions can "make meaning" by allowing you to choose your perspective on whatever you're defining. Depending on who's looking at it, a rock can be a paperweight, a building material, a garden decoration, or a weapon. Similarly, a definition can place something ordinary into a new context, so that readers see it in a new way. Think of the many ways in which people might define a shopping mall:

- a place for meeting friends
- a competitor for downtown businesses
- an all-weather walking track
- a retail site
- a source of jobs

In the following reading selection, author Beverly Coyle defines malls in an especially surprising way—a place where racial barriers began to break down.

READING TO WRITE: FIRST STEPS TO INTEGRATION

In "The Minister's Daughter," author Beverly Coyle reminisces about growing up as a white female in racially segregated Florida. Shopping centers were a new concept then, and Coyle notes that they helped to break down traditional barriers between the races.

Before you begin reading, freewrite a paragraph that "makes meaning" by describing some of your own experiences at shopping centers and malls.

Your freewriting:

Vocabulary:

Jim Crow   (noun) laws denying civil rights to African-Americans

Shopping Centers
from "The Minister's Daughter" by Beverly Coyle

Shopping centers gave blacks and whites space to hang out together, after a fashion. And I think it was here that I saw my first images of blacks in families, in units like my own. We all still maintained our traditional, segregated shopping areas close to where we lived. Shopping centers were neutral ground. They sprang up out of a field that was on no particular "side of town."

If one really wanted to maintain Jim Crow, shopping centers were a big mistake. If two different families could walk around eating ice cream cones together in this relatively new common space, then why could one such family sit down at a counter and the other not? Shopping centers were spaces that caused me to see what I had previously been unable to see, having been born into what looked like peaceful, agreed-upon separation of blacks and whites.

Collaborative Activity: Define Terms Differently

Instructions: Meet with a small group of other students to write new definitions for familiar terms—as Beverly Coyle did when she wrote about shopping malls as cradles of integration. For example, a thrift shop could be defined as a museum of American culture rather than a place to purchase used items. The World Wide Web can be defined as an electronic tool that brings democratic ideas to dictatorships.

Writing Assignment: Write a New Definition

Instructions: Select one of the new definitions your group developed in the previous Collaborative Activity, and develop it into a paragraph. When you are finished, read your definition to your group members.

In the following paragraph, historian Daniel Boorstin defines two terms—"hero" and "celebrity"—for a persuasive purpose: He hopes to inspire readers to make their own contributions to society. Notice that Boorstin uses contrasts to make his point:

> The hero is known for achievements, the celebrity for well-knownness. The hero reveals the possibilities of human nature. The celebrity reveals the possibilities of the press and media. Celebrities are people who make news, but heroes are people who make history. Time makes heroes but dissolves celebrities.

Writing Assignment: What's a Hero?

Instructions: Write a paragraph defining your concept of what a hero is. When you have finished, meet with two or three other students to compare your definitions. What characteristics did you agree upon? In what ways do your definitions differ?

A CLOSER LOOK AT DEFINITIONS

College and professional writing tasks often involve definitions. Job descriptions are actually definitions that help orient new employees to the tasks they will be doing; effective definitions ensure that the division of labor in a workplace is clearly understood by everyone. In college, a professor's definition of such terms as "research paper," "lab report," and "plagiarism" can have lasting impact on your grade-point average.

Definitions often have an informative purpose, but they can also be descriptive or persuasive. You can entertain your readers by writing a funny definition of a football fan, including descriptions of the costumes, attitudes, and behaviors of people who are fanatics about their favorite team. Or a definition can be persuasive, painting a vivid picture of what you think a term like "love" or "professionalism" should mean. An effective definition can inspire readers to strive for excellence in performing a task or playing a role—or it can be persuasive, asserting your opinion about what a term should mean. At the end of this chapter, you will read a definition of "American" by Richard Rodriguez that encourages Americans to focus on their contemporary culture as well as the culture of their immigrant families.

Collaborative Activity: Define Your Terms

Instructions: Imagine that you were hired to write a handbook for first-year students enrolling in your college for the first time. Working with a small group of other students, list at least ten terms that should be defined in the handbook. Work out definitions for at least four of the terms your group selected.

TIPS FOR WRITING DEFINITION PARAGRAPHS AND ESSAYS

1. Often it's helpful to start by placing your term into a general category and then narrow it down. For example, you could define a "role model" as an admirable person (general) whom people watch and imitate (specific).

2. "Make meaning" by staying focused on your purpose. If your definition is primarily descriptive or informative, make sure you provide sufficient facts and details. If you're writing persuasively, make sure your supporting evidence is vivid and convincing.

3. Develop your definition with details and descriptions. Use your "writer's eyes" to help readers imagine the qualities you're describing. Use stories if appropriate.

4. Choose appropriate language. "Jargon" (terms understood only by specialists) may be clear to you, but readers struggling with your definition may be confused by terms they don't know. If you must use a term your readers may not understand, put a definition into parentheses (as I did for "jargon" above).

Two Students Write Definitions

The next two selections were written by students. In the first paragraph, a student named Gene defined his job as a computer lab assistant: His supervisor had asked for a job description that could serve as a training tool for future student workers. Gene's purpose is primarily informative, so he began with a general description of his job and added details about specific tasks.

Job Description for a Computer Lab Assistant

A computer lab assistant is a student worker who ensures that students, staff, and instructors obtain satisfactory results in the computer center. General duties involve answering questions, offering instruction, solving problems, and keeping equipment functioning.

In accordance with the college mission statement, service to students is the computer center's first priority. Lab assistants help students in three major ways: answering questions, offering instruction, and troubleshooting machines. Lab assistants are expected to wear their nametags, respond promptly and courteously to requests for help, and walk among the computers frequently to spot potential problems. Providing these services to instructors and staff is the second priority. Because the college offers many courses and workshops in computer skills, assistants are not expected to provide lengthy instruction. They are encouraged to teach particular skills and offer tips that will help users get the most benefit from the computers. Assistants should know where the instruction manuals for each program are stored.

In addition, lab assistants are expected to keep the electronic equipment functioning smoothly. The printers and photocopy machine should always be stocked with paper and checked regularly to ensure that they are online. Assistants should replace ink cartridges as needed and clear paper jams promptly. When a warning message appears on a piece of equipment, an assistant should report the message and the machine number to the lab supervisor. A warning sign should be posted when a piece of equipment is offline.

Lab assistants are expected to keep adding to their computer skills. When time allows, assistants should teach new skills to one another.

Other tasks include securing items left behind in the lost-and-found cabinet under the check-in counter, monitoring the recycling bins, and performing routine maintenance tasks on the equipment. Assistants on duty when the computer lab first opens should boot up the computers and turn on the printers and photocopy machine. Assistants on duty at closing time should shut down all equipment.

Writing Assignment: Write a Job Description

Instructions: Write a job or role description. Choose a job, paid or unpaid, that you have held, or describe a role you have played—parent, big brother, friend, employee, volunteer.

A Student Defines a Scientific Term

The paragraph that follows is a definition with a persuasive purpose, written by a science major named Joan. She had noticed that some of her friends rejected scientific information on the grounds that it was only a "theory." In her paragraph, she tried to convince them to take scientific theories more seriously:

Not "Just a Theory"

Because scientific issues are in the news so often, it's important to know how to read the statements that scientists make. I've noticed that many of my relatives and friends have trouble with the word "theory" because its everyday and scientific meanings are different. In everyday life, a "theory" is a guess that hasn't been tested. For example, you might have a theory about why your friend Bill didn't come to class this morning—perhaps his aging car broke down again. But scientists use a different term for that kind of guessing: "hypothesis." They reserve "theory" for a more complex situation. In science, a "theory" is a complex system of knowledge, such as Mendel's theory of heredity, Newton's gravitational theory, and Einstein's theory of relativity. Theories allow scientists to make accurate predictions of events and phenomena. For example, Newton's gravitational theory led scientists to explain how the solar system is organized. As a result, eclipses can be foreseen hundreds of years before they occur. Using Einstein's theory of relativity, J. Robert Oppenheimer predicted the discovery of collapsed stars called "black holes" long before astronomers were able to prove their existence. Biologists have developed many new varieties of plants by working with Mendel's theory of heredity. When you hear scientists talk about "quantum physics theory" or "the theory of evolution," remember that they're talking about a system of knowledge rather than a "hypothesis" or "guess."

Writing Assignment: Write a Definition

Instructions: Think of a word or phrase important to you that can be defined in several ways. In five to ten sentences, define the term as *you* see it. Include examples in your definition.

READING TO WRITE: THINKING ABOUT SCIENCE

Because science is so exacting, scientists require precise definitions of the terminology they're using. You're about to read an extended definition of the "scientific method" that scientists use to solve problems. Before you begin reading, spend a few minutes writing informally about the strategies you use in your own life to solve problems. Then write your own informal definition of the scientific method. (If it's been a while since you've taken a science course, write your own impression of how scientists work.)

    Your strategies:

    Your ideas about the scientific method:

The Scientific Method
from Critical Thinking: How to Prepare Students for a Rapidly Changing World
by Richard W. Paul, edited by Jane Willson and A. J. A. Binker

Scientific thinking is not a matter of running through a set of steps once. Rather it is a kind of thinking in which we continually move back and forth between questions we ask about the world and observations we made and experiments we devise to test out various hypotheses, guesses, hunches, and models. We continually think in a hypothetical fashion: "If this idea of mine is true, then what will happen under these or those conditions? Let me see, suppose we try this. What does this result tell me? Why did this happen?"

Responding to What You Have Read

1. List the strategies a scientist might use when solving a problem.
2. Does the definition you just read match your previous beliefs about what scientists do? Why or why not?
3. Briefly describe a situation in which you used scientific strategies to solve a problem successfully.
4. Many people think that scientists are always right because the scientific method guarantees absolute truth. Do you think Paul would agree or disagree? Why?

Writing Assignment: The Scientific Method

Instructions: Choose one of the following topics and write a paragraph about it.

Topic 1: Recall a scientific experiment you performed, at school or elsewhere. Did your experience match Paul Willson, and Binker's description of the scientific method? Why or why not?

Topic 2: Recall a time when you wish you had solved a problem more effectively. What strategies from the previous selection could you have used to devise a better solution? Be specific about the steps you might have used.

A STUDENT WRITES AN INFORMATIVE DEFINITION

The following essay was written by Kelly, a student who had been closely associated with several alcoholics. Notice that Kelly considered her audience and purpose as she planned, wrote, and revised her essay. Kelly knew she was writing for students who might not have had much experience with alcoholism. She tried to present useful information about alcoholism in an interesting, readable essay.

Not What You Might Think

I'm an expert about a topic I wish I'd never heard of: alcoholism. I'm not a doctor or counselor, and my expertise has never earned me a dime. I don't even have a college degree (although I'm working on one). My expertise comes from life experience. Both my mother and my ex-husband are alcoholics. I've also had two bosses who were alcoholics. While I was trying to save my marriage, I attended Al-Anon meetings for several years. (Al-Anon is a support group for family and friends of alcoholics.) Only then did I learn what the word "alcoholic" really meant.

For years I thought an "alcoholic" was a man who's always falling down drunk. Like most people, I didn't even think about women alcoholics, yet my mother was one. Her three children didn't recognize it for years because we kept looking for the wrong things. I made the same mistake with my husband, who never got drunk in public and was a successful insurance agent and a faithful churchgoer. And both my alcoholic bosses fooled me (but only for a while) the same way.

I now know that many alcoholics seem perfectly normal unless you know what to look for. Many completely hide their drinking. My mother used to go to bed early, too "sick" with headaches to check homework or kiss us goodnight. Years later I realized she didn't want us to smell her breath. Behind her locked bedroom door she could drink herself into a stupor. My father didn't interfere because my parents divorced when I was a baby.

Alcoholics have many problems besides heavy drinking. When I was married to George, I thought he was a terrific person except for his weekend binges. After I started going to Al-Anon, things began to look different. I saw that an alcoholic's whole life revolves around the bottle, even when there's no alcohol around. George didn't have any real friends, and he only pretended to care about me. He spent the whole week looking forward to Friday evening, when he would drink until late Saturday night. On Sunday he started drinking again right after church. We could never make plans, solve problems, or enjoy each other. Liquor was his life.

After I divorced George, I hoped I'd never meet another alcoholic. But in the last eight years I've had to quit two good jobs because of problems with bosses who were alcoholics. The first boss was a woman who did many of the same things my mother and George did. She pretended to care about the office and her staff, but it was all empty talk. She actually did very little work and often disappeared behind her locked office door. My second alcoholic boss was a man and very different in some ways. He flew off the handle easily and told many lies about big and small job issues. Eventually, though, I saw the same alcoholic behavior. The bottle—not his job or employees—was the most important thing in his life.

Because I didn't know what an alcoholic was for so many years, I wasted a lot of time and energy trying to save my marriage all by myself. Those jobs would have been disasters too if I hadn't educated myself about alcoholism. I now realize that it takes two committed people to make a partnership at home and in the workplace. At Al-Anon I learned that many alcoholics do turn their lives around. Perhaps many more could be helped if everyone had a better understanding of the complex term "alcoholic."

Exercise 1: Analyze Kelly's Essay

1. Summarize Kelly's essay by listing the main points she makes about alcoholics.
2. Evaluate her introduction and conclusion. Did they suit her purpose?
3. Did Kelly use transitions effectively?
4. Did Kelly omit anything important? Do you feel she explained the term "alcoholic" adequately? Why or why not?

Writing Assignment: Write a Definition

Instructions: Plan, draft, and revise an informative definition of a term that other students might find interesting. (The suggestions on page 241 may be helpful.) Choose a term that you know well enough to develop with stories and descriptive details. When you are finished, share your essay with a group of other students, and consider incorporating their suggestions into a revision.

READING TO WRITE: WHAT'S AN AMERICAN?

The United States has often been called a "melting pot" because so many people from around the world have been blended into American life. Brainstorm a list of members of ethnic and national groups you have encountered. (If you are an international student, list the encounters you have had while living in the United States.)

Your list:

Richard Rodriguez, the son of Mexican-American immigrants, grew up in the United States. In the following selection, he explains why he defines himself as an "American" rather than a "Hispanic"—and what the term "American" means to him.

Vocabulary:

predominantly   (adjective) mostly

inevitable   (adjective) unavoidable

intact   (adjective) whole, unchanged

Who am I
adapted from "The Chinese in All of Us" by Richard Rodriguez

Last year, I was being interviewed by Bill Moyers. "Do you consider yourself American or Hispanic?" he asked.

"I think of myself as Chinese," I answered.

A smart-aleck answer, but one that is true enough. I live in San Francisco, a city that has become, in my lifetime, predominantly Asian, predominantly Chinese. I am becoming like them. Do not ask me how, it is too early to tell. But it is inevitable, living side by side, that we should become like each other. So think of me as Chinese.

Oh, my critics say: Look at you, Mr. Rod-ree-guess. You have lost your culture.

They mean, I think, that I am not my father, which is true enough. I did not grow up in the state of Jalisco, in the western part of Mexico. I grew up here, in this country, amongst you, I am like you.

My critics mean, when they speak of culture, something solid, something intact. You have lost your culture, they say, as though I lost it at the Greyhound bus station. You have lost your culture, as though culture is a coat I took off one warm afternoon and then forgot.

I AM MY CULTURE. Culture is not something opposite us, it is rather something we breathe and sweat and live. My culture? Lucille Ball is my culture. (I love Lucy, after all.) And Michael Jackson. And Benjamin Franklin is my culture. And Elvis Presley and Walter Cronkite. Walt Disney is my culture. The New York Yankees.

My culture is you. You created me; if you don't like it, if I make you uncomfortable now by being too much like you, too bad.

Responding to What You Have Read

Write a brief summary of this reading selection.

READING TO WRITE: SMALL STEPS TO EXCELLENCE

You're about to read a definition of a Japanese work—*kaizen*—from *Awaken the Giant Within* by Anthony Robbins, an author and business consultant who helps people overcome problems and achieve their full potential. Before you begin reading, freewrite about the word "improvement." Here are several questions you might answer. What successful improvements have you made in your life in the past? What improvements do you think you would like to make in the future? What strategies work best for you? Do you think striving for constant improvement is helpful or harmful to people's lives?

Vocabulary:

Deming	(noun) Dr. W. Edwards Deming, and American business consultant who helped Japan rebuild its economy after World War II.
refinements	(noun) subtle, delicate improvements
compounded	(adjective) multiplied
enhancements	(noun) improvements
befallen	(verb) happened to

Kaizen

from Awaken the Giant Within *by Anthony Robbins*

The beliefs that we hold in business and in life control all of our decisions, and therefore our future. One of the most important global beliefs that you and I can adopt is a belief that in order to succeed and be happy, we've got to be constantly improving the quality of our lives, constantly growing and expanding.

In Japan, they understand this principle well. In fact, in Japanese businesses, as a result of Deming's influence, there is a word that is used constantly in discussions about business or relationships. That word is *kaizen.* This word literally means constant improvement, and the word is constantly used in their language. They often speak of the *kaizen* of their trade deficit, the *kaizen* of the production line, the *kaizen* of their personal relationships. As a result, they're constantly looking at how to improve. By the way, *kaizen* is based upon the principle of gradual improvement, simple improvements. But the Japanese understand that tiny refinements made *daily* begin to create compounded enhancements at a level that most people would never dream of. The Japanese have a saying: "If a man has not been seen for three days, his friends should take a good look at him, and see what changes have befallen him." Amazingly, but not surprisingly, we have no equivalent word for *kaizen* in English.

The more I began to see the impact of *kaizen* in the Japanese business culture, I realized that it was an organizing principle that made a tremendous impact in my own life. My own commitment to constantly improve, to constantly raise my own standards for a quality life is what's kept me both happy and successful.

Responding to What You Have Read

1. Based on what you just read, write your own definition of *kaizen.*
2. Why do you think the English language has no word equivalent to *kaizen?*
3. Do you think American businesses are committed to constant improvement? Why or why not? Give examples from your own experience.
4. Are the people you know committed to constant improvement in their relationships? Why or why not? Give examples from your own experience.
5. Why do you think Robbins emphasizes the importance of small, gradual refinements rather than large, dramatic changes?
6. Robbins begins this selection by explaining that our beliefs control both our decisions and our future. Do you agree or disagree? Why or why not? Give examples to support your answer.

Writing Assignment: Experiment with Kaizen

Instructions: Think of ways you could apply *kaizen* to an important area of your own life. (If constant, gradual improvement is already part of your value system, write about how you've applied this idea.)

Writing Assignment: An Important Word

Instructions: Robbins says that the word *kaizen* is used frequently in Japanese life. Think of a word you hear often—perhaps in a certain setting such as school, work, home, or church, or with a particular group of friends. Define the word and tell several stories to demonstrate its importance.

SUMMARY

1. Definitions are important in academic, personal, and professional life.
2. A definition explains the meaning of a term and clarifies it with specific examples.
3. An effective definition places a term into a category and adds details and examples for clarification.

LOOKING AHEAD

Now that you're experienced with the writing process and several ways to organize essays, you're ready to sharpen your sentence skills. In Part Three, Editing Skills, you will focus on two important areas: writing interesting sentences and avoiding sentence errors.

PART THREE

EDITING SKILLS

CHAPTER SIXTEEN

Writing Effective Sentences

Preview

Editing and proofreading are important parts of the revision process. When you "edit," you rewrite sentences to make them more effective than the previous versions. When you "proofread," you eliminate misspellings, punctuation mistakes, and other usage errors. Careful editing can make your sentences strong and interesting—especially thesis statements and topic sentences.

THE IMPORTANCE OF EDITING

Clear, interesting, well-written sentences are vital to the success of a writing project, for two reasons. They effectively convey your ideas to readers, and they demonstrate that you're serious about writing. In the remaining chapters of this book, you will review punctuation rules and other usage principles related to sentence writing.

Successful writers usually wait until the last stage of the writing process—"editing"—to make these changes. As you've already seen, larger concerns such as audience, purpose, and organization should be tackled first. After you've written an advanced draft, you can begin looking for ways to improve individual sentences. If you start editing too soon, you may spend a great deal of time correcting sentences that won't appear in your final draft.

"Proofreading"—correcting misspelled words, punctuation mistakes, and other usage errors—should also be delayed until you're satisfied with the overall structure of your essay. Don't try to correct sentence errors until you've written an advanced draft of your essay. A proofreading checklist appears at the end of this chapter. You'll learn more about correcting sentence errors in Chapter Seventeen and in the last six chapters of this book.

IMPROVING THESIS STATEMENTS AND TOPIC SENTENCES

When you edit your work, make sure your most important sentences—the *thesis statement* and *topic sentences*—are working as hard as you want them to. Small, careful changes can make these sentences more professional and more powerful than your first versions.

One useful guideline is to think of the beginning of a sentence as its "engine." Important sentences (thesis statements, for example) should begin with interesting, specific words. Compare the following sentence pairs:

> An experience that changed my life was when I spent a night in jail. WEAK THESIS STATEMENT
>
> The night I spent in jail last summer led to three important changes in my life. BETTER

Although both sentences are grammatically correct, the second is stronger. The first begins vaguely: "An experience that changed my life was when . . ." Readers have to take in eight words before the sentence becomes interesting: ". . . I spent a night in jail."

The next two sentence pairs illustrate the same principle. Notice that the first sentence in each pair starts slowly; the second conveys the same message, but it has a more powerful "engine" at the beginning.

> A place I enjoy visiting is Walt Disney World. WEAK THESIS STATEMENT
>
> I always have fun visiting Walt Disney World. BETTER
>
> Someone who has helped me improve my basketball game is Coach Giles. WEAK THESIS STATEMENT
>
> Coach Giles has helped me improve my basketball game. BETTER

Another way to give sentences a powerful "engine" is to avoid beginning them with *there is* or *there are*. When possible, put a noun (a thing) and an active verb (action) near the beginning of the sentence. Compare these sentence pairs:

> There is an important problem, global warming, that more nations need to work together to solve. WEAK THESIS STATEMENT
>
> More nations need to work together to solve the problem of global warming. BETTER
>
> There are many poor children who live in dilapidated welfare hotels. WEAK THESIS STATEMENT
>
> Many poor children live in dilapidated welfare hotels. BETTER

Exercise 1: Powerful Sentences

Instructions: Rewrite the following thesis statements to make them more forceful. *Hint:* Try substituting other verbs (action words) for *is, are, was,* and *were.* (You can learn more about verbs in Chapter Twenty-Two.)

1. The high school experience that I remember most vividly was being chosen captain of the chess team.
2. There is a piece of advice I think about often, "Put yourself into the other person's place."

3. One of my biggest dreams is to own an educational software business.

4. There is one subject, reading, that needs more attention in high schools.

5. A pastime that taught me a lot when I was younger is keeping tropical fish.

6. A career in sports medicine is my ambition.

7. Watching professionals play basketball on television is one way to improve your skills on the court.

8. Tending a garden is good therapy for many people after a stressful day.

9. There are still unexploded bombs and mines from World War I hidden in the French countryside.

10. There are three problems to watch for when you buy a used car.

CLARITY IN THESIS STATEMENTS AND TOPIC SENTENCES

Besides lacking power, weak thesis statements and topic sentences can confuse your readers. If you're writing an essay that challenges a popular belief or widespread misinformation, make sure you've stated your viewpoint clearly. Avoid vague thesis statements like this one:

Many college students expect their first year to be easy. WEAK THESIS STATEMENT

Does the writer agree with these college students? It's impossible to tell. But in the version below, the word *although* immediately clarifies the writer's opinion:

Although many college students expect their first year to be easy, they soon discover that their old study techniques don't work. BETTER

Beware of writing thesis statements and topic sentences that join ideas with *and*. Although *and* is a useful and important word, it can be misleading if it isn't used carefully. In this example, for instance, *and* blurs the relationship between two ideas:

Poverty and homelessness afflict many American families. MISLEADING THESIS STATEMENT

This sentence is poorly written because it makes poverty and homelessness sound like unrelated problems. It should be revised to show that poverty is a *cause* of homelessness:

Poverty, which leads to homelessness, is destroying the hopes of many American families. BETTER

As you saw in Chapter Six, when you write a thesis statement or topic sentence, you should avoid the neutral words *change, different,* and *affect*. Substitute more definite words that clearly state your attitude or intention. Note these examples:

My boss should change his attitude towards women. VAGUE

My boss should treat women more respectfully. BETTER

I want to live in a different climate. VAGUE

I want to live in a warmer climate. BETTER

Patsy's irresponsibility is affecting her children. VAGUE

Patsy's children are starting to imitate her irresponsible habits. BETTER

Collaborative Activity: Rewrite Weak Thesis Statements

Instructions: Fifteen thesis statements appear below. Seven clearly state a viewpoint; eight do not. Working with a small group of other students, identify the eight that need more clarity, and rewrite them for greater effectiveness. Be as creative as you wish.

1. I make extra money every month from the aluminum cans and glass bottles I find in my neighborhood, and I enjoy recycling.
2. Because many entry-level workers are unskilled, employers are relying heavily on automation.
3. Many students are thrilled when they receive their first credit card in the mail.
4. My eating habits have changed since I started living in a college dorm.
5. I'm glad campus rules are more liberal than they were twenty years ago.
6. Some young tennis players are so caught up in the glamour of professional tennis that they miss important lessons about growing up.
7. Poor sleeping habits can affect your grade-point average.
8. Many students believe they have no control over the way they spend their time.
9. Americans are more health conscious, and they are doing less social drinking.
10. Watching a baseball game on TV is different from watching it in a ballpark.
11. Many young parents think making a will is not important.
12. When energy reserves began to dwindle in the 1950s, many people turned down the thermostats in their homes and businesses.
13. Many boxing fans are bewildered by Olympic boxing because they don't understand the scoring system.
14. We need to find new strategies to fight child abuse.
15. Recent changes in professional football regulations have made the games more interesting.

MAKING EFFECTIVE WORD CHOICES

Good writers make their words "work"—every word has a job to do. Empty words and phrases can weaken your message and make sentences drag. As you read the following list, notice how many words and expressions you hear regularly that don't "work":

- blue in color, small in size: "blue" and "small" don't need explaining; omit "in color" and "in size."
- the month of July: isn't July always a month?
- for the purpose of, in order that, in order to: just write *to*.
- for the reason that: just write *because*.
- really, very: often you can omit these.
- being that: just write *because*.
- a personal friend, I personally feel: omit "personal" and "personally": all friends and feelings are personal.
- at this point in time: just write *now*.
- end result, final result: just write *result*.
- true fact: just write *fact*; if it's not true, it's not a fact.

Even useful words can be overused, as you can see in these sentence pairs:

reason:

a) The reason I was late is because my alarm clock stopped. WORDY

b) I'm late because my alarm clock stopped. BETTER

individual:

a) Individual members should volunteer for a committee by November 1. WORDY

b) Members should volunteer for a committee by November 1. BETTER

now:

a) We are now remodeling our photography lab. WORDY

b) We are remodeling our photography lab. BETTER

back:

a) I returned the engagement ring back to Gary. WORDY

b) I returned the engagement ring to Gary. BETTER

Repetitious words weaken your writing by slowing the pace of your ideas and examples. Study these examples:

Last year I shocked my parents by entering a local beauty contest. The beauty contest increased my self-confidence and paid a semester's college tuition. REPETITIOUS

Although my parents were shocked when I entered a local beauty contest, it increased my self-confidence and paid a semester's college tuition. BETTER

The first African-American to chair the Joint Chiefs of Staff was General Colin Powell. General Powell was also the youngest person ever to hold that office. REPETITIOUS

General Colin Powell, the first African-American to chair the Joint Chiefs of Staff, was also the youngest person ever to hold that office. BETTER

Exercise 2: Make Every Word Work

Instructions: Omit unneeded words as you rewrite these sentences.

1. A library card is an important necessity for any serious student who wants to be successful in college.
2. Hurrying at a fast speed, Geoffrey jumped onto the train just before it pulled out of the station.
3. My mother gave me an expensive briefcase for my birthday because carrying a briefcase will make me look and feel successful.
4. After an electric storm, all the clocks in my house start blinking, and I can't stand that blinking.
5. Individual citizens should urge their lawmakers to make highway safety a priority this year.
6. The President of the United States can't read each and every letter that's sent to the White House.
7. Something I never see anymore is a fountain pen; fountain pens disappeared when ballpoints became popular.
8. Having room service in a hotel is the ultimate luxury for me; room service makes me feel rich and pampered.
9. Since the computers were purchased for use by students, they should be available during convenient times.
10. The university has been in existence since 1953.
11. To tell you the truth, I was just now writing you a letter when yours arrived in the mail.
12. I have a question about why student parking permits aren't sold in the Student Services Building during the time period designated for registration.
13. During the winter season, college students make extensive use of local sports facilities such as the ice-skating rink and ski slopes.
14. What many people are concerned about is the need for worthwhile leisure activities for teenagers.
15. The picture of Franklin D. Roosevelt on our dime was drawn by Selma Burke; Burke is an African-American who also drew the picture of Rosa Parks on the fifty-cent piece.

USING AN APPROPRIATE TONE

If you've taken a speech course, you understand the importance of having an appropriate "tone" in your voice. If your tone is wrong—too angry, too silly, or too weak—listeners may reject your message. Written words have a "tone" also, even though there's no physical voice. Slang, colloquialisms, and cliches send inappropriate messages to readers, making the "tone" of your writing too clumsy, juvenile, or trite.

Slang includes nonstandard words and expressions such as "ain't" and "snuck." *Colloquialisms* are casual expressions that may be acceptable in everyday speech but sound awkward in college writing. If you eavesdrop on a friendly conversation, you're likely to hear sentences like this: "Well, I was talking to this weird guy, you know?" While a sentence like that is acceptable in ordinary conversation, it has the wrong "tone" for a college essay. *Cliches* are overused expressions that lost their effectiveness long ago. Writing "It was raining cats and dogs" or "Don't put the cart before the horse" gives the impression that you have no fresh ideas to share with your readers.

Exercise 3: Slang, Colloquialisms, Cliches

Instructions: Carry an index card with you for a day and list ten examples of slang, colloquialisms, and cliches that you heard.

Collaborative Activity: Learn More about Tone

Instructions: Meet with a small group of other students to prepare a master list of slang, colloquialisms, and cliches from the index cards you prepared for Exercise 3. Then prepare another list of substitute words and expressions that would be suitable for college and professional writing.

Collaborative Activity: Write a Dialogue

Instructions: Working with another student, invent a short conversation between two people, using slang, colloquialisms, and cliches. Then rewrite the conversation in a style acceptable for college writing.

IDENTIFYING COMMON USAGE ERRORS

The final task in the writing process is "proofreading"—looking for and correcting misspelled words, punctuation mistakes, and other usage errors. These problems can be hard to spot because your mind is more interested in ideas than small (but important) details like omitted and reversed letters. As a result, you're likely to miss proofreading errors when you check the final draft of your paper.

One good strategy is placing a ruler beneath each line of writing as you read. Because your attention is focused on only that line, you're more likely to catch small errors. You can also try proofreading your essay from bottom to top. The ideas you're reading won't make sense, but usage mistakes may jump out at you. Finally, you can make a photocopy of your essay and have a friend read it aloud while you check your original for errors.

Use the checklist on the following pages to check for errors that often appear in college essays. Although the list may seem long at first, with practice you can become a skilled and efficient proofreader. The numbers in parentheses refer to pages in this text.

USAGE CHECKLIST

1. Are all sentences complete?

   (Fragments are most likely to appear in thesis statements and supporting ideas. See Chapter Seventeen.)

2. Does every sentence end with a period or question mark?

   (Make sure you didn't incorrectly join sentences with *then, next, however, therefore, consequently,* or similar words.)

3. Are sentences combined correctly?

   (Sentence patterns are reviewed in Chapters Eighteen and Nineteen.)

4. Are all capital letters correct?

   (Sometimes capital letters incorrectly appear after a transition word or a semicolon. See page 292.)

5. Are all commas correct and consistent?

   (See Chapter Nineteen.)

6. Are all apostrophes correct?

   (With few exceptions, apostrophes should be used only with contractions and possessive nouns. See Chapter Twenty-One.)

7. Did you make effective word choices?

   (See pages 256–257.)

8. Did you avoid errors with other pronouns?

   (The "thumb rule" will help you avoid problems with the pairs *I* and *me, he* and *him, she* and *her, we* and *us, they* and *them.* For more information about pronouns, see Chapter Twenty-Four.)

9. Are verb tenses correct?

   (Verb endings and abrupt changes between past to present can create problems. See Chapter Twenty-Two.)

10. If the verb *would* appears in your paper, is it used correctly?

    (*Would* usually appears when you're writing about possibilities. It can also be used— sparingly—with repeated past actions.)

11. Did you avoid confusing words that look or sound alike? (Check the dictionary for easily confused words such as *its* and *it's, their, there,* and *they're.* See Chapter Twenty-Three.)

12. Are descriptive words and phrases placed correctly? (See Chapter Seventeen.)

SUMMARY

1. Careful editing can make thesis statements and topic sentences clear and interesting.
2. Eliminating repetition and unnecessary words can make your sentences lively and powerful.

LOOKING AHEAD

In Chapter Seventeen, you'll practice identifying and correcting four kinds of sentence errors: fragments, fused sentences, comma splices, and dangling modifiers.

CHAPTER SEVENTEEN

Avoiding Sentence Errors

Preview

Even superior writing can be marred by sentence errors. This chapter will help you avoid four common sentence problems: writing incomplete sentences (fragments), running sentences together (fused sentences), using a comma instead of a period (comma splices), and writing sentences with misplaced phrases and clauses (dangling modifiers).

WRITING COMPLETE SENTENCES

Sentence fragments (incomplete sentences) are serious writing errors. You can avoid them by applying the following principles as you write:

1. *Make sure every sentence has a main subject and verb.* In these pairs, the first example is a fragment. The second example is correct because it has a subject and verb (underlined).

   > Striving to succeed as a professional soccer player. FRAGMENT
   > <u>Jack is</u> striving to succeed as a professional soccer player. CORRECT
   > The menu on the top half of the computer screen. FRAGMENT
   > <u>I scanned</u> the menu on the top half of the computer screen. CORRECT

2. *Make sure every subordinate clause is attached to a complete sentence.* (See pages 282–283 for more information about subordinate clauses.) "If," "when," "because," and "although" are the four subordinate conjunctions you're likely to hear most often. When a group of words begins with one of these conjunctions, make sure a complete sentence is attached either in front or in back. In the following pairs, the first example is a fragment. The second example is correct because a complete sentence (underlined) has been added.

   > Because my college studies take up more time than I had expected. FRAGMENT
   > <u>I've had to change my work schedule</u> because my college studies take up more time than I had expected. CORRECT

Because my college studies take up more time than I had expected, <u>I've had to change my work schedule.</u> CORRECT

If my parents don't visit during Homecoming Week. FRAGMENT

<u>I'll be disappointed</u> if my parents don't visit during Homecoming Week. CORRECT

If my parents don't visit during Homecoming Week, <u>I'll be disappointed.</u> CORRECT

3. Don't start a sentence with *who* or *which* unless it's a question.

<u>Who</u> broke Gordie Howe's goal-scoring record. INCORRECT

<u>Who</u> broke Gordie Howe's NHL goal-scoring record? CORRECT

I just read an article about hockey player Wayne Gretzky, <u>who</u> broke Gordie Howe's NHL goal-scoring record. CORRECT

4. If you're working from an outline, make sure it's written in complete sentences. If your thesis statement and supporting ideas are written as fragments, they may reappear in your final draft without your knowing it. The ideas in the following outline are incomplete sentences:

Outline (written in fragments)
Making the college dance team. THESIS
First, choosing music for my demonstration dance.
Second, choreographing an original routine.
Most of all, practicing dance steps in the gym every afternoon.

The following outline is written in complete sentences:

Outline (written in sentences)
I was thrilled when I made the college dance team. THESIS
First, I struggled to find a good piece of music for my demonstration.
Second, I spent hours choreographing an original dance.
Most important, I practiced dance steps in the gym every afternoon.

Because the second outline is written in complete sentences, fragments are less likely to occur when it's expanded into an essay.

Exercise 1: Correct Sentence Fragments

Instructions: Correct any fragments (incomplete sentences) below.

1. Although I'm glad to recycle all the glass bottles in our house.
2. Have to admit being bothered by the sounds of shattering glass at the recycling bin.
3. Last month I read a fascinating magazine article about a top model.

4. Which describes one of her typical working days.
5. Spends two hours applying makeup to look natural.
6. Because technology is so popular today, many people overlook the usefulness of inexpensive and ordinary devices.
7. Easier to keep track of appointments in a pocket calendar than a computer notebook.
8. Many Internet users who swear by their computers.
9. Surprised when librarians quickly find information in reference books.
10. Although many people assume that over-the-counter medications are always safe.
11. Popular headache remedies can have serious side effects.

Exercise 2: Correct Fragments in an Essay

Instructions: Read the following essay, which was drafted from an outline written in fragments rather than complete sentences. Underline the fragments, and rewrite them on a sheet of paper as complete sentences.

The Thrift Shop

Tasks I performed working as a clerk in a thrift shop when I was in high school. Although I expected the job to be easy, I soon discovered otherwise. My duties challenged me to grow in ways I hadn't expected.

First, assisting customers with their shopping. I answered questions about our merchandise, prices, return policy and delivery schedule. During the first month I was often embarrassed because I didn't understand a customer's questions or had forgotten what the store manager told me. One afternoon I had to visit her office seven times to ask about the store's policies. I realized I needed to develop better listening skills and a sharper memory.

In addition, helping with store upkeep. I sorted and priced donated merchandise, straightened clothing racks and rearranged window displays. Because I didn't bother much about neatness at home, I didn't think it was important at the store either. The manager had to convince me that the store would be more successful if our merchandise looked attractive. After the first month, I began to take pride in the way our store looked.

Most important, handling money responsibly. At first I often made errors with change and entered incorrect wrong amounts into the cash register. I used to chatter with customers instead of concentrating on the money in my hand. One afternoon a customer insisted that she'd given me a twenty-dollar bill. I thought she'd given me only a ten, but I couldn't be sure. To avoid an argument, I made change for a twenty. At the end of the day, the cash register was short and I had to make up the difference myself.

Luckily I was a quick learner, and I soon became a valuable worker. Two years ago I was hired as assistant manager at a clothing store; retailing fascinates me, and I'm hoping to own a store of my own someday. The long hours I spent at the thrift shop taught me important lessons that I expect to use throughout my career.

FUSED SENTENCES

When two sentences are mistakenly run together, they are called *fused* or *run-on* sentences. Like fragments, fused sentences are serious writing errors. The simplest correction is to insert a period at the end of the first sentence:

> Children are the main victims of war they are killed, disabled, and dispossessed in huge numbers. FUSED SENTENCE
>
> Children are the main victims of war. They are killed, disabled, and dispossessed in huge numbers. CORRECT
>
> My father loves his pocket-size computer I think it's just an expensive notebook with batteries. FUSED SENTENCE
>
> My father loves his pocket-size computer. I think it's just an expensive notebook with batteries. CORRECT

Chapter Eighteen, "Achieving Sentence Variety," will give you opportunities to practice other ways to combine sentences.

Some fused sentences can also be called *comma splices*. A comma splice occurs when a comma is incorrectly placed between two sentences instead of the period that belongs there.

> Cable TV increases viewing choices, even more channels are available with a satellite dish. COMMA SPLICE
>
> Cable TV increases viewing choices. Even more channels are available with a satellite dish. CORRECT

Exercise 3: Correct Fused Sentences and Comma Splices

Instructions: Fused sentences and comma splices appear below, along with several correct sentences. Make any needed corrections.

1. Five years ago my mother desperately wanted a microwave now she uses it only for heating water.
2. Many people haven't been taught basic oral hygiene they needlessly lose teeth that could have been saved.
3. Of course I cherish the right to privacy, our society should also emphasize individual responsibility.
4. According to some political leaders, future generations may not enjoy the freedoms we take for granted.
5. Americans shouldn't be forced to choose between preventing crime and punishing it, both approaches are important.
6. By narrowly focusing on a single career goal, students may find themselves unprepared for other opportunities.

7. Studies show that Americans can expect to change careers three times before retirement.

8. Automatic teller machines save money for banks because machines are less expensive than human workers.

9. The extra leaf was in the dining-room table when I came home obviously we're expecting company.

10. Everyone I've talked to remembers a beloved stuffed animal from childhood.

Exercise 4: Correct Sentence Errors

Instructions: Some of these sentences require periods; others have unnecessary commas; still others are correct. Make any corrections needed.

1. There's no "cents" symbol on my computer keyboard, that reveals something interesting about our economy.

2. My mother rarely uses her ironing board years ago she spent long hours standing over it.

3. Giving a cat medicine isn't easy, wrapping the cat in a big towel sometimes works.

4. I'm finding that dorm life has both advantages and disadvantages that I didn't expect.

5. Sedatives seem like a good solution to insomnia, they prevent normal dreaming and restful sleep.

6. Because I'm watching my weight, I'd rather receive flowers than candy on Valentine's Day.

7. My florist talked me into buying a bouquet for my boyfriend, I was disappointed that Gene didn't like it.

8. Having many responsibilities and too little time, Jaffa uses her car as a mobile office.

9. I used to hate wearing stockings with seams now I enjoy them because they're different.

10. Two years ago I started to learn line dancing, then last year I signed up for clogging lessons.

WORDS THAT DON'T JOIN SENTENCES

Be careful not to join sentences with adverbs (such as *now*, *then*, and *next*) or adverbial conjunctions (such as *however*, *nevertheless*, and *consequently*). End the sentence with a period, and capitalize the adverbial conjunction to begin a new sentence. (Many writers use semi-colons instead of periods with these words. To learn more about adverbial conjunctions, see page 285.)

> Most college students are eligible to vote, nevertheless, many take no interest in current events. COMMA SPLICE
>
> Most college students are eligible to vote. Nevertheless, many take no interest in current events. CORRECT

I finally bought an electric razor, now I don't cut myself shaving. FUSED SENTENCE

I finally bought an electric razor. Now I don't cut myself shaving. CORRECT

I'm having Muffy spayed tomorrow, therefore, she won't add to the pet overpopulation problem. FUSED SENTENCE

I'm having Muffy spayed tomorrow; therefore, she won't add to the pet overpopulation problem. CORRECT

Exercise 5: Correct Fused Sentences

Instructions: Correct any fused sentences that appear below.

1. Domestic pets can harm songbirds and other wildlife, therefore pets should be confined in a home or yard.
2. Amateur wildlife photographers also disturb birds, which feel threatened when a photographer tracks them for a picture.
3. Officials for the tobacco industry used to say the nicotine in cigarettes isn't addictive.
4. Many Americans learned more about Japan when the 1998 Winter Olympics were held there.
5. The country of Wales is very different from the rest of the United Kingdom it's a fascinating place to visit.
6. Because I've always lived in Florida, I can't imagine how it feels to ride a bobsled.
7. Many Americans have never been poor, moreover they don't have any friends who live below the poverty line.
8. I don't have room to store old calendars, so at the end of the year I frame the pictures I like best.
9. I was surprised to learn that badminton, ping-pong, and soccer are popular in China.
10. Study and work are my first priorities, then I schedule recreation and relaxation.

MISPLACED MODIFIERS

What is wrong with this sentence?

I saw two shoe stores walking down the street. INCORRECT

It contains a "misplaced modifier"—a description that is out of place in the sentence. Here's the corrected version:

Walking down the street, I saw two shoe stores. CORRECT

To correct a misplaced modifier, rearrange the sentence so that the description is placed logically. In the previous sentence, Walking down the street should be placed next to I. Compare the following sentence pairs. The first sentence in each pair is incorrect; the second has been rearranged so that the modifier is placed correctly.

> Nurses used to be afraid to question physicians' decisions, forgetting that patients' welfare comes first. INCORRECT
>
> Forgetting that patients' welfare comes first, nurses used to be afraid to question physicians' decisions. CORRECT
>
> Barking happily, George threw a frisbee to his dog. INCORRECT
>
> George threw a frisbee to his dog, barking happily. CORRECT
>
> Bill narrowly missed hitting a tree driving recklessly down the country road. INCORRECT
>
> Driving recklessly down the country road, Bill narrowly missed hitting a tree. CORRECT

When you're editing something you've written, read each sentence thoughtfully. Ask a friend or family member to help, looking especially for sentences that don't make sense, like this one:

> Max chewed on his pencil struggling with a math problem. INCORRECT

This sentence is incorrect because it sounds as if the pencil is struggling with a math problem. Here is the corrected version:

> Struggling with a math problem, Max chewed on his pencil. CORRECT

In the previous example, the "misplaced modifier" contained a word ending in *ing*. When you're editing, pay particular attention to all phrases that begin with *ing* words, like these:

> The police officer chased down the pickpocket, <u>blowing his whistle loudly.</u> INCORRECT
>
> <u>Flapping in the breeze,</u> the cadets saluted the flag. INCORRECT

These sentences are correct:

> <u>Blowing his whistle loudly,</u> the police officer chased down the pickpocket. CORRECT
>
> The cadets saluted the flag, <u>flapping in the breeze.</u> CORRECT

Exercise 6: Correct Misplaced Modifiers

Instructions: Rewrite the following sentences to make them more clear and logical.

_____ 1. Driving to work this morning, the radio had a report about Nigeria.
_____ 2. I put the salad into the refrigerator that we hadn't eaten.
_____ 3. After three spectacular years on the varsity team, the coach recommended Steve for an athletic scholarship.
_____ 4. While still in elementary school, my mother taught me tennis skills.

____ 5. Rusty and battered, they bought the old convertible for a low price.

____ 6. Every night before he goes to sleep, I read Jake a bedtime story.

____ 7. Patiently explaining all the examples in the text, everyone passed Professor Kiley's final.

____ 8. Working through the night, the crew repaired the machinery.

____ 9. Dreaming of an Olympics medal, Clare worked with a famous figure-skating coach.

____ 10. Shabby after years of neglect, we faced the unwelcome task of remodeling the house.

Review Exercise: Practice What You've Learned

Instructions: Rewrite the sentences below so that they are correct. (Often the sentence can be correctly written in several ways.) Look for fragments, fused sentences, comma splices, and misplaced modifiers.

1. Wake up at two o'clock in the morning with strange thoughts racing through my brain.

2. The faculty wants students to read, however each dorm room has only one small book-case.

3. Looking for places to stack all these books, my dorm room is never neat.

4. I almost always buy a T-shirt when I go to a concert or museum.

5. Which quickly tells other people about my interests and enthusiasms.

6. I bought my favorite T-shirt at the Museum of Fine Arts in Boston, displaying a beau-tiful Monet painting.

7. Because I made an A in English last semester, I was selected for the Student Partner-ship Team.

8. Which links successful students with others needing assistance.

9. Although there aren't enough A students for everyone wanting a partner.

10. Plant explorer David Fairchild gave hand lenses to his children and their friends, it opened up the world of nature to them.

11. Adults value interesting pastimes, they forget that children also need worthwhile ways to spend their time.

12. Architect Frank Lloyd Wright said his interest in buildings began when he played with geometric wooden blocks in kindergarten.

SUMMARY

Fragments, fused sentences, comma splices, and misplaced modifiers are serious sentence errors.

LOOKING AHEAD

In Chapter Eighteen, "Achieving Sentence Variety," you'll learn how mastering several sentence patterns can add clarity and interest to your writing.

CHAPTER EIGHTEEN

Achieving Sentence Variety

Preview

Successful writers express their ideas in a variety of sentence patterns. Sentence variety connects your ideas, clarifies them, and makes them more readable. Mastery of sentence patterns helps you avoid monotony and choppiness. Each sentence pattern has a special set of words called conjunctions, and each has its own usage rules.

INTRODUCING SENTENCE VARIETY

Successful writers express their ideas in a variety of sentence patterns. Mastery of these patterns makes your style more professional, and it helps you communicate your ideas more effectively to readers. Each sentence pattern is used with a special set of words called conjunctions. (The usage chapters of this book offer detailed instructions about writing these sentences correctly.) Since you already use most of these patterns and conjunctions in everyday conversations, you have already taken the first step toward mastering them.

The following examples will introduce you to a variety sentence patterns. The first two sentences about Jacques Cousteau are short and choppy; there's no attempt to connect them. Notice how much better the sentences sound when they have been connected with joining words (called *conjunctions*). The numbers in parentheses direct you to the pages that will teach you how to punctuate these sentence patterns.

> Jacques Costeau advocated respect for marine life. He was not able to stop the pollution of our oceans. CHOPPY

1. Combined with the coordinate conjunction *but* (page 286)

   Jacques Cousteau advocated respect for marine life, *but* he was not able to stop the pollution of our oceans.
2. Combined with the subordinate conjunction *although* (pages 282–283)

   Although Jacques Cousteau advocated respect for marine life, he was not able to stop the pollution of our oceans.
3. Combined with a semicolon (pages 292–295)

Jacques Cousteau advocated respect for marine life; he was not able to stop the pollution of our oceans.

4. The same sentence with the conjunctive adverb *however* (page 285)

Jacques Cousteau advocated respect for marine life; *however*, he was not able to stop the pollution of our oceans.

5. Combined with the relative pronoun *who* (pages 287–288)

Jacques Cousteau, *who* advocated respect for marine life, was not able to stop the pollution of our oceans.

In this chapter you will practice using these five sentence patterns to add variety to your style:

1. Sentences with a coordinate conjunction (*for, and, nor, but, or, yet, so*)
2. Sentences with a subordinate conjunction (*if, when, because, although,* and similar words)
3. Sentences with a semicolon
4. Sentences with a semicolon and conjunctive adverb (*nevertheless, however, therefore, moreover,* and similar words)
5. Sentences with a relative pronoun (*who, which,* and *that*)

You can see the benefits of sentence variety in the two paragraphs below. The sentences in the first paragraph are monotonous and unconnected; the second uses several sentence patterns. Notice how the variations enhance the second paragraph.

a) Without sentence variety:

Lost Childhood

Childhood isn't much fun for some of the boys and girls I know. Their parents constantly pressure them to achieve. These children have been taught to value competition. They've never known the fun of imaginative play. After school, they have private instruction in sports and the arts. Evenings are devoted to academic work. They don't play tag or hide-and-seek. They never have time to ride bicycles or push doll carriages. Their parents want them to have a full life. These children aren't learning how to enjoy living.

b) With sentence variety:

Lost Childhood

Childhood isn't much fun for some boys and girls I know, whose parents constantly pressure them to achieve. Because they have been taught only to value competition, these children have never known the fun of imaginative play. After school, they have private instruction in sports and the arts; evenings are devoted to academic study. They don't play tag or hide-and-seek, and they never have time to ride bicycles or push doll carriages. Their parents want them to have a full life, but these children aren't learning how to enjoy living.

Exercise 1: Recognize Sentence Variety

Instructions: Decide which of the two paragraphs below uses a variety of sentence patterns, and explain your choices.

Frustrations

I expected to enjoy college. It's not working out the way I expected. Many times I find myself saying "no" to things I'd like to do. First, I don't have enough money. I can't afford to attend the plays and concerts on campus. I hoped to have exciting new cultural experiences in college. It's not working out. My other problem is time. I'm working behind a lunch counter to pay my car expenses. I don't have enough study time and failed two quizzes last week. I haven't had time to develop close friendships with other students. I feel cut off from campus life. College should be exhilarating and enriching. I feel exhausted and impoverished.

Whiter than White?

I'm learning how to wash my own clothes, and it's been disheartening. Since I moved into the dorm, my laundry mistakes have ruined several outfits. Clothing labels are one part of the problem. When I sorted my clothes, I didn't notice that a sweater and blouse had to be washed separately. My sweater shrank, and the dye from my blouse ruined a white dress. My other problem is bleach, which I foolishly thought would make my clothes sparkling clean. But I used too much and now have a streaky wardrobe. I wish the college had a course called Elementary Laundry 101.

Collaborative Activity: Discuss Sentence Patterns

Instructions: Meet with a small group of other students to discuss the two paragraphs you just read. Underline each conjunction and label each sentence pattern.

USING SENTENCE PATTERNS FOR CLARITY

Conjunctions provide important clues to your readers, making your ideas easier to understand. As you read the incomplete sentences below, notice that you can predict what will appear after the conjunction:

Joe planned to see the math tutor this afternoon, but

_____.

Joe planned to see the math tutor this afternoon because

_____.

Skilled writers use conjunctions frequently because they help readers anticipate ideas. Words like *but, although, however,* and *nevertheless* introduce contrasting ideas, as in these examples:

> I studied all night *but* failed my test.
> *Although* I studied all night, I failed my test.
> I studied all night; I failed my test, *however.*
> I studied all night; *nevertheless,* I failed my test.

And and *moreover* tell your reader that additional related information is coming.

> My car needs a new battery, *and* the tires are getting worn.
> My car needs a new battery; *moreover,* the tires are getting worn.

So, because, consequently, and *therefore* tell readers to expect a logical consequence:

> *Because* my dancing has improved, I'm having more fun.
> My dancing has improved; *consequently,* I'm having more fun.
> My dancing has improved; *therefore,* I'm having more fun.

Exercise 2: Understand Conjunctions

Instructions: Paying close attention to conjunctions and their meanings, use appropriate ideas to complete the following sentences. Be as creative as you wish.

1. Elise couldn't get her car started although _____

   _____.

2. Elise couldn't get her car started; moreover, _____

   _____.

3. Our new line of sportswear is popular, and _____

   _____.

4. Our new line of sportswear is popular; nevertheless, _____

   _____.

5. Betty and Harold feel confident that the stock market will rise; consequently, _____

   _____.

6. Betty and Harold feel confident that the stock market will rise; however, _____

   _____.

7. Soccer is not popular in the United States, so _____

   _____.

8. Soccer is not popular in the United States because _____

_____.

9. I'm hoping to visit Europe after graduation, but _____

_____.

10. I'm hoping to visit Europe after graduation; therefore, _____

_____.

USING SENTENCE VARIETY IN PARAGRAPHS

In the selections below, several professional writers used sentence variety to make their ideas more interesting. (The topic sentences have been underlined.) Mastery of sentence variety can empower your ideas in the same ways.

1. In *A Brief History of Time,* Stephen Hawking used a *which* clause to introduce a definition of "entropy":

   The nondecreasing behavior of a black hole's area was reminiscent of the behavior of a physical quantity called entropy, which measures the degree of disorder within a symptom. It is a matter of common experience that disorder will tend to increase if things are left to themselves. (One has only to stop making repairs around the house to see that!) One can create order out of disorder (for example, one can paint the house), but that requires expenditure of effort or energy and so decreases the amount of ordered energy available.

2. In "A Plea for the Chimps," Jane Goodall's *but* clause emphasizes the contrast between the chimps' togetherness and the loneliness they suffered later.

   The chimps had each other for comfort, but they would not remain together for long. Once they were infected, probably with hepatitis, they would be separated and placed in another cage. And there they would remain, living in conditions of severe sensory deprivation, for the next several years. During that time, they would probably become insane.

3. In *Thriving on Chaos,* Tom Peters used an *if* idea to plunge his readers into the future:

   If the word excellence is to be applicable in the future, it requires wholesale redefinition. Perhaps: "Excellent firms don't believe in excellence—only in constant improvement and constant change." That is, excellent firms of tomorrow will cherish impermanence—and thrive on chaos.

Exercise 3: Identifying Effective Sentences

Instructions: Underline each sentence that uses an effective sentence pattern to state a position. Briefly explain your choices.

1. I get tired of sorting glass and bundling newspapers; recycling is important to me.

2. Because many entry-level workers are unskilled, employers are relying heavily on automation.

3. Garage sales may not be popular with most students, but my friends and I explore them every weekend.

4. People who haven't studied time management are likely to be disappointed in their business careers.

5. Some amateur boxers concentrate on powerful punching, and some focus on balance and footwork.

6. Americans are more health-conscious than they used to be; therefore social drinking is declining.

7. Since the 1950s, both energy reserves and luxury cars have become smaller.

8. There are many busy young people today who think making a will is not important.

9. I registered as a Republican although my family has always supported Democratic candidates.

10. Child abuse, which affects every economic class in America, has resisted all our efforts at eradication.

Collaborative Activity: Sentence Variety in Paragraphs

Instructions: The following paragraphs contain a variety of sentence patterns. Working with a small group of other students, find two sentences that contain:

- a subordinate clause
- a coordinate clause
- a relative pronoun

1. From "Scott Joplin: Black-American Classicist" by Rudi Blesh

    Although creatively far ahead of his time and place, Joplin was also imprisoned in it. Beyond the publishing of piano rags, and, perhaps, money and a certain circumscribed fame, where could he go? Even in Sedalia he was limited to the black world. If his conceptions were those of genius, still his genius wore a black skin.

2. From *Child Star,* by former actress Shirley Temple Black:

No longer a cuddly child, I increasingly needed to establish my appeal to adult audiences. Yet the less I remained a child, the less my charm could be sustained for a new generation of children. Although Zanuck crammed me backwards in time into childish molds, no practiced eye could fail to sense onrushing puberty.

3. From "University Days" by James Thurber

I passed all the other courses that I took at my university, but I could never pass botany. This was because all botany students had to spend several hours a week looking through a microscope at plant cells, and I could never see through a microscope. I never once saw a cell through a microscope.

4. From *The Woman Warrior* by Maxine Hong Kingston

On a farm near the sea, a woman who tended her appearance reaped a reputation for eccentricity. All the married women blunt-cut their hair in flaps about their ears or pulled it back in tight buns. No nonsense. Neither style blew easily into heart-catching tangles. And at their weddings they displayed themselves in their long hair for the last time.

Exercise 4: Learn More about Sentence Variety

Instructions: Complete the activities below.

1. Photocopy a short essay from a newspaper or magazine that you enjoyed reading. Find three sentences in which the author used a conjunction to help readers anticipate the idea or information coming next.
2. From an essay or book you liked, copy three topic sentences similar to the sentence patterns in this unit.
3. Reexamine an essay you've already written, underlining sentences that could be combined for sentence variety. Rewrite one paragraph of the essay so that its sentence patterns are more varied.

Writing Assignment: Enhance Your Writing

Instructions: Write an essay about one of the following topics. During the revision step, concentrate on using a variety of sentence patterns.

1. The good (or bad) side of being a child today
2. A profession that needs to dedicate itself to excellence
3. A scientific concept that interests you
4. A challenge you've faced in college
5. Your transition from childhood to adolescence
6. Your transition from adolescence to adulthood

SUMMARY

1. Mastering a variety of sentence patterns adds polish and clarity to your writing.
2. Skillful writers use many kinds of words to connect their ideas: subordinate and coordinate conjunctions, relative pronouns, and conjunctive adverbs.
3. Each group of joining words has its own punctuation rules.

LOOKING AHEAD

In Part Four, Reviewing Punctuation, you will develop confidence and skill with commas, semicolons, apostrophes, and other important punctuation marks.

PART FOUR

REVIEWING PUNCTUATION

CHAPTER NINETEEN

Using Commas Correctly

Preview

Commas are important punctuation marks that make your writing easier for readers to understand. Although commas can be used in many ways, their rules aren't difficult to learn. You probably know many of these rules already:

1. Use commas in a series of three or more items.
2. Use commas with introductory clauses, phrases, and words.
3. Use commas with coordinate conjunctions.
4. Use commas with quotation marks.
5. Use commas with interrupters.
6. Use commas to separate cities and states, to write dates, and to address a person directly.

COMMA RULES

1. Use commas in a series of three or more items.

Use commas to separate items in a series (a list of three or more items):

> I'm taking courses in English, chemistry, and algebra this semester. EXAMPLE

Professors and editors disagree about the comma before *and*. Some require it, while others insist that it be omitted like this:

> I'm taking courses in English, chemistry and algebra this semester. COMMA OMITTED

Since English handbooks allow both points of view, follow your instructor's guidelines about this comma.

A final reminder about commas in series: Do not use a comma in a sentence listing only two items:

> Mark has studied French in Montreal and Paris. NO COMMA

Exercise 1: Commas in a Series

Instructions: Insert commas into the following sentences.

1. The Martin Luther King Jr. National Historic Site in Atlanta contains civil rights archives a library King's crypt and an exhibition hall.
2. Federal income tax deductions include charitable donations mortgage interest and medical expenses.
3. Yesterday afternoon Amy and I tasted snowflakes made snow angels and threw snow-balls at each other.
4. Every season has its special chores such as shoveling snow sprinkling grass seed pulling weeds and raking leaves.
5. My great-grandmother's music collection includes gramophone cylinders long-play records and compact disks.
6. *In the Line of Fire Dirty Harry* and *Unforgiven* are my favorite Clint Eastwood movies.
7. Jerry bunted singled and struck out in Saturday's game against the Pistols.
8. Fax machines photocopiers and cellular phones have revolutionized business practices.
9. Bubble baths hot-fudge sundaes and perfume are my favorite luxuries.
10. Thirteen weeks in boot camp at Parris Island made me stronger thinner and more mature.

2. Use commas with introductory clauses, phrases and words.

Use a comma when a sentence begins with introductory material. Reading aloud may help you hear the difference between an introduction and the main clause that follows. Read the following sentences aloud, noting the commas:

Before Wal-Mart opened a new store in Central Florida, it agreed to reserve part of its land as habitat for an endangered bird species. EXAMPLE

In an election year, public officials are highly sensitive to the wishes of citizens in their districts. EXAMPLE

Because government support for the arts is shrinking, private citizens must make up the difference. EXAMPLE

A *clause* is a word-group containing a subject and a verb. *Subordinate clauses* begin with a subordinate conjunction, such as *if, until, when, while, whether, because, since, as, so that, although.* Each sentence below begins with a subordinate clause: Notice where the commas are placed.

Because circus performers spend so much time traveling, they view the circus train as their home. EXAMPLE

When I heard my daughter imitating an obnoxious TV character, I started paying more attention to the programs she watches. EXAMPLE

If I don't finish this book report today, I'll have to work on it over the weekend. EXAMPLE

Note that the next two sentences, which have subordinate clauses at the back, do not have commas:

> I started paying more attention to the programs my daughter watches *when I heard her imitating an obnoxious TV character.* EXAMPLE

> I'll have to work on this book report over the weekend *if I don't finish it today.* EXAMPLE

Exercise 2: Insert Commas into Sentences

Instructions: Insert commas into the following sentences.

1. Although flight attendants serve meals and drinks their primary responsibility is passenger safety.
2. When I was only a few weeks old my parents started saving for my college education.
3. Many American churches and synagogues faced a crisis when their female members began asking for leadership roles.
4. Dorm security improved after the Campus Safety Committee completed its study.
5. I'm going to play volleyball again next year unless my courses are too demanding.
6. Since ice dancing is an Olympic sport I guess it's all right to have ballroom dancing in the Olympics too.
7. You'll have to take organic chemistry if you plan to apply to medical school.
8. As hockey increases its popularity in the United States more TV stations are broadcasting hockey games.
9. I listen to public radio while I'm commuting to and from the university.
10. Whether you enjoy writing or not it's essential to your success.

Exercise 3: Add Commas Where Needed

Instructions: Complete the following sentences with ideas of your own. Add commas where needed. (Noting where the subordinate clause is located in the sentence will be helpful.)

1. Because college is different from high school _____

   _____.

2. _____

   _____ when I graduate from college.

3. _____

   _____ until I looked at my watch.

4. Unless you have another suggestion _____

   _____.

5. _____

_____ so that I can accomplish my goal.

6. If my plans work out _____

_____ .

7. _____

_____ when I feel discouraged.

8. _____

_____ since we always disagree.

9. Although I can usually control my temper _____

_____ .

10. As I glanced down the road _____

_____ .

a) Commas with introductory phrases

A *phrase* is a word-group that lacks either a subject or verb. You may use a comma whenever a phrase appears before the main subject and verb of a sentence.

> *Stressing commitment,* the coach demands the most from every player on the team. EXAMPLE

> *Confused by terms like "Shift Lock Override,"* I haven't learned how to program my car radio. EXAMPLE

> *Still breathing hard,* Abel began the next race. EXAMPLE

Exercise 4: Insert Commas Where Needed

Instructions: Insert commas into the following sentences.

1. With a microwave oven you can prepare meals quickly and efficiently.
2. Answering questions rapidly she demonstrated her competence to the nominating committee.
3. Every morning I force myself to leave the comfort of my warm bed.
4. For many people discovering the high interest they've been paying on their credit cards is a terrible shock.
5. Sprinkled on cereal wheat germ is a superb source of vitamins and minerals.
6. In the movie *Down and Out in Beverly Hills* Nick Nolte ate real dog food.
7. The best-selling fashion doll in history Barbie is more popular than ever.
8. As a teenager Michael Jordan was cut from his high-school basketball team.
9. On and off the court Jordan sets high standards for himself.

10. In recent years medical schools have been putting more emphasis on pain relief.

b) Commas with introductory words, such as introductory adverbs
Use a comma after conjunctive adverbs such as *however, nevertheless, therefore, consequently, subsequently,* and *moreover.* (Note that these words cannot, by themselves, combine sentences.)

> New baseball equipment can reduce the risk of injuries. *However,* many youth organizations lack the funds to switch to this new equipment. EXAMPLE
>
> A new, lower-impact baseball can prevent serious head injuries to players struck by the ball. *Moreover,* new face guards, face cages and helmets are available to protect young athletes. EXAMPLE
>
> Breakaway bases help runners avoid foot, ankle, and knee injuries. *Therefore,* many parents are asking local teams to stop using traditional bolted bases. EXAMPLE

Exercise 5: Insert Commas Where Needed

Instructions: Insert commas into the following sentences.

1. The Jewish Talmud is a diverse collection of sixty-three ancient books. However all the volumes are united by their emphasis on the virtue of compassion.
2. George Lucas had made only two feature films before he directed *Star Wars.* Nevertheless *Star Wars* is one of the most successful films ever made.
3. I'm never sure how much to tip in a restaurant. Consequently I always feel nervous when it's time to pay the bill.
4. The attack on Pearl Harbor in 1941 created a huge demand for trained soldiers. Therefore the army sent photographers into combat to make training films.
5. This filming mission was a dangerous one. Consequently twenty-five percent of the photographers died in combat.

Review Exercise 1: Practice What You've Learned

Instructions: You have learned how to use commas in sentences with series and with introductory phrases and clauses. Using what you have learned, insert commas into the following sentences.

1. When the first Kentucky Derby was run in 1875 all except one of the jockeys were African-Americans.
2. However racism soon forced out the African-American jockeys.
3. I did well on my physics test although I didn't have time to answer all the questions.
4. For the most part college life is what I expected it to be.
5. Overall I miss my mother's cooking the most.
6. Even in its earliest years the Salvation Army encouraged women to become preachers.
7. If you try line dancing you'll probably like it as much as I do.

8. Nevertheless I think you should try square dancing first.
9. I never paid much attention to timepieces until Jeff gave me a Cinderella watch.
10. When he put it on my wrist I suddenly remembered that I'd wanted this watch as a child.

3. Use commas with coordinate conjunctions.

Coordinate conjunctions include the words *and, but, or, nor, for, so* and *yet*. Use a comma before the conjunction when one of these words combines two sentences:

> I have a frequent shopper card**,** but I don't go to the mall as often as I used to. EXAMPLE
>
> I budget more carefully now**,** and I use my spare time for studying instead of shopping. EXAMPLE
>
> I have a frequent shopper card but don't go to the mall as often as I used to. NO COMMA
>
> I budget more carefully now and use my spare time for studying instead of shopping. NO COMMA

Exercise 6: Use Commas with Coordinate Conjunctions

Instructions: Insert commas where needed into the following sentences. Remember to look for a complete sentence both before and after the coordinate conjunction.

1. My study hours are long but I set aside time to work out every afternoon.
2. I can't apply nail polish neatly so I have a manicure twice a month.
3. Renting a video is more convenient than going to a movie theater and often costs a lot less.
4. I often use a calculator to balance my checkbook but can also do the computations accurately with a pencil and paper.
5. Caron says she doesn't own a TV nor does she need one.
6. I'll sign up for the introduction to government course in the spring or take it over the summer.
7. My mother's dog growls at mail carriers and mine behaves the same way.
8. A weapon and a uniform used to be the only essential equipment for police officers but now laptop computers are often issued as well.
9. I can lend you my copy of *The Prophet* by Kahlil Gibran or you can borrow it from the library.
10. I had hoped my new planning calendar would turn my life around but no dramatic change has happened so far.

4. Use commas with quotation marks.

Use commas with direct quotations (a person's exact words). Commas and periods are placed inside quotation marks. If you're quoting a complete sentence, capitalize the first letter of the quotation. Study these examples:

A quotation at the end of a sentence:

> Norman Cousins said, "More and more, the choice for the world's peoples is between world warriors or world citizens."

An interrupted quotation:

> "Everybody is ignorant," said Will Rogers, "only on different subjects."

A sentence that begins with a quotation:

> "Bad officials are elected by good citizens who do not vote," said George Jean Nathan.

Exercise 7: Punctuating Quotations

Instructions: Insert commas, capital letters and quotation marks into the following sentences.

1. The time has come the Walrus said to talk of many things.
2. Linus Carl Pauling said science is the search for truth—it is not a game in which one tries to beat his opponent, to do harm to others.
3. Wisdom is knowing when you can't be wise said Paul Engle.
4. Samuel Taylor Coleridge said common sense in an uncommon degree is what the world calls wisdom.
5. Bernard Shaw said my method is to take the utmost trouble to find the right thing to say, and then to say it with the utmost levity.
6. Groucho Marx said military intelligence is a contradiction in terms.
7. In an address at Cooper Union in New York, Lincoln suggested that conservatism was adherence to the old and tried rather than the new and untried.
8. General Omar Bradley said ours is a world of nuclear giants and ethical infants.
9. John W. Gardner said one of the reasons mature people stop learning is that they become less and less willing to risk failure.
10. Everything should be made as simple as possible said Albert Einstein but not simpler.

5. Use commas with interrupters.

An *interrupter* is a group of words that break the normal flow of a sentence. When an interrupter appears in the middle of a sentence, it's attached with a comma in front and another at the back:

> Sonograms, popular with expectant parents who want to know their baby's sex, are no longer covered by most health insurance. EXAMPLE
>
> Sacagawea, a Native American woman, served as a guide when Lewis and Clark explored the Northwest Territory. EXAMPLE

When an interrupter is attached to the end of a sentence, only one comma is used:

> I've just learned the words to "Lift Every Voice and Sing," often called the "African-American national anthem." EXAMPLE

Do not use commas for essential information that belongs in a sentence and does not "interrupt" it:

> A cocker spaniel named Corky seized illegal substances worth over $18 million dollars for the United States Customs Service. EXAMPLE

[The dog's name is essential to the sentence; no commas are used.]

> Snacks high in cholesterol or salt increase the risk of disease. EXAMPLE

[The type of snack is essential information here.]

Use commas when you add descriptive words after the name of a person or place:

> Most Elvis Presley fans have heard of Colonel Tom Parker, *Elvis's manager.* EXAMPLE

> Few know that Parker, *who was never a colonel at all,* was once an illegal alien from Holland. EXAMPLE

> Children usually enjoy visiting Sagamore Hill, *the Long Island home of Theodore Roosevelt and his family.* EXAMPLE

Exercise 8: Use Commas with Interrupters

Instructions: Insert commas where needed.

1. Every major-league baseball team has a "closer" a relief pitcher who tries to strike out the last few batters in a game.
2. W. C. Fields whose movies still make audiences break into laughter was both a gifted comedian and a superb juggler.
3. The vacuum cleaner I used in college isn't powerful enough to clean my new shag carpeting.
4. Administrators should impose stiff penalties on teenagers who drive at top speed in school parking lots.
5. The Super Bowl which should be the most interesting football game of the year often becomes boring after the first quarter.
6. An English professor who teaches at the University of Pennsylvania believes that rap music can be an effective educational tool.
7. The microwave I desperately wanted five years ago sits on my kitchen counter unused.
8. Punctuality a quality I should cultivate does not come easily to me.
9. Pitcher Jim Abbott who has only one hand was named the top amateur athlete in the United States when he was a student.
10. Clock-watching an incurable habit of mine may cause problems in my career later on.

Exercise 9: Use Commas with Interrupters

Instructions: Insert commas where needed.

1. We all wore uniforms last year at Bishop Falwell High School.
2. However the wealthier students still managed to set themselves apart with gold jewelry and expensive watches.

3. Football kickers who usually train as soccer players spend most of the game sitting on the bench.

4. Since they use their feet to play however I think they have a right to be called "football players."

5. Perspiration leaves ugly stains on our living-room furniture which we bought only a month ago.

6. Consequently I'm not allowed to sit in the living room right after tennis practice.

7. Starting a small business a long-time dream of mine sometimes seems impossible.

8. I'm doing everything I can nevertheless to prepare for a business career.

9. I've been reading such books as *Growing a Business* and *A Passion for Excellence*.

10. I've been investigating in addition the business opportunities in my city.

6. Use commas to separate cities and states, to write dates, and to address a person directly.

a) Commas separating cities from states:

Ralph Waldo Emerson and Bronson Alcott lived in Concord, Massachusetts. EXAMPLE

Fairchild Tropical Garden is located in Coral Gables, Florida. EXAMPLE

b) Commas separating days from years:

Dr. Who, the world's longest-running science fiction show, was first broadcast in Great Britain on November 22, 1963. EXAMPLE

Donald Duck made his first appearance in the Sunday comics on December 16, 1934. EXAMPLE

Accused murderer Lizzie Borden was born on July 19, 1860. EXAMPLE

c) Commas with direct address:

"Direct address" means using a person's name when talking directly to him or her. Use a comma after the person's name.

"Lucy, you can't go into show business!" shouted Ricky. EXAMPLE

Use a comma in front and one in back if the name interrupts the sentence:

"I need the money, *Alice,* or I'll miss my big chance," said Ralph Kramden. EXAMPLE

Do not use commas if the name is not a direct address:

Fred Flintstone told Wilma that he was going bowling no matter what. EXAMPLE

Ricky struggled endlessly to keep Lucy out of show business. EXAMPLE

Exercise 10: Comma Practice with Dates, Places, and Direct Address

Instructions: Insert commas where needed in the following sentences.

1. Visitors to the Normandy coast in France still talk about the D-Day invasion of June 6 1944.

2. Mr. and Mrs. Borden were brutally murdered in Fall River Massachusetts on August 4 1892.

3. We're worried Andy because Barney's awful voice might spoil the spring concert for the whole town of Mayberry North Carolina.

4. Barney Fife used to spend his vacations at the YMCA in Raleigh North Carolina.

5. The *Andy Griffith Show* was first broadcast on October 3 1960.

6. Gail did you watch the first *Mr. Ed* show on January 5 1961?

7. Sybil and Basil Fawlty run a hotel in Torquay England.

8. Mary Martin flew across the television screen as Peter Pan for the first time on December 8 1960.

9. On November 1 1945 the first issue of *Ebony* was published.

10. "Hurry up Beaver before Mom starts asking questions," said Wally.

Review Exercise 2: Practice What You Have Learned

Instructions: Use all the rules in this chapter to insert commas where needed in the following sentences.

1. George Santayana said the wisest mind still has something yet to learn.

2. Opponents of abortion hope to overturn Roe vs. Wade the Supreme Court decision that legalized abortion in the United States.

3. Few ballet enthusiasts know that Rudolph Nureyev one of the great dancers of our time was the child of Muslim parents.

4. Students who park in a fire lane may not be able to find their cars when classes are over for the day.

5. I was wondering Bill what you would do if you couldn't watch reruns on cable.

6. My cousin is attending Gaullaudet University an institution of higher education for hearing-impaired students.

7. Barbara Harris an African-American priest was named the first female Episcopal bishop on January 19 1989.

8. The mambo bolero and West Coast swing are all favorites of professional ballroom dancers.

9. Genetic theory which I studied in biology doesn't help me understand why I'm so different from my parents.

10. My mother's high-school photos which depict her in saddle shoes and poodle skirts look hysterically funny today.

SUMMARY

1. Use commas in a series of three or more items.

2. Use commas with introductory clauses, phrases, and words.

3. Use commas with coordinate conjunctions.
4. Use commas with quotation marks.
5. Use commas with interrupters.
6. Use commas to separate cities and states, to write dates, and to address a person directly.

LOOKING AHEAD

In Chapter Twenty, "Using Semicolons and Colons Correctly," you'll practice writing and punctuating with these two punctuation marks.

CHAPTER TWENTY

Using Semicolons and Colons Correctly

Preview

Use a semicolon (;) when you want to combine two related sentences into a longer one. Use a colon (:) when a sentence is followed by explanatory information or ideas.

INTRODUCING THE SEMICOLON

Use a semicolon (;) instead of a period when you want to combine two sentences into one long one. Use a lower-case letter after the semicolon (unless it's a word that normally needs a capital letter, such as a person's name).

Here are two sentences ending with periods:

> Baking my own dog biscuits was supposed to save me a lot of money. After a year, however, I've saved very little.

Here they've been combined with a semicolon. Notice the lower-case *a* on *after:*

> Baking my own dog biscuits was supposed to save me a lot of money; after a year, however, I've saved very little. SEMICOLON SENTENCE

Here are two more examples:

> I need to do more to prepare for the future. Dr. Monahan described some of the challenges we will face later on. SENTENCES ENDING WITH PERIODS
>
> I need to do more to prepare for the future; Dr. Monahan described some of the challenges we will face later on. SENTENCES COMBINED WITH A SEMICOLON [Notice the capital *D* on Dr.]

Since you can always end a sentence with a period or question mark, semicolons are never required. But they're a useful option when you want to add sophistication to your writing. In the second sentence pair below, notice how the semicolon enhances the sentence:

When I watch old situation comedies, it's easy to see how Americans' values have changed. Characters in today's situation comedies no longer smoke the way Lucy and Desi once did. NO SEMICOLON

When I watch old situation comedies, it's easy to see how Americans' values have changed; characters in today's situation comedies no longer smoke the way Lucy and Desi once did. SEMICOLON

Exercise 1: Combine Sentences with Semicolons

Instructions: Use semicolons to combine the following sentence pairs. Be sure to use lower-case and capital letters correctly.

1. I used to love a party game that involved dropping clothespins into a milk bottle. However, clothespins and milk bottles have disappeared from most homes today.
2. The game of dominoes is popular with children. An imaginative child can also use dominoes to make fences and buildings.
3. Many Americans think Henry David Thoreau lived like a hermit at Walden Pond. The truth is that he went to his mother's home almost every day for lunch.
4. My friends insist that there's more to country music than trucks and broken hearts. Jeremy loves the wordplay in Dolly Parton's "Rocking Years."
5. Cody tells great stories about her job in a music store. She says sometimes it's hard to keep a straight face when customers hum or sing a song they want to buy.
6. Other jobs are unbearably boring. I spent hours wrapping silverware in napkins when I worked in a cafe last summer.
7. Sometimes I think home schooling is a great idea. At other times I think children should be in a classroom with their friends.
8. I've learned that children love to get mail. Consequently, I always send postcards to my best friend's two sons when I'm out of town.
9. Balloons aren't just for children anymore. Several businesses in town send balloons and flowers on special occasions.
10. I wish my fiance, Anna, didn't insist on having a dozen roses delivered on St. Valentine's Day. The price of roses always goes up on February 13.

INTRODUCING THE COLON

A colon (:) is used when a complete stop in a sentence is followed by explanatory information, such as an idea, a fact or a list of examples:

According to Frank M. Potter, Jr., "Environmental concerns are no longer the private preserve of the birdwatchers: The same bell tolls for us all." EXAMPLE

Compare the following pairs of sentences to see how the colon is used:

a) My dressing table no longer has room for all the products I need to do my nails, such as undercoat, nail polish, topcoat, drying agent, buffer, nail file, cuticle remover, polish remover, cotton, and manicure scissors. NO COLON

b) My dressing table no longer has room for all the products I need to do my nails: undercoat, nail polish, topcoat, drying agent, buffer, nail file, cuticle remover, polish remover, cotton, and manicure scissors. COLON

a) I've always thought that journalists have the perfect job: asking interesting questions of fascinating people. COLON

b) I always thought that journalists have the perfect job because they ask interesting questions of fascinating people. NO COLON

Usually a lower-case letter appears after a colon. When a colon is followed by a complete sentence, you may begin it with either a capital or a lower-case letter. (If your instructor has a preference, follow his or her instructions.) Notice that both sentences below are correct:

Here's a simple and low-cost way to quit smoking: Place dirty ashtrays all over your house, and display a drawing of a human lung next to each one. EXAMPLE

Here's a simple and low-cost way to quit smoking: place dirty ashtrays all over your house, and display a drawing of a human lung next to each one. EXAMPLE

Exercise 2: Use Colons in Sentences

Instructions: Use a colon as you rewrite each of the following sentences.

1. Libraries are much nicer than they used to be. I walked into the children's room last week and saw fifteen boys and girls laughing at a puppet show.

2. Houseplants offer many benefits. They remove impurities from the air, brighten a dreary room, and stimulate our nurturing instincts.

3. I was surprised when Nekkia took a job as a nanny, but now I understand. She's spending the summer in Europe, all expenses paid, with two delightful little girls.

4. I decided not to work with a personal trainer. I'm self-disciplined enough to improve my fitness level on my own.

5. Salad bars don't always offer low-calorie nutrition. Salt, fat, and sugar are found in many dressings and condiments.

SUMMARY

1. Use a semicolon when you want to combine two related sentences into one large sentence. Use a lower-case letter after the semicolon unless the word is normally capitalized.

2. Use a colon when a sentence is followed by explanatory information or ideas. If the follow-up is a complete sentence, you may begin it with a capital letter.

LOOKING AHEAD

In Chapter Twenty-One, "Using Apostrophes Correctly," you'll learn how to place apostrophes in contractions and in possessive words.

CHAPTER TWENTY-ONE

Using Apostrophes Correctly

Preview

Apostrophes have two important uses. They signal that letters have been omitted (haven't, o'clock), and they show possession (Mary's car, someone's book.)

APOSTROPHES THAT SIGNAL OMITTED LETTERS

Use apostrophes to show that letters have been omitted in contractions (two words run together and shortened). For example, *did not* becomes *didn't*. Study these examples:

> I *don't* enjoy movies much because *there's* so much talking during the main feature. EXAMPLE
>
> Recently, during an exhausting evening in the kitchen, I discovered that making home-made fudge *isn't* as much fun as I thought it was. EXAMPLE

The apostrophe replaces omitted letters:

$$do\ not = don\cancel{o}t = don't$$
$$is\ not = isn\cancel{o}t = isn't$$
$$it\ is = it\cancel{i}s = it's$$

Here are some of the most common contractions:

we're = we are	she's = she is
we'll = we will	he's = he is
they're = they are	wouldn't = would not
they've = they have	shouldn't = should not
they'll = they will	couldn't = could not
you're = you are	I've = I have
you've = you have	I'm = I am
doesn't = does not	don't = do not

Notice that *it's* is a contraction of *it is*. (The possessive form, *its,* does not have an apostrophe. See page 322 in Chapter Twenty-four to learn more about possessive pronouns like *its*.)

The omitted letters signaled by an apostrophe may not be obvious. The contraction *won't* stands for *will not,* and *twelve o'clock* means *twelve of clock.*

Exercise 1: Apostrophes in Contractions

Instructions: Insert apostrophes where they're needed in the following sentences.

1. The servers in this restaurant dont come around often enough with coffee refills.
2. On a busy day its not difficult to be so distracted that you lock your keys in your car.
3. Whats not easy is locking your keys in the car three times in a single day, as I did.
4. Im still not sure how I managed to do that.
5. Weve been talking about abstract art in my humanities class.
6. Yesterday several of us suddenly realized that abstract paintings dont mystify us anymore.
7. Because Mothers Against Drunk Driving has been so persistent, drinking and driving arent taken as lightly as they once were.
8. Two friends who are doing community service say theyre never going to drink and drive again.
9. Luis told me hes going to buy a face shield for his motorcycle helmet.
10. He learned that if he doesnt wear a face shield when it rains, the raindrops feel like stinging needles.

APOSTROPHES THAT SIGNAL POSSESSION

Use apostrophes to show possession (an "of" idea). Study these examples:

Mary's car is in the shop. EXAMPLE
I like Doris' way of explaining math concepts. EXAMPLE
A month's vacation would feel good right about now. EXAMPLE
Men's suits will be on sale until the end of the week. EXAMPLE

When you see an apostrophe in constructions like these, look for an "of" idea:

the car of Mary (Mary's car)
the way of Doris (Doris' way)
vacation of a month (a month's vacation)
suits of men (men's suits)

Because there is no "of" idea in the following sentence, no apostrophe is used.

The Powells gave me a ride home from the football game. NO APOSTROPHE

In possessive constructions, the "s" means *of*. It *does not* mean more than one.

Mary's car is in the shop. (Only one "Mary" owns the car.)

Exercise 2: Look for "Of" Ideas

Instructions: Put a check in front of each sentence containing an "of" idea, and underline the word or name that requires an apostrophe. Don't try to place the apostrophes yet.

_____ 1. I was touched when I found a "Get Well" card from the Browns in my mailbox.
_____ 2. Bettys brother is going to be my blind date this weekend.
_____ 3. Manufacturers should design womens shoes that are both comfortable and stylish.
_____ 4. I enjoyed Louis speech about ice hockey.
_____ 5. When my sisters toddler is visiting, I never seem to have a minutes peace.

Placing Apostrophes Correctly

When an apostrophe is needed in a possessive word, place it behind the last letter in the owner's name (or ownership word). Study these examples:

pay of a day = a day's pay
sleep of a night = a night's sleep
books of children = children's books
bottle of a baby = baby's bottle
toys of babies = babies' toys

When a name or word ends in *s*, and an "of" idea is present, place the apostrophe after the *s*, as in these examples:

cat of Dennis = Dennis' cat
car of the boss = the boss' car
office of Miss Jones = Miss Jones' office

When a possessive word or name ends in *s*, as these do, you may add an additional *s* at the end if you wish:

Dennis's cat
the boss's car
Miss Jones's office

Three "special" plurals require special attention. Fortunately they are easy to memorize:

men's women's children's

When you use an apostrophe with these words, place it *before* the *s*. This rule also applies to "grandchildren" and "stepchildren":

I enjoyed my grandchildren's visit last week. EXAMPLE

Remember to omit the apostrophe when no "of" idea is present:

The puppies are up to date on their vaccinations. NO APOSTROPHE
I invited the Townleys for dinner on Friday night. NO APOSTROPHE

Exercise 3: Practice Inserting Apostrophes

Instructions: These are the same sentences you saw in Exercise 2. Insert apostrophes where needed.

1. I was touched when I found a "Get Well" card from the Browns in my mailbox.
2. Bettys brother is going to be my blind date this weekend.
3. Manufacturers should design womens shoes that are both comfortable and stylish.
4. I enjoyed Louis speech about ice hockey.
5. When my sisters children are visiting, I never seem to have a minutes peace.

Exercise 4: Insert Apostrophes

Instructions: Insert apostrophes where needed in these sentences.

1. Hank Aaron broke Babe Ruths home run record on April 8, 1974.
2. Although many baseball fans were thrilled by Aarons achievement, others wish Babe Ruths record had continued to stand.
3. Few sounds irritate me the way childrens whining does.
4. Whining adults infuriate me even more.
5. When I was little, the tire swing in my familys back yard was one of my favorite playthings.
6. After the Johnsons divorce, they set up a joint custody agreement that seems to be working well.
7. They don't want their childrens lives to be disrupted by the divorce.
8. Elvis Presleys backup group, the Jordanaires, deserves part of the credit for his success.
9. Will kitchens in the next century be equipped with vending machines rather than appliances?
10. For me, winters biggest headache is getting my car started on subzero mornings.
11. Both families vacations were cut short by emergencies.

12. At graduation, one students mortarboard carried a grateful message: "Thanks, Mom and Dad!"

13. County libraries budgets were increased again this year.

14. A few teachers requests for new computer software had to be delayed.

15. Did you know that Dionne Warwick is Whitney Houstons cousin?

Review Exercise: Practice What You Have Learned

Instructions: Insert apostrophes where needed in the sentences below.

1. Malls are popular gathering places in many communities because theyre safe, clean, and interesting.

2. The mall in my town serves free coffee to mall walkers who dont mind getting up early for their daily exercise.

3. I wont be joining the mall walkers for a while because I like the colleges jogging track.

4. No matter how you choose to exercise, its important to persist until you get the benefits youve been working for.

5. My grandchildrens school encourages fitness by sponsoring noncompetitive track meets four times a year.

6. The Thompsons commuter marriage seems to be working well although Ben and Arlene work in different cities.

7. My mothers vintage Chevy convertible may be cute, but it isnt very comfortable on cold or windy days.

8. Since I first tried on a pair of black canvas hightops two years ago, Ive refused to wear any other shoes for sports or recreation.

9. Our communitys after-school program provides security, academic assistance, and recreation for boys and girls in grades one through eight.

10. Im impressed that Kathys thank-you notes arrived only two weeks after her graduation.

SUMMARY

1. Apostrophes indicate that one or more letters have been omitted in contractions such as I'm, can't, and wouldn't.

2. Apostrophes are used with the letter *s* to indicate possession: Mary's book, an hour's delay, the puppies' toys.

LOOKING AHEAD

In Part Five, "Avoiding Common Errors," you'll learn how to identify and correct errors in verbs, word choice, and pronouns.

PART FIVE

Avoiding Common Errors

CHAPTER TWENTY-TWO

Using Verbs Correctly

Preview

1. Verbs are words that show action (such as *go, work, think,* and *hurry*) and existence (such as *am, is,* and *was*).
2. The effective use of verbs adds vitality and interest to your writing.
3. It's important to be able to use verb forms correctly, both in writing and speaking. Listeners and readers may quickly notice whether you use *do* and *does, went* and *gone, is* and *are,* and other verbs correctly.

PRESENT TENSE VERB FORMS

Present tense verbs are used for actions that are happening now or that happen regularly. Use an *s* ending when one person or thing is the subject of the sentence. Do not add the *s* ending when the subject is *I, you,* or a plural person or thing. Study these examples:

Algebra is difficult for me.

I always enjoy my weekends at the beach.

Dale loses his temper easily.

Lisa and Carl teach scuba diving.

You inspire me with your enthusiasm about learning.

We work the same shift at the hospital.

The technicians eat dinner with us almost every evening.

They have a demanding job.

Exercise 1: Use Verbs Correctly

Instructions: Choose the correct form of the verb in each sentence.

1. Sometimes my dog (eat, eats) my homework.
2. My wife always (change, changes) the radio station in the bathroom.
3. I (change, changes) it right back.

4. My mother and her friends (exercise, exercises) to music from the fifties.
5. You (seem, seems) unusually happy today.
6. My grandfather (make, makes) coffee the old-fashioned way, with eggshells.
7. He never (tell, tells) anyone the purpose of the eggshells.
8. I secretly (buy, buys) myself a chocolate bunny every spring.
9. My health-minded parents (is, are) against candy.
10. You (understand, understands) the appeal of chocolate, though.

Exercise 2: More Practice with Verb Endings

Instructions: Choose the correct form of the verb in each sentence.

1. Some men (thinks, think) that wives (is, are) replacement mothers.
2. Successful people (operates, operate) on a long-range plan.
3. Many people (thinks, think) that on-the-job drug testing (is, are) an invasion of privacy.
4. Linda and David (doesn't, don't) know whether they (wants, want) children.
5. A student (needs, need) a big block of time to write a draft of my research project.
6. My grandmother (cries, cry) at every family wedding.
7. We (wants, want) to form a chapter of Students Against Drunk Driving here on campus.
8. I (feels, feel) angry when I (hears, hear) about the destruction of the rain forests.
9. You (seem, seems) doubtful about that blind date.
10. Ricky (fall, falls) in love every other week.

Exercise 3: Insert the Correct Verb

Instructions: The subjects are missing from the following sentences. Insert names or suitable words in the spaces provided.

1. _____ watch *Dirty Dancing* again every time it's on television.
2. _____ wants to do a mambo like Patrick Swayze's.
3. _____ teaches Latin dancing.
4. _____ enjoy teaching the children in our family the stroll and the shag.
5. _____ avoids parties with live bands and dancing.
6. _____ consider dancing a safe and enjoyable form of exercise.
7. _____ tries to imitate John Travolta in *Saturday Night Fever*.
8. _____ like to watch Fred Astaire and Ginger Rogers on the dance floor.
9. _____ thinks the frug is still a terrific dance.
10. _____ prefers to sit and watch.

Adding the *S* Ending

Some verbs require extra care because the *s* ending is often overlooked in writing and speech: *lifts, costs, asks, trusts,* and similar verbs. Read the following examples aloud, being careful to pronounce the final *s:*

> Oprah Winfrey <u>hosts</u> a popular talk show. EXAMPLE
>
> The final examination <u>tests</u> your understanding of photosynthesis. EXAMPLE

Exercise 4: Choose the Correct Verb

Instructions: Choose the correct form of the verb for the sentences below:

1. The program guide (lists, list) all the movies on Home Box Office this month.
2. Because metal (rusts, rust) so quickly, regular maintenance (is, are) important.
3. My brother and his wife (fasts, fast) once a month.
4. I'm going to invest in this stock because I (trusts, trust) your judgment.
5. The attorney (rests, rest) her case.
6. After a visit to my uncle's bakery, we (feasts, feast) on fancy breads, pies, and cookies.
7. Several purple martins (nests, nest) there every spring.
8. Officer Kraft (dusts, dust) for fingerprints with this kit.
9. You always (asks, ask) difficult questions, but I (enjoys, enjoy) trying to answer them.
10. Barbara's plants (looks, look) beautiful because she (mists, mist) them every day.

USING VERBS WITH *HERE* AND *THERE*

Here and *there* often appear at the beginning of a sentence, but they never function as subjects. In the following sentences, the subjects are underlined:

> Here comes <u>the bride</u>. EXAMPLE
>
> There are <u>your photocopies</u>. EXAMPLE
>
> There is <u>a problem</u> with this equipment. EXAMPLE

The subject in these sentences always appears *after* the verb. You can find the correct verb by reversing the word order:

> Here ***come*** the football players.
> (The football players ***come*** here.)
> Here ***comes*** the bride.
> (The bride ***comes*** here.)
> There ***are*** your photocopies.
> (Your photocopies ***are*** there.)

There *is* a problem with this equipment.

(A problem with this equipment *is* there.)

Exercise 5: Choose the Correct Verb

Instructions: Underline the correct verb in parentheses.

1. There (is, are) three important formulas in the next unit of your algebra text.
2. Here (is, are) the scuba-diving equipment you ordered.
3. There (stands, stand) the woman who inspired me to come to college.
4. Here (comes, come) the train.
5. There (goes, go) our chance to win the championship.
6. Here (lies, lie) many heroes from the invasion of Normandy on June 6, 1941.
7. There (hangs, hang) an unusual painting by Rembrandt.
8. Here (is, are) the letters that Keith sent me before we broke up.
9. There (speaks, speak) a man who understands the pressures of college life.
10. Here (comes, come) a new problem for us to solve.

CHOOSE EFFECTIVE VERBS

Many writers overuse *There is* and *There are*. Try to vary your sentences. Whenever possible, substitute an action (such as *dance, work, think, solve*) for *is* and *are*. Compare the following sentence pairs:

There are several excellent examples in your paper. WEAK
You included several excellent examples in your paper. BETTER

There are two reasons why Larry's photograph won first prize. WEAK
Larry's photograph won first prize for two reasons. BETTER

There is a delicious recipe for curried rice in this magazine. WEAK
I found a delicious recipe for curried rice in this magazine. BETTER

Exercise 6: Choose Effective Verbs

Instructions: Choose either *is* or *are* in the sentences below. Then rewrite each sentence so that it doesn't begin with *There is* or *There are*. Be as creative as you wish. The first sentence is done for you.

1. There (*is, are*) a problem with my new Honda.
   I'm having trouble shifting into third gear with my new Honda.
2. There (*is, are*) several changes needed in this insurance policy.

_____.

3. There (*is, are*) three errors in the letter that Kay typed.

   _____.

4. There (*is, are*) five students waiting to talk to Professor Riley.

   _____.

5. There (*is, are*) an important task for us to do.

   _____.

VERBS AND PREPOSITIONAL PHRASES

Be especially careful when a verb is preceded by a prepositional phrase. Prepositions are words (usually small ones) that indicate direction or purpose: *by, for, to, on, under, of, with, in,* and similar words. A word-group starting with a preposition is called a *prepostional phrase* (which usually ends in a noun: *in the kitchen, to Dairy Queen*).

Since a prepositional phrase can never be the subject of a sentence, you must always look for the subject elsewhere and make it match your verb. In the following examples, the prepositional phrase is underlined:

> Thirty students from the graduating class are planning medical careers. EXAMPLE
> One of the eggs is broken. EXAMPLE
> The prices in that advertisement are valid until Thursday. EXAMPLE

Here are the same examples with the subjects and verbs underlined:

> Thirty students from the graduating class are planning medical careers. EXAMPLE
> One of the eggs is broken. EXAMPLE
> The prices in that advertisement are valid until Thursday. EXAMPLE

Exercise 7: Choose the Correct Verb

Instructions: Choose the correct verb in the sentences below.

1. The use of slide rules and calculators (is, are) permitted on some college tests.
2. The services provided by this agency (does, do) not meet state requirements.
3. Errors in punctuation (lowers, lower) your final grade.
4. Motorcyclists without head protection (endangers, endanger) the lives of others.
5. A mailbag full of letters for Don Johnson (arrives, arrive) here every morning.
6. That plant with three shiny leaves (looks, look) like poison ivy.
7. The papers for Dr. Curtis (is, are) ready to be picked up.
8. A panel of experts about spouse abuse (is, are) scheduled to speak here tonight.
9. Airfare to many European cities (costs, cost) more now.

10. The officers of our computer club (supports, support) this policy.
11. Interest in the roots of rock and roll music (is, are) increasing.
12. Disregard for people's feelings (is, are) the sign of immaturity.
13. Enthusiasm for the Smurfs (disappears, disappear) when children enter junior high.
14. Wishing for happiness and prosperity (isn't, aren't) enough.
15. Excellence in business (is, are) rare, according to Tom Peters.

Choosing Specific Verbs

In each of the following pairs, the second sentence is more interesting than the first because it tells specifically what the person *does*.

> Greg is friendly.
> Greg smiles at everyone he sees.

> Ellen is independent.
> Ellen pays all her own college expenses.

> Diane is compassionate.
> Diane volunteers at Meadowbrook Hospital on weekends.

The words *friendly, independent,* and *compassionate* are adjectives. To make words like these come to life, write sentences with *active* verbs—*smiles, pays, volunteers. (Is* and *are,* as you saw on page 303, are *existence* verbs.)

Verb choices are important to both college and professional writing. In college, well-chosen, specific verbs bring clarity and interest to your writing. Business supervisors and managers often use active verbs to write evaluations of their employees. It's not enough to describe a person as *creative, responsible, incompetent,* or *dishonest.* Specific examples are necessary:

> Barbara Jones is responsible. WEAK
> Barbara Jones *manages* a ten-thousand-dollar equipment account. BETTER

> Calvin Thompson is creative. WEAK
> Calvin Thompson's "Employee of the Month" idea *increased* productivity and company loyalty. BETTER

> Dennis Frasch is incompetent. WEAK
> Dennis Frasch *embarrasses* customers who try to return defective merchandise. BETTER

> Faye Oliver is dishonest. WEAK
> Faye Oliver *takes* credit for work completed by other employees. BETTER

As you revise your own writing, look for opportunities to bring adjectives to life with active verbs.

Exercise 8: Write Effective Sentences

Instructions: Read each sentence below, choosing the correct verb. Then write a second sentence showing a specific, appropriate action. The first one is already done for you.

1. Paul McCartney (*is,* are) concerned about animal welfare.
   Paul McCartney is a member of People for the Ethical Treatment of Animals.

2. Gloria Estefan (*is, are*) a talented performer.
   _____.

3. Diane Simmonds (*is, are*) an efficient office manager.
   _____.

4. Ken Duran and Sally Jones, our customer service representatives, (*is, are*) helpful.
   _____.

5. Carole Chan, the head teller, (*is, are*) trustworthy.
   _____.

6. Experimenting with drugs (*is, are*) dangerous.
   _____.

7. My college courses (*is, are*) challenging.
   _____.

8. Ken Griffey Jr. and Andre Agassi (*is, are*) superb athletes.
   _____.

9. Watching television (*is, are*) relaxing.
   _____.

10. Housework (*is, are*) tiring.
    _____.

Exercise 9: Write Sentences of Your Own

Instructions: Write five sentence pairs of your own, similar to those in Exercise 7. Make your first statement general, using *is* or *are* as your verb. Make your second sentence specific. The following suggested topics may help you get started:

sports	popular music	a close friend
your favorite college subject	fast-food restaurant	entertainer

CHOOSE CORRECT VERB FORMS

Many people mistakenly use nonstandard verb forms: *gone* instead of *went* with a "helping" verb, for example. Study these examples:

Bill <u>has went</u> with Sharon to the movie. INCORRECT (*Has* is a helping verb that must be used with *gone*, not *went*.)

Bill <u>has gone</u> with Sharon to the movie. CORRECT.

Here are three sentences with mistakes in the past tense of the verb:

James <u>done did</u> his math homework already. INCORRECT

(Correct version: James <u>did</u> his math homework already.)

The Johnsons <u>have went</u> to every Super Bowl game since 1987. INCORRECT

(Correct version: The Johnsons <u>have gone</u> to every Super Bowl game since 1987.)

I <u>seen</u> Aunt Mary at the mall this morning. INCORRECT

(Correct version: I <u>saw</u> Aunt Mary at the mall this morning.)

Whenever you're doubtful about the past tense of a verb, check the dictionary. The second part listed is used by itself; the third part must be used with a helper (*am, is, are, was, were, be, have, has, had*). For example, the dictionary lists three parts for the verb go: *go, went, gone*. Use *went* by itself, and use *gone* with a helper.

We <u>went</u> to Atlanta for the Summer Olympics in 1996. CORRECT

My father <u>has gone</u> to the Summer Olympic games for over twenty years. CORRECT

We <u>saw</u> a good science-fiction movie last week. CORRECT

I <u>have seen</u> *Star Wars* twelve times. CORRECT (*"Have" is a helping verb.*)

When you're doubtful about the correct form of a verb, check the dictionary. For example, *sneaked* (not *snuck*) is the correct past tense of *sneak*. And *brought* (not *brang*) is the correct past tense of *bring*.

Exercise 10: Choose the Correct Verb Form

Instructions: Insert the correct verb form into the blank spaces in these sentences. The verbs to be used appear in capitals at the end of each sentence. Refer to the dictionary if necessary.

1. The music of Scott Joplin, which _____ composed at the turn of the century, _____ still popular today. BE

2. When Terri and Joshua first _____ three years ago, they _____ not expect to fall in love. MEET, DO

3. Last year, every morning after I _____ breakfast, I _____ twenty minutes on my tracking machine. EAT, SPEND

4. I have _____ curry in several restaurants, and I like the Thai version best. EAT

5. Joni has _____ out three pairs of designer jeans already this year. WEAR

6. She _____ them to every class and campus event. WEAR

7. I _____ to be serious about school this year because I hadn't _____ appropriate academic courses in high school. BEGIN, TAKE

8. My son has _____ me crazy all week asking what he's getting for his birthday. DRIVE

9. Louise _____ in the outfield after she had _____ the fly ball. FALL, CATCH

10. Dale _____ hands with everyone at the meeting, so she was _____ when someone complained that she was unfriendly. SHAKE, SHAKE

Review Exercise: Practice What You Have Learned

Instructions: Insert the correct verb into each sentence.

1. I haven't yet _____ any results from my new fitness program. SEE

2. Today, for a change, Andy _____ happier with his grade in chemistry than I _____. BE, BE

3. After Cory _____ to see his professor a few times, he _____ better in his math course. GO, DO

4. The college course schedule _____ only two sections of intermediate algebra. LIST

5. The college _____ a big softball tournament every spring. HOST

6. Sally always _____ well under pressure. DO

7. Every year Coach Brock _____ the entire volleyball team at a banquet. HONOR

8. Brenda _____ so well because she has _____ with an award-winning chorus since she _____ eleven. SING, SING, BE

9. I _____ into the gym late last night to watch my friends practice for the cheerleading tryouts. SNEAK

10. Wesley _____ college would be easy, but a few bad experiences this semester have _____ him otherwise. THINK, TEACH

SUMMARY

1. Verbs are words that show action and existence.
2. Effective verbs add vitality and interest to your writing.
3. It's important to be able to use verb forms correctly, both in writing and speaking.

LOOKING AHEAD

In Chapter Twenty-Three, "Choosing the Right Word," you'll take a close look at words that are often confused and misused.

Choosing the Right Word

Preview

The English language has many words that look or sound alike. It also contains words and expressions that people often use incorrectly.

WORDS OFTEN CONFUSED

Many words in English look or sound alike and must be used with caution. Review this list to see which words are likely to create problems for you. Write the words and their meanings on index cards to study, or keep a list in a notebook to refer to when you're writing a paper. Use the dictionary for more information if needed.

accept—to receive
except—but

affect—to change
effect—a change; to cause

all together—in a group
altogether—completely

brake—to stop a car; the stopping mechanism in a car
break—to interrupt; an interruption

capital—first-rate; money owed or invested; the town, city or district where governing is conducted
capitol—a building where legislative bodies meet

cite—to quote, point out
sight—vision
site—location

coarse—rough
course—program of study; path; the expression "of course"

complement—complete or accent
compliment—praise

die—to end life
dye—agent to change color; act of coloring

fair—just; outdoor festival
fare—transportation expense

forth—ahead
fourth—number four

hear—to listen
here—in this place

hole—opening
whole—entire

hour—sixty minutes
our—belonging to us

its—belonging to it
it's—contraction of *it is*

know—to have information
no—negative

maybe—perhaps
may be—might be

meat—animal product
meet—to encounter; a competition

passed—went beyond; completed a course of study
past—before

patience—willingness to wait
patients—persons under medical care

peace—harmony
piece—portion

plain—without decoration; flat, grassy area
plane—vehicle that flies; flat surface in geometry

presence—being here
presents—gifts

principal—amount owed on a loan; head of a school; important
principle—rule

stationary—not moving
stationery—paper

steal—to rob
steel—metal

than—comparison
then—time

their—belonging to them
there—place
they're—contraction of *they are*

threw—past tense of throw
through—between

to—preposition indicating direction or purpose
too—excessive; also
two—the number

who's—contraction of *who is*
whose—possessive of who

your—belonging to you
you're—contraction of *you are*

Exercise 1: Choose the Correct Word

Instructions: Choose the correct word from each pair in parentheses.

1. If (you're, your) one of the people who want a world at (piece, peace), you should work for social justice.
2. (It's, Its) not enough to have good intentions: action is important (to, too, two).
3. (Their, There, They're) are many people who are willing to get involved when (their, there, they're) asked to help.
4. My world history (course, coarse) has made me see that (their, there, they're) are (no, know) easy answers.
5. I learned not to (steal, steel) when I was very small and tried to take a candy bar without paying for it.
6. The change from high school to college can (affect, effect) a student in many ways.
7. Many athletes who aren't asthma (patience, patients) say asthma medicine helps them in competitive events.

8. But some observers think healthy athletes use the asthma medication more (than, then) they should.

9. The business my mother started two years ago has doubled (it's, its) profits in the (passed, past) three years.

10. My father often (compliments, complements) her on her business achievements.

ADDITIONAL WORDS TO STUDY

Here are more words that look or sound alike. Review the meanings of these words and practice pronouncing them, using a dictionary if necessary.

advice—recommendation
advise—to recommend

breath—intake of air
breathe—to inhale and exhale air

choose—to select
chose—past tense of choose

clothes—apparel
cloths—pieces of fabric

conscience—inner sense of right and wrong
conscious—aware

desert—to abandon; sandy, barren area
dessert—sweet dish at the end of a meal

formally—politely, properly
formerly—previous

lose—to misplace
loose—not snug

quiet—silent
quite—very

sense—feeling
since—because; time indicator

though—but
thought—idea

thorough—complete
threw—past tense of throw

weather—climatic condition
whether—if

wear—to don clothing
were—past tense of are
where—indicates a place

which—introduces a description
witch—evil female magician

Exercise 2: Choose the Correct Word

Instructions: Choose the correct word from each pair in parentheses.

1. When I first came to college, I used to (lose, loose) my way at least twice a week.
2. Now that many people own computers, privacy issues have become (quiet, quite) important.
3. Every year some parents (desert, dessert) their children.
4. Dr. Robert Coles is a psychologist who is interested in the way children develop a (conscience, conscious) that helps them make moral decisions.
5. New (clothes, cloths) and a new image are part of the fun of college.
6. The ancient wisdom of yoga teaches how to (breath, breathe) in ways that reduce stress.
7. I like any kind of (desert, dessert) as long as it's made of chocolate.
8. Many physicians wonder (weather, whether) the United States will eventually adopt socialized medicine.
9. I mistakenly (though, thought, thorough) choosing a major would be easy once I started college.
10. I've been (threw, through) many kinds of career testing but still haven't made up my mind.

WORDS OFTEN MISUSED

Many words and expressions in English are commonly misspelled or used incorrectly.

a) The phrases *used to* and *supposed to* usually end in *d.*

   I was supposed to meet Millie at six, but my car broke down. CORRECT

   When we lived in Orlando, we used to go to Disney World often on weekends. CORRECT

b) *All right* and *a lot* are often misspelled. In the United States they must be written as two words. (In the British Isles, *all right* is often written as one word, and you may see it that way in books. But in the United States, the one-word spelling is not acceptable.)

c) Avoid awkward or unnecessary words and phrases.

"Only" is often misplaced. Position it next to the word it describes:

Janelle <u>only</u> has three college credits so far. INCORRECT

Janelle has <u>only</u> three college credits so far. CORRECT

Notice how the meaning of a sentence can change as the position of "only" changes:

I <u>only</u> work here. (Implied: I don't have any management responsibility.)

I work <u>only</u> here. (Implied: I don't have another job.)

Avoid ending sentences with *at*:

I don't know where she's <u>at</u>. AWKWARD

I don't know where she is. BETTER

Where are your books <u>at</u>? AWKWARD

Where are your books? BETTER

Substitute "couldn't care less" for "could care less" in sentences like these:

Glen didn't invite me to his party, but I could care less. AWKWARD

Glen didn't invite me to his party, but I couldn't care less. BETTER

When possible, omit "couldn't care less," which is overused, and choose other words:

I'm not angry that Glen didn't invite me to his party. IMPROVED

Avoid double negatives like *don't have none* and *couldn't hardly*:

The chorus didn't have hardly any members after the first rehearsal, so Mr. Werner asked us to recruit our friends. INCORRECT

The chorus had hardly any members after the first rehearsal, so Mr. Werner asked us to recruit our friends. CORRECT

I'd be glad to lend you some cash, but I don't have none with me. INCORRECT

I'd be glad to lend you some cash, but I don't have any with me. CORRECT

Exercise 3: Correct the Errors

Instructions: Cross out and correct the errors in the sentences below.

1. I didn't have hardly any understanding of psychology when I came to college, but now it's my favorite subject.

2. Can you tell me where the Student Service Center is at?

3. I only have enough money to buy my holiday gifts at the thrift store.

4. I use to think I couldn't learn math, but now I know better.

5. Calvin is suppose to call me after basketball practice is over.

6. You'd better wash the dishes because we don't have no clean ones for dinner.

7. I managed to water all the plants without scarcely wetting any of the carpet.

8. Dale said he only missed a few questions on his exam.

9. I don't have a date for tomorrow's dance, and I could care less about it.

10. Please take this document to where the notary is at.

Review Exercise 1: Practice What You Have Learned

Instructions: Choose the correct words from the pairs in parentheses.

1. Everyone in class (accept, except) me seems to (know, no) more about chemistry (than, then) I do.
2. (Maybe, May be) a tutor (whose, who's) blessed with (patience, patients) can give me the help I need.
3. Sometimes I'm (to, too, two) embarrassed to ask questions in class.
4. My friends tell me they went (threw, through) college chemistry successfully, and I can be successful (to, too, two).
5. If I (passed, past) chemistry with a C, I would (accept, except) their (complements, compliments) gratefully.
6. I understand the (principals, principles) well, but I'm not (all together, altogether) sure how to do the math problems.
7. Can you (advice, advise) me (wear, where) to find a tutor (who's, whose) effective with students like me?
8. (Since, Sense) chemistry is difficult for me, I need a (through, thorough) review of some basic concepts.
9. I don't want to (lose, loose) my chance at graduating with honors.
10. If I succeed with chemistry, I'm (quiet, quite) sure I'll have a good grade-point average.

Review Exercise 2: Practice What You Have Learned

Instructions: Correct any errors in the sentences below.

1. I had know trouble learning the definitions for today's sociology assignment.
2. Where suppose to memorize more then twenty definitions for next week's quiz.
3. Its been a long time sense I've had to learn anything so difficult.
4. I use to have trouble because my study skills where so poor.
5. Gail only scored seventy-one on the test this passed week.
6. I didn't have hardly any difficulty scoring a ninety.

    7. French verbs is were my problems are at.

    8. I only memorized half the verb in the forth chapter.

    9. Were suppose to no them all by Monday.

  10. Altogether their are fifty verbs to memorize.

SUMMARY

It's important to recognize words and expressions that are often confused and misused. Referring to a dictionary during the proofreading step of the writing process can help you avoid word-choice errors.

LOOKING AHEAD

In Chapter Twenty-four, you will practice using pronouns (words like *he, I, you,* and *they* that take the place of nouns).

CHAPTER TWENTY-FOUR

Using Pronouns Correctly

Preview

1. Pronouns are words such as *he, she, I,* and *you* that take the place of nouns.
2. The "thumb rule" often is helpful in choosing the correct form of a pronoun.
3. Possessive pronouns such as *his, hers,* and *yours* never have apostrophes.
4. Care is needed to avoid sexism when using pronouns.

INTRODUCING PRONOUNS

Pronouns are words such as *I, he, you,* and *they* that take the place of nouns. It's easier to write, "Cinderella lost *her* glass slipper on the stairs," instead of "Cinderella lost Cinderella's glass slipper on the stairs." The word that a pronoun refers to is called its "antecedent." In the example above, *Cinderella* is the antecedent of *her.*

Pronoun usage in academic and professional English is stricter than in everyday speech. This unit will help you review the most important rules.

THE "THUMB RULE"

In academic and professional writing, you must be careful to use the pronouns *I* and *me* correctly. Try choosing the correct pronoun in these examples:

The Spice Girls' latest album surprised Linda and (I, me).
My brother and (I, me) replaced our cassettes with compact disks.
The Spice Girls' latest album surprised Linda and **me.** CORRECT
My brother and **I** replaced our cassettes with compact disks. CORRECT

The "thumb rule" is an easy and effective aid for choosing the correct pronoun in sentences like these. Find the *and* phrase in the sentence and cover it with your thumb. Then read the sentence without the *and* phrase and choose the correct pronoun.

The Spice Girls' latest album surprised ~~Linda and~~ (I, me).

The Spice Girls' latest album surprised Linda and **me.** CORRECT

~~My brother and~~ (I, me) replaced our cassettes with compact disks.

My brother and **I** replaced our cassettes with compact disks. CORRECT

You can apply the "thumb rule" in any sentences that have an "and" phrase followed by a pronoun. Study these examples:

Larry and (she, her) did an excellent presentation about the greenhouse effect for our biology class.

~~Larry and~~ (she, her) did an excellent presentation about the greenhouse effect for our biology class.

Larry and **she** did an excellent presentation about the greenhouse effect for our biology class. CORRECT

Exercise 1: Apply the "Thumb Rule"

Instructions: Underline the correct pronoun in the sentences below.

1. Susan and (I, me) often buy designer jeans.
2. But sometimes the labels confuse Susan and (I, me).
3. Donald says that his wife Anne and (he, him) have the same problem.
4. Donald and (she, her) find that the size marked on the label can be misleading.
5. Although Anne and (I, me) both wear size ten jeans, some brands and styles don't fit us.
6. Donald says that Anne and (he, him) have the same philosophy about jeans.
7. Designer jeans are all right for their teen-aged son and (they, them), but their six-year-old wears store brands.
8. Susan and (I, me) agree.
9. Our husbands and (we, us) budget our money carefully.
10. My friend Carl, who has five children, always buys store brands for himself and (they, them).

POSSESSIVE PRONOUNS

Pronouns that show possession, such as *his, hers, ours, yours, theirs, mine,* and *its,* never have apostrophes. Study the following examples:

The medical school has <u>its</u> own library, parking lot, and security system.

<u>Ours</u> is the best college volleyball team in the state.

I want my hook shot to be as accurate as <u>hers</u>.

My family, like <u>yours</u>, loves to celebrate holidays.

Exercise 2: Possessive Pronouns

Instructions: Choose the correct pronoun in each sentence from this list: *his, hers, theirs, yours, ours, its.* Remember that apostrophes never appear in possessive pronouns.

1. Caroline was sitting here a minute ago, so these books are probably _____.
2. The company doubled _____ profits this year.
3. If I bring my canoe on Saturday, and you bring _____, we'll have room for every-one.
4. Ben is angry because Julie forgot _____ birthday.
5. We're hoping _____ will be the best dance routine in the competition.
6. I'm supposed to pick up my parents' luggage, but I'm not sure which bags are _____.

PRONOUN AGREEMENT

A pronoun must "agree" with its antecedent. This means that singular pronouns should be used with singular words, and plural pronouns should be used with plural words. Study these examples:

> The teacher gave each mother a photograph of *her* child.
> The students handed in *their* research papers yesterday.
> Every football player invited *his* parents to the banquet.

The first example uses the pronoun *her* because the antecedent "mother" is singular. In the second example, *their* is correct because the antecedent "students" is plural. "Football player" in the third example is singular; therefore *his* is correct.

Because the following words are singular, use them with a singular pronoun (*he, she, it, his, her, its*):

every	everyone	everybody	someone	no one
somebody	each	anyone	anybody	another
nobody	either	neither	one	

Study these examples:

> Somebody left *his* face mask in the men's locker room.
> Another father told me about *his* children's problems this morning.

Plural pronouns (*we, they, our, their, ours, theirs*) should be used only with plural words.

Study these examples:

All of the boxers are preparing for *their* next bouts.

Many directors say *they* like the challenge of working with modern drama.

Exercise 3: Pronoun Agreement

Instructions: Underline the correct pronoun in each sentence.

1. Every ballerina was fitted for (*her, their*) costume this morning.
2. Many dancers had trouble keeping (*his, their*) balance on the slippery dance floor.
3. Each hockey player bought a corsage for (*his, their*) date to wear to the awards banquet.
4. Every young actress says that (*she, they*) yearns to play the role of Juliet in Shakespeare's play.
5. Several professors invite guest speakers to (*her, their*) classes.
6. All the nuns who teach at my sister's college say that (*she, they*) have seen many changes in religious life.
7. My uncles enjoy sharing (*his, their*) memories of growing up on my grandparents' farm.
8. Every rooster crows when (*he, they*) sees the sun coming up.
9. Each of the Girl Scouts proudly wore (*her, their*) uniform to the ceremony.
10. Many coaches monitor (*his, their*) athletes' academic performance closely.

AVOIDING SEXISM WITH PRONOUNS

"Sexism" is a language error that involves using masculine words to refer to both sexes. The following sentence is an example of sexist language:

Many policemen use laptop computers to write their reports. SEXIST

This non-sexist version is better:

Many police officers use laptop computers to write their reports. BETTER

When a sentence is about a man, it is correct to use masculine pronouns:

John bought *his* daughter a slice of pizza. CORRECT

But when a sentence could be about either men or women, or both, choose nonsexist language. For example, the words *firefighter* and *server* are better than the sexist words *fireman* and *waitress*. And you should avoid using *his* and *he* when a sentence might refer to both men and women:

Every student should ensure that *he* has allowed enough time to complete his research assignment. SEXIST

Every student should ensure that *he or she* has allowed enough time to complete his or her research assignment. BETTER

Writers use several techniques to avoid sexism with pronouns. One possibility—used in the previous example—is to expand *his* to *his and her*:

Everyone showed *his or her* student identification card at the door. CORRECT

Another possibility is to change a sentence from singular to plural:

The patients said *they* benefited from the experimental drug. CORRECT

A third possibility is to omit the pronoun "his" altogether:

Somebody left *a* book in the physics lab. CORRECT

Exercise 3: Avoiding Sexist Language

Instructions: Rewrite these sentences to eliminate sexist language.

1. A good physician answers his patients' questions in language they can understand easily.

2. The policeman looked sternly at the young woman who had driven her car recklessly.

3. Every telephone operator is taught emergency procedures so that she can assist callers who need help.

4. A postman who delivers mail on foot gets plenty of exercise walking his route every day.

5. Each nurse receives excellent benefits when she signs a contract to work at this hospital.

USING PRONOUNS IN COMPARISONS

Students often wonder which pronoun is correct in sentences like these:

Bonnie handles her money better than (*I, me*).
After watching the Skyhawks at practice, the coach said our team is better than (*they, them*).

You can be sure of choosing the correct pronoun if you "finish the sentence" with an appropriate verb—usually *am, are, is, was, were, do, does,* or *did*. Reading the sentence aloud will often help you hear the correct verb. Read these examples aloud:

Bonnie handles her money better than (I, me) do.

Bonnie handles her money better than I. CORRECT

After watching the Skyhawks at practice, the coach said our team is better than (they, them) are.

After watching the Skyhawks at practice, the coach said our team is better than they. CORRECT

Exercise 4: "Finish the Sentence"

Instructions: Choose the correct pronouns by "finishing the sentence."

1. Ray is more interested in nutrition than (I, me).
2. He keeps track of his fat intake more faithfully than (I, me).
3. But Linda says she eats more sensibly than (he, him).
4. Linda and Ray say I don't exercise as much as (they, them).
5. But I can run a mile faster than (they, them).

Review Exercise: Practice What You Have Learned

Instructions: Underline the correct pronouns in the sentences below.

1. Janet and (I, me) are thinking about signing up for computer dating.
2. She will probably be luckier than (I, me) when she meets her computer choices.
3. Drama students like Dennis and (she, her) have an advantage when meeting new people.
4. I want to be as self-confident as (they, them).
5. But majoring in drama has (its, it's) problems too.
6. When I talk to student actors, I realize that my life is easier than (theirs, their's).
7. An actor who wants to play Hamlet or Macbeth must expect (his, their) share of disappointments.
8. Every actress knows that (she, they) chose a demanding profession.
9. When Dennis and Janet are rehearsing a play, they get much less sleep than (I, me).
10. But they say that the excitement of acting makes up for (its, it's) disadvantages.

SUMMARY

1. Pronouns are words that take the place of nouns.
2. The "thumb rule" can help you choose the correct pronoun.
3. Possessive pronouns never have apostrophes.
4. Avoid sexism when using pronouns.

Credits

Index